The Process of

Writing News

R. Thomas Berner
The Pennsylvania State University

Allyn and Bacon
Boston • London • Toronto • Sydney • Tokyo • Singapore

Series Editor: Stephen Hull
Senior Editorial Assistant: Amy Capute
Editorial-Production Administrator: Rowena Dores
Editorial Production Service: Editorial Inc.
Cover Administrator: Linda Dickinson
Composition Buyer: Linda Cox
Manufacturing Buyer: Megan Cochran

Library of Congress Cataloging-in-Publication Data
Berner, R. Thomas.
   The process of writing news / by R. Thomas Berner.
     p. cm.
   Includes bibliographical references and index.
   ISBN 0-205-13523-4 :
   1. Journalism—Authorship. 2. News writing. I. Title.
PN4775.B445 1992
808'.06607—dc20   91-39926
                                   CIP

 This book is printed on recycled, acid-free paper.

Credits
Preface
Page *xiii.* "Hogan Remains a Presence at 77," by Jaime Diaz. From
  The New York Times, May 20, 1990. Copyright © 1990 by The New
  York Times Company. Reprinted by permission.

Credits continued on page 321, which constitutes an extension of the copyright
page. Other copyrighted material is acknowledged where it appears.

Printed in the United States of America
10 9 8 7 6 5 4 3 2 1   96 95 94 93 92 91

For Paulette

in the Advising Center

Contents

Preface

This is a different kind of newswriting text. I have tried to write a book that relates to what beginning journalism students really do. Most do not cover five-alarm fires, gory accidents and gangland slayings. New to the business, they must first learn the craft of newswriting from the ground up. The basics. The techniques. The audience. How to sign on to the computer.

I don't want to make a special claim for uniqueness, for I am merely building on the work of others (cited in the "Endnotes" and "Sources and Resources" sections of each chapter). I have relied on the work of others in my capacity as a writing coach to my students and to professionals. In addition to teaching since 1975, I have been a consultant for several newspapers, where I have held workshops on how to improve writing. I have also attended several sessions on coaching writing at the Poynter Institute for Media Studies in St. Petersburg, Florida (although, alas, never in the winter). I have put my knowledge and hands-on experience into this book.

What I do here is focus on the *process* of writing news rather than the outcome of that process. Whereas most newswriting texts offer the user an industry model of journalism—a finished product, a story—and urge imitation, I examine the steps journalists take to create that product.

The reader will not find chapters on how to cover a speech or how to cover a fire or how to cover a meeting. The principles of writing about those events are the same. What the reader will find is much about gathering information and then writing it. And while I do not distinguish between the subjects of stories—the speech, the fire, the meeting—I do distinguish between the purposes of stories. I admit to the validity of a basic news story. Most news stories are structured like an inverted pyramid. After that, I look at modifications to that formula, modifications based on the intention of the story. The metaphor for my approach is the corkscrew; the reader keeps going deeper and deeper into the principles of writing.

Also important to the beginning journalist is an understanding that revising is part of writing. Revision gets a chapter to itself, although one could argue that anytime I write about changing a story, I am talking about revision. Even then, is rewriting any different from writing? As the writer Larry Gelbart once said of the rewriting he does, "I don't even think of it as rewriting anymore. I think of it as the writing process."[1]

I have also tried to mix print and broadcast examples (one chapter deals only with broadcasting) and to refer to the "news media" rather than "the press," which connotes print journalism only. Journalism students should not think of themselves as only print or only broadcast writers, but should consider journalism first a process of gathering information and only then a technologically divided process of disseminating information. I believe a journalist should gather information without regard for which outlet it will appear in.

Having said that, I admit that my preferences run to print. Still, the writing principles are the same, though applied differently. Understanding the principles comes before application. For example, when broadcast journalists mix their own words and the voices of their sources, are they not doing the same as print journalists do when they to insert a direct quotation into a story? The addition of pictures forces the writer to see as he writes—nothing writers haven't been doing for years.

Regardless of the outlet, the writing must be clear, concise, interesting and accurate. Accuracy is the backbone of all journalism. "The first duty of a newspaper is to be accurate," Herbert Bayard Swope said before radio and television news existed. "If it be accurate, it follows that it is fair."

Furthermore, all the news media need good writing. "Press, radio and television are being tested as never before," Claude Sitton told a group of journalism educators and students at the University of Georgia. "We compete for the attention of a public whose busy lifestyle leaves little free time. We contend with pressures from within and without that threaten our credibility. We convey news to an audience whose ability to comprehend is sometimes dulled by a lack of interest or a lack of learning or both. We cope with a demand for content that not only fills the wants and needs of readers but does so in a vibrant and compelling way."[2]

From a different podium, Richard O'Mara argued that maybe one of the reasons newspapers were not attracting young readers was because of bad writing and bad story selection. "Newspaper reporters and writers are as inclined to the use of clichés as addicts are to needles," O'Mara wrote. "Inappropriate metaphors, clumsy similes, meaningless modifiers abound."[3]

So the focus on writing is timely. A critical rather than an accepting attitude is what journalism students need. They need to understand the process and how they fit into the process. Too often, hewing to the inverted pyramid structure is billed as the sole requirement for objective newswriting. But we know that the form of the story does not make the story objective. Why teach that? One thing I do in my newswriting and reporting classes is to make students aware of their prejudices, as a way of making them better journalists. The first myth to fall is that newswriting can be totally objective. That then allows me to teach my students how to write.

Some of the examples in this book were written by my students. While I could have gotten plenty of examples from the news media, I use some of my students' work to demonstrate what beginning journalists are capable of writing. To novice journalists reading this book, I say this: If you are serious about writing, you don't need to write for 20 years before turning out something good. You can do it now.

Acknowledgments

If I were to credit all the people who inspired me or helped me write this book, I could write another book filled only with their names. Since that would not work, let me give as much credit as I can here.

First, I acknowledge the encouragement of Gordon T.R. Anderson, who at the time I met him was executive editor of the College Book Division of Longman Inc. Gordon was the first editor willing to discuss my idea about a book on the process of newswriting, and in a letter to me in October 1988, he said, "We are in accord in philosophy and approach."

On August 10, 1990, Gordon died. He was 50. He cared about textbooks and writing and students, and he deserved a longer life.

After I had completed a draft of this book, I served as a writing coach at the *York* (Pa.) *Daily Record*. The reporters and editors were responsive and thoughtful, and that helped me clarify my ideas. Some of the solutions that the *Record*'s staff provided show up in this book unacknowledged.

A few months later, I served as a visiting faculty member at the Poynter Institute, coaching and lecturing on writing. Institute faculty and participants helped me focus my ideas in revising the book.

Also helpful were the students in my beginning newswriting classes. Professors, like students, enjoy positive reinforcement, and the students who have weaned me away from fact sheets and rewarded me with better stories through rewriting gave me reinforcement of the best kind.

A Note to Instructors

As I slowly evolved from a product-oriented instructor to a process-oriented instructor, several things happened in my newswriting classes. These are the kinds of things potential converts to process over product need to know.

First, I stopped relying on fact sheets. They do not reflect the way journalists really gather information and they had become a crutch for me. I knew what the best story could be given a certain fact sheet, and so I began to look for that story—that product—and accepted little else. With live assignments—even routine speeches on campus and by classroom visitors—I can take fresh interest in each article because I don't know how it will turn out.

I use as few fact sheets as possible in the beginning classes and none in the advanced classes. I assign my beginning students to cover on-campus events and then to write and rewrite. As the great professional golfer Ben Hogan once said, "A teacher can tell you something, but unless you go out and practice it for hours, you can't prove it."[4] If we have enough notice, I ask them to write advance stories based on library research. One successful assignment focused on a late-semester speech by Helen Suzman, then a member of South Africa's parliament and an opponent of apartheid. Assignments included an advance, coverage of an in-class news conference by a white South African who was a graduate student on campus at that time, and coverage of Suzman's speech. In addition, one student wrote an in-depth article on apartheid and was able in the rewrite to draw on crowd response to Suzman's speech as a lead-in to her article. Most of this work was written as ungraded drafts, with only the rewrites getting a grade. That enabled the students to write first drafts without penalty and, where possible, to do more reporting, even just reexamining notes to see what they might have overlooked. Mixed in with all this writing work are style and language skills exercises.

I also use videotapes. We often videotape speeches or other programs from television or on campus and use them in class. I have taped several hours of "The People's Court," which has become an excellent replacement for fact sheets. Students must pay attention; they must get names spelled correctly; they must separate the wheat from the chaff. Despite the fact that the stories based on one Judge Wapner decision run no more than 250 words, students find the tapes challenging, and I find they produce scores of opportunities to talk about the process of reporting and writing.

And talk I do. I've always done a little warming up before letting students write. But it soon occurred to me that just throwing them into the water and letting them sink or swim was not teaching. Now we discuss possible leads and story organization. We talk about an outside assignment before writing it. To those who think this is giving students the answers, I respond: "Nonsense!" It helps the average students get better and the better students get good. In any case, I don't write the story for them; writing remains the solitary act it should be. Of course, near the end of the semester, I become less involved. At some point, the birds need to fly solo.

In the meantime, my students do a lot of rewriting. We discuss stories as a class and then rewrite, or I may critique each story and ask for rewrites. This is where computers come in handy. Computers have reduced the pain of rewriting by making it so easy. They have also made grading easier: Students provide me with electronic versions of their stories, which I evaluate on my computer. I make more comments than I would with pencil. I have created a glossary of answers to common problems.

The process of drafting and rewriting also occurs with a news feature that requires library research and local interviews. (I include at least one topic reflecting cultural diversity.) I evaluate the drafts but do not grade them. Then I put two (or three) grades on the final paper. I explain that this is my attempt to help them all get A's. This is where our future journalists blossom; they take advantage of the opportunity to improve.

Endnotes

1. Jaime Diaz, "Hogan Remains a Presence at 77," *The New York Times,* May 20, 1990, VIII, 7.
2. Mervyn Rothstein, "Is There Life after 'M★A★S★H'?" in *The New York Times Magazine,* October 9, 1989, 54. Copyright © 1989 by The New York Times Company. Reprinted by permission.
3. Claude Sitton, Ralph McGill Lecture, The University of Georgia, February 16, 1990, 3.
4. Richard O'Mara, "The Flight from Newspapers," *The Quill* (March 1990): 34.

Sources and Resources

Brown, Betsy E. "Reflections on Recent Research in Composition." *English Journal* (September 1983): 51–54.
Rowan, Katherine E. "New Examples Improve Understanding of Story Types." *Journalism Educator* 44, no. 4 (Winter 1990): 27–30.
Zurek, Jerome. "Research on Writing Process Can Aid Newswriting Teachers." *Journalism Educator* 41, no. 4 (Spring 1986): 19–23.

The Process Is Prologue

Ten Steps in the Writing Process

Most news stories begin life in written form. True, broadcast journalists give occasional on-the-spot and last-minute live reports, but usually a news story is written before it is presented. Newswriting, I want to stress, does not mean only the physical act of putting words on paper. Rather, it is a process, 90 percent of which is not putting words on paper. I see the process as having ten steps.[1]

1. The first step is reporting.

No journalist writes about nothing or makes something up out of thin air. A journalist cannot fashion a news story without first doing some reporting, that is, gathering all the relevant information, getting details, finding examples and visualizing the story. A good story should not be based on one source. Journalists rely on a variety of sources in gathering the information for a story. Information is gathered through interviews, by observation and at libraries, which I define broadly to include electronic databases.

2. The second step is thinking.

I call this analysis aforethought. The journalist needs to think about what the story is and how to shape it before writing begins. Even the live broadcast report does not reach the public's ears without analysis aforethought.

Part of the thinking occurs during note taking. A journalist covering a long governmental meeting may use a lull in the action as an opportunity to review notes and highlight important aspects of the meeting. On stories for which information is gathered over a period of time, a journalist should take some time at the end of each day to highlight notes. I once told a journalist on deadline to go to a nearby cafeteria and drink a cup of coffee. She used the time to think about her story and produced an above-average account of an unusual accident.

Thinking extends beyond the initial analysis. Thinking is a continuum in which the journalist reconsiders what the story is as he or she gathers new information.

3. The third step is organizing.

A good journalist organizes a story before beginning to write. Although making outlines may sound tedious, the fact remains that the journalist who loses time in outlining makes it up in writing. An organized journalist can write faster and better, and knows where the story has been and where it is going. Although some novice journalists may believe that after they put down the first sentence, a story writes itself, most journalists find that a story writes itself only after the journalist has planned it.

Good organization results from first knowing what the story is about. Once the theme is established, the most natural way to organize facts is logically. Keep related facts together; put one fact after another in a logical way. Put good detail into the body, and wherever possible, show, don't tell. Good examples strengthen any piece of writing.

4. The fourth step is getting the mechanics right.

A good journalist gets the mechanics right because that is what the audience understands. The mechanics of our language are conventions, and the journalist follows the conventions of the audience—standard punctuation and grammar. Nothing idiosyncratic to cloud understanding.

5. The fifth step is crafting the style.

Style is the flavor, quality, spirit, and personality of a written piece. Style is the sum of a writer. In part, it is an attitude: A good journalist wants to write well and interestingly and to use original language. Avoid clichés. Avoid jargon. Be original. Write the story as it has never been written before.

The next three steps are concerned with forming the main parts of the story: the lead, the body and the ending. Together these provide the story's unity. If they are not properly connected, the story falls apart.

6. The lead or first paragraph engages the audience.

Leads can be of various types—shocking statement, narrative, description, summary, information, direct address, quotation, question, surprise, teaser, and so on—but what the journalist should really appreciate about a lead is that it should be determined by the content. Don't decide to write a particular lead because it is the middle of the month and it is time for such a lead; write a lead that comes naturally from the information you have gathered.

7. The body conveys the main facts.

This is where the seed of good reporting grows. If the reporter has failed to gather enough or the right kind of information, the body of the story will lack clarity. If the reporter fails to organize the facts, the body of the story will suffer.

8. The ending closes the story appropriately.

News stories usually give the facts in descending order of importance, so the ending of a news story normally contains the least consequential information. But feature stories, in-depth articles, editorials and columns need more punchy endings—endings that summarize the story's content with an apt fact or a clever turn of phrase or thought. A story should conclude naturally, not with some pious summary by the journalist. If a story has a good ending, its impact will continue after the reader has put the story aside.

9. The ninth step is evaluating one's own work.

A good writer is also a good editor, as difficult as that is when you are editing your own work. Editing your own copy is almost like seeing your own or your children's faults—it is very difficult to be objective.

Writing is discovery, and most discoveries are made in the evaluation stage. Those who do not evaluate their own writing well do not discover much from having written. One important test at this stage is asking if the story lives up to its intention. If not, perhaps rewriting or re-reporting is necessary.

10. The tenth step is rewriting and re-reporting the story. Every piece of writing can benefit from rewriting. Rewriting allows a journalist to focus a story more sharply and perhaps note non sequiturs or a missing fact, which the journalist may need to obtain through re-reporting (for instance, calling a news source again).

Writing is hard work. It is not like memorizing multiplication tables. Once you know them, you are over the hump. Two times two is always four. But writing does not get easier the next time you do it. Those who write clearly do toil. But the good result that comes from hard work is worth it. Excellence is its own reward.

Endnote

1. Adapted from R. Thomas Berner, *Writing Literary Features* (Hillsdale, N.J.: Lawrence Erlbaum Associates, 1988), 13–16. Reprinted with permission of the publisher.

Chapter 1

News

Chapter Objectives

In this chapter you will find a brief history of journalism. You will get a sense of journalism's antecedents and of its role in modern society. Then you will learn about the many and varied elements of news. You will read about the role of the audience in helping an editor or producer determine what is newsworthy, and how editors and producers aim to provide timely and interesting information that they believe their readers and listeners should have or want to have. You will learn that news can also be a human interest story.

Introduction

Writing has long been a means of getting news to the public. Historians credit Julius Caesar with publishing handwritten news sheets titled *Acta Senatus, Acta Publica,* and *Acta Diurna* to provide a summary of what the Roman government was doing. *Acta Diurna* means "Daily Acts," and the Latin word *diurnal,* "daily," is the antecedent for the word *journalism.* Two thousand years later the news media are still engaged in telling readers and listeners what is happening in their world.

The Role of the News Media in Society

"We in the press," editorial writer Jean Otto once said, "create one of this nation's common denominators—shared information. We unify. We create the base upon which our nation's diversities can co-exist without destroying themselves and each other."[1] In that light, journalism is something of a mission. Journalists generally do not see themselves as holding down a job but as following a calling, much the way someone who takes religious vows might. Journalists seek to convey a larger truth about the world, to shed light where there are shadows, to make the sun shine through the clouds of government obfuscation.

The sharing and distribution of information has always been important. History records many cultures and countries finding ways to obtain public information. *The Travels of Marco Polo* is but one of many examples of somebody providing information about exotic places. Even in modern times, travelers who have visited a closed society can provide information.

With the invention of the movable type printing press by Johannes Gutenberg about 1450 came the rise of censorship, that is, attempts by government to silence journalists. In England during the reigns of Mary Tudor and Elizabeth I, the Crown established a monopoly on printing through the Stationers Company and then proceeded to censor content. Elizabeth also established the infamous Star Chamber, which prosecuted, among others, printers who failed to submit to her editing pencil. The licensing system that attempted to keep printers and others in line and negative information away from the public lasted for a century.

In the American colonies some people attempted to provide information not controlled by the Crown or its agents. One of the first newspapers was the *News-Letter*. Published in Boston in 1704, it proclaimed it was published "for the Publick Good, to give a true Account of All Foreign & Domestick Occurrences, and to prevent a great many false reports of the same."

One of the best-known journalists in the colonies was Benjamin Franklin, who published the *Pennsylvania Gazette* in Philadelphia. In the early days of journalism, the owners of the newspapers did everything: They gathered information, set type, ran the presses, delivered the papers, sold advertising and kept the books in order. As technology improved, those jobs were split among many people. Today, interestingly enough,

Figure 1.1 From Nova Reperta (New Discoveries of the Middle Ages and the Renaissance. *Plate 4, "Printing books—just as one voice can be heard by a multitude of ears, so single writings cover a thousand sheets." This interior of a printing shop represents the possible appearance of Gutenberg's own shop. At the right are two screw presses. In the background a printer applies ink with two daubers. At the left compositors set type while an apprentice gathers the sheets. The proofreader wears an early form of spectacles. One of a series of drawings by Jan van der Straet, 1523–1605, who worked in Florence. He sent his drawings by courier to Antwerp for engraving and publication by Theodor Galle, who issued this print in 1638. Notes by Ben Dibner in a 1953 reissue of the print by the Burndy Library. Courtesy Burndy Library, Norwalk,*

one person with a personal computer can effectively follow in the steps of those early owners, for the personal computer allows one person to write and correct the information, design and print the pages (if necessary), distribute the information electronically (if desired), and, with a modest spreadsheet program, keep the accounts.

Franklin was one of many bold journalists. "If all printers were determined not to print anything until they were sure it would offend nobody," he once wrote, "there would be very little printed." Franklin

Figure 1.2 Engraving, "Franklin takes home his paper." From The Life of Benjamin Franklin, *Philadelphia, 1836. Courtesy American Philosophical Society.*

made that comment before the First Amendment protection of freedom of the press and speech had been firmly established. A milestone in establishing this protection was the 1735 trial and acquittal of the New York editor John Peter Zenger, charged with seditious libel for criticizing the colonial governor in print. But legal protection did not guarantee safety for journalists.

Boldness often came with a price. Napoleon once had a printer executed. Still later, another newspaper condemned the general, leading him to refer to the press as "the fifth great power." Around the same time in England, Edmund Burke supposedly referred to the press as the Fourth Estate,[2] and Thomas Macaulay saw the press as the equal of the three estates of the realm: the Lords Spiritual, the Lords Temporal and the Lords Common.[3] Neither Burke nor Macaulay was happy with the power of the press. And Napoleon observed, "A journalist is a grumbler, a censurer, a

THE

New-York Weekly JOURNAL

Containing the freſheſt Advices, Foreign, and Domeſtick.

MUNDAT November 12, 1733.

Mr. *Zenger.*

INcert the following in your next, and you'll oblige your Friend,
CATO.

Mira temporum felicitas ubi ſentiri quæ velis, & quæ ſentias dicere licit.
Tacit.

THE Liberty of the Preſs is a Subject of the greateſt Importance, and in which every Individual is as much concern'd as he is in any other Part of Liberty : Therefore it will not be improper to communicate to the Publick the Sentiments of a late excellent Writer upon this Point, ſuch is the Elegance and Perſpicuity of his Writings, ſuch the inimitable Force of his Reaſoning, that it will be difficult to ſay any Thing new that he has not ſaid, or not to ſay that much worſe which he has ſaid.

There are two Sorts of Monarchies, an abſolute and a limited one. In the firſt, the Liberty of the Preſs can never be maintained, it is inconſiſtent with it ; for what abſolute Monarch would ſuffer any Subject to animadvert on his Actions, when it is in his Power to declare the Crime, and to nominate the Puniſhment ? This would make it very dangerous to exerciſe ſuch a Liberty Beſides the Object againſt which thoſe Pens muſt be directed, is

their Sovereign, the ſole ſupream Maiſtrate ; for there being no Law in thoſe Monarchies, but the Will of the Prince, it makes it neceſſary for his Miniſters to conſult his Pleaſure, before any Thing can be undertaken : He is therefore properly chargeable with the Grievances of his Subjects, and what the Miniſter there acts being in Obedience to the Prince, he ought not to incur the Hatred of the People ; for it would be hard to impute that to him for a Crime, which is the Fruit of his Allegiance, and for refuſing which he might incur the Penalties of Treaſon. Beſides, in an abſolute Monarchy, the Will of the Prince being the Law, a Liberty of the Preſs to complain of Grievances would be complaining againſt the Law, and the Conſtitution, to which they have ſubmitted, or have been obliged to ſubmit; and therefore in one Senſe, may be ſaid to deſerve Puniſhment, So that under an abſolute Monarchy, I ſay, ſuch a Liberty is inconſiſtent with the Conſtitution, having no proper Subject in Politics, on which it might be exercis'd, and if exercis'd would incur a certain Penalty.

But in a limited Monarchy, as *England* is, our Laws are known, fixed and eſtabliſhed. They are the ſtreigh Rule and ſure Guide to direct the King, the Miniſters, and other his Subjects : And therefore an Offence againſt the Laws is ſuch an Offence againſt the Conſtitution as ought to receive a proper adequate Puniſhment ; the ſevere
Conſtit

Figure 1.3 Front page of John Peter Zenger's New York Weekly Journal, *November 12, 1733. The lead says, "The Liberty of the Press is a Subject of the greatest Importance. . . ." At Zenger's trial for seditious libel two years later, Alexander Hamilton stepped from among the spectators to take over Zenger's defense, arguing for the right to print matters "supported with truth." Truth as a defense against criminal libel was not established in U.S. and British constitutional law until the 19th century.* `North Wind Picture Archives.

Figure 1.4 Frontispiece from John F. Trow's Alton Trials, *New York, 1838, depicting a mob attacking an Alton, Illinois, warehouse where Elijah Lovejoy's printing press was stored. Lovejoy, an abolitionist and the editor of* The Observer, *died in this attack on November 7, 1837, while protecting his press. Courtesy Library of Congress, Rare Book and Special Collections.*

giver of advice, a regent of sovereigns, a tutor of nations. Four hostile newspapers are more to be feared than a thousand bayonets."[4]

In the United States, newspapers began as extensions of political parties, their distribution through the mail subsidized by the federal government, and it was not until the 1830s that newspapers shifted from party ownership to private ownership, signaling what is considered the rise of the penny press. Communications scholar Michael Schudson says it was then that fact gained prominence over opinion in news stories. Schudson also notes changes in the names of newspapers, away from commercial names such as *Advertiser* to functional ones such as *Herald* or *Tribune*.[5]

Schudson also credits the press with taking advantage of the technology of the time. One major advance was the steam press, which enabled publishers to reproduce thousands of copies of a multiple-page newspaper in a short time. Before the steam press, newspapers had been printed on presses with movable type. They did not have many pages, yet printing them consumed much of the publisher's labor.

Also popular with the press was the telegraph, which enabled newspapers to get information quickly across great distances. The telegraph first proved its worth to newspapers during the Civil War when correspondents at the sites of battles could quickly send their stories to waiting editors in major cities.

By the end of the 19th century, newspapers had become more democratic, more egalitarian and more middle class. The mass distribution of newspapers meant that many people not only read the news stories but also the advertisements. Thus was born the mass market. A larger audience shared information. Furthermore, Schudson notes, the newspaper changed "from something to be borrowed or read at a club or library to a product one bought for home consumption."

Also born at the century's close, according to Schudson, was the formal position of reporter. The division of labor common for most of the 20th century had arrived. Some workers, such as the printers, became unionized, usually under the International Typographical Union. Where once travelers provided information to the local editor, reporters were now hired full time to gather news and write stories. Some of those early reporters went on to become masters of American literature. Realism was a major element in the American novel at that time, and scholars today trace that to the journalistic work that predated the novels.

After World War I, with the Depression just beginning, American journalism broadened its outlets. One such addition was *Time* magazine, a combination of news and interpretation in each story. One of *Time*'s founders, Henry R. Luce, disdained those who spoke of objectivity: "Show me a man who thinks he's objective, and I'll show you a man who's deceiving himself," he said. Other magazines followed.

Then came the rise of radio. Suddenly, Americans could hear firsthand the words of the president of the United States or of a foreign dictator. Broadcast stations created networks and hired their own reporters. Edward R. Murrow assembled a team to cover the war in Europe. Murrow would broadcast live to the United States during German bombing raids on London.

Murrow went on to present equally intensive and exciting journalism on television. The newscast evolved someone sitting behind a desk reading the news to a 15-minute program with two anchors to the longer

Figure 1.5 Time *magazine cover, July 30, 1923 (vol. 1, no. 22), picturing the Italian actress Eleanora Duse. Copyright © 1923 Time Warner Inc. Reprinted by permission.*

interpretive programs we see and hear today. Live coverage of both parties' presidential conventions helped advance the careers of some broadcast journalists.

Today, news junkies have much to choose from. If they have the time, they can read at least three newspapers distributed nationally—*The Wall Street Journal, The New York Times* and *USA Today*—as well as a local newspaper. If they live in an area served by cable television, they can watch news from NBC, CBS, ABC, CNN, PBS, and Fox, and at least one C-SPAN channel. They probably also have access to some local radio stations and a couple of regional television stations that provide some local news as well as a videotext on one of the cable channels.

All these outlets, in the tradition of Julius Caesar, inform people about current events. But they also do what Jean Otto talked about: They create

Figure 1.6 "Years of Crisis" CBS radio broadcast, January 3, 1954. Left to right: Eric Sevareid, Howard K. Smith, George Herman, Edward R. Murrow, Richard C. Hottelet, David Schoenbrun, and Alexander Kendrick. Courtesy of CBS Inc.

an environment of shared information from which we, a diverse people, derive some measure of unity.

Ample local coverage exists as well. In a study of what makes smaller newspapers excellent, journalism professor Thomas Connery noted thorough coverage of the community, original reporting, in-depth reporting, and a strong editorial voice. One editor told Connery:

> Our job is to make our readers care. Not just about government, but about the way people live, about the way the world lives. Our job is to see that they know the facts and figures, but the human stories, too, and to do it honestly and responsibly.[6]

Implicit in this statement is a view of the press that agrees with a 1947 study, known generally by the name of chairman of the commission that issued the study, Robert M. Hutchins. The Commission on Freedom of the Press named five expectations for the communications media:[7]

1. A truthful, comprehensive and intelligent account of the day's events in a context which gives the meaning.
2. A forum for the exchange of comment and criticism.
3. The projection of a representative picture of the constituent groups in the society.
4. The presentation and clarification of the goals and values of the society.
5. Full access to the day's intelligence.

Expressing what is called the social responsibility theory of the press, the preceding expectations have driven the news media since 1947. Some would argue that the pace of the drive has been slow. But the news media are not monolithic, although they are referred to collectively as "the press" or "the media." Each outlet—each newspaper, magazine, radio station and television station—holds its own opinions and behaves as it wants. That means each outlet does not necessarily measure up to the expectations of the Hutchins Commission. Still, the commission's expectations continue to influence views of what the news media should do in our society. The assumption of this book is that the Hutchins Commission's expectations are good guidelines for modern journalists.

News Values

Deciding what constitutes news is not easy. For the beginning newswriter, news can be rising tuition and dorm fees, unwanted pregnancy, sexually transmitted diseases, a noisy dorm floor, a cutback in library hours, the scheduled appearance of a favorite musical group on campus or the success or failure of an athletic team. For others, news can be increasing taxes, the rising cost of medical care, the inefficiency of the trash collection system, the infrequency of police patrols in a neighborhood, the plans for a new (and expensive) school. News is information that is fascinating and interesting to readers and listeners.

Events by themselves are not news. News is a construct, the product of a social process. The social process occurs in classrooms and newsrooms as educators and editors discuss and decree what is newsworthy. Thus, a beginning journalist could examine the back issues of newspapers or tapes of newscasts and figure out what editor or producer considered newsworthy at the time. Aware of this societal consensus, the journalist could spend his or her career imitating past practices. But possibly news so based would not be very useful to a democratic society, since it would tend to merely reinforce past practices and ignore new ideas.

Anyone who has examined the process of writing news soon realizes that news really is a construct, that far from having some inherent quality, news is whatever the journalist writes and the editor prints or the producer broadcasts and the audience listens to. That's not necessarily bad *as long as everyone including readers and listeners recognizes this characteristic of news.* News sometimes gets tangled up in a web of disputes when some try to say it is something it is not. While news is based on fact, it does not replace truth, and it is not an objective account of events, although journalists strive to be fair and balanced.

Journalism students learn what constitutes newsworthiness in a variety of ways. Textbooks usually list what their authors consider the attributes of news. The lists vary. Professor Wallace B. Eberhard of the University of Georgia compiled terms from 14 newswriting textbooks. He found the following listed as attributes of news: timeliness, proximity-nearness, prominence-eminence, change, action, audience, impact, unusualness, conflict, significance, magnitude, human interest, consequence–probable consequence, sex, children, animals, tragedy, oddities-bizarreness-novelty-rarity, interest, importance, economic impact, familiarity, humor, pathos–pathos/bathos, currency, emotional stimulus–emotion, accuracy, certainty, explanation, clarity, sensationalism, suspense, objectivity, conciseness, irony, drama, surprise, identification, concreteness, personality, progress, disaster, news balance.[8] As Eberhard pointed out, editors know that it is more than a list of conditions, elements and qualities that determines what is newsworthy.

News comes with a variety of definitions. Lord Northcliffe once described news as "something someone wants to suppress." The classic definition says that when a dog bites a man, that isn't news; but when a man bites a dog, that is. (The author's files contain a story that details the successful efforts of a man to give mouth-to-muzzle resuscitation to a

Dalmatian. Perhaps that kind of story will become the more humane version of man bites dog.)

John Chancellor of NBC News defined news as "a chronicle of conflict and change." Implicit in that description is that peace and stability are not news. News organizations seem to detail war more than peace, just as history courses focus on wars rather than on the periods of peace between the wars. News can be stories about ongoing tension or the resolution of tension. Given Chancellor's description, one can understand why underrepresented groups in our society have found it necessary to become confrontational and hostile; it has seemed the best way of getting attention from the news media.

Wrongly, news has been geocentric and ethnocentric, reflecting biases good journalists overcome. To overcome these biases, journalists have had to create a diverse newsroom. Editors have realized that ethnic and gender variety in the newsroom diversifies the news and creates a newspaper or broadcast more relevant to the population. Stories are no longer projected through the narrow prism of one ethnic group or one gender. Thanks to an increasing number of women in the newsroom, editors have been made aware of the news value of stories on childcare and women in the workplace. The arrival of ethnic minorities in the newsroom gave rise to broader reporting on social issues. Does welfare work? What are the conditions among the disenfranchised? How does racism hold people back?

The news media are often criticized for focusing on personalities rather than issues. The head of *The Wall Street Journal*'s Washington bureau, Albert R. Hunt, once wrote:

> Legitimate complaints about the national press corps abound. We often overemphasize the politics of a development and underestimate the policy significance. . . . We sometimes lack discipline and are swept away by the passions of the moment. Some important issues and ideas get little attention.[9]

A similar point is made by journalism professor James Brann. "The press covers what is familiar," he writes. "What if it is the unfamiliar that does us in?"[10] Brann is arguing for journalists to look deeper and harder into new places. Don't always go back to the sources that produced the last story.

Other critics raise questions that cannot always be answered but should be kept in the mind by all journalists when they create news. Political scientist Lance Bennett, for example, wonders if news isn't an advertisement for the system. In other words, news reinforces the status quo. And sociologist Herbert Gans says news is "often the highlights of highlights."[11]

Journalists are the ones who decide what the highlights of the highlights will be. The mayor of a city in Pennsylvania, one of the few in the nation with independent competing newspapers, once observed that new ownership of one of the newspapers had resulted in increased coverage of local government. It wasn't that local government had done anything more newsworthy; it was that the new blood in an old competitive situation had redefined news in this city.

Some journalists have claimed that the news media merely reflect society, but the truth is that many journalists often write stories for other journalists (especially for editors), journalists often conform to stereotypes, and journalists often come to a news event predisposed to a story line rather than with an open mind. Journalists are hardly the objective fact-gatherers and presenters that they claim to be. Depending on the audience, the story is constructed differently. Writing about broadcast news executives, Edward Epstein says: "They more or less operated on the assumption that a news story could be shot, edited and narrated in a number of different ways, and that the producer was responsible for reconstructing it along lines that met the standards and policies of the network."[12]

The same is true of newspapers. Here are excerpts from a *New York Times* story about the governor of New York testifying before a House committee.[13]

> WASHINGTON, July 17—Governor Cuomo took his case against President Reagan's tax revision plan to Congress for the first time today, calling the arguments of the President and his supporters "palpably contradictory" and shaking some legislators with his sharp tongue.
>
> . . .

"Let me answer that with some questions of my own," declared Mr. Cuomo, one of the most prominent opponents of repealing the state and local deductions.

. . .

Governor Cuomo, however, was the star of the show, and the audience that packed the hearing room had clearly come to see his performance.

. . .

After weeks of desultory tax hearings in which business executives, labor leaders and other special pleaders have pressed their claims in an often dreary and sometimes obsequious fashion, the legislators seemed unprepared for Governor Cuomo's quick retorts.

Here are excerpts from *The Wall Street Journal*'s account of the same event:[14]

WASHINGTON—New York Gov. Mario Cuomo topped a list of politicians from all levels of government who pleaded with the House Ways and Means Committee to preserve the deduction for state and local taxes.

. . .

The Reagan administration's proposal to repeal the deduction, which annually costs the federal government billions of dollars in lost revenues, has become the most controversial provision of its tax-overhaul plan. "No other provision has stimulated such broad-based concern," said Rep. Dan Rostenkowski (D., Ill.), chairman of the panel.

. . .

Gov. Cuomo, a Democrat, asserted that the repeal was included in the tax bill solely to raise revenue to finance lower tax rates.

. . .

The administration found its champion in Republican Gov. Richard Thornburgh of Pennsylvania, who said that an overhaul to bring down tax rates would benefit most Americans, even if the deduction for state and local taxes is repealed. Gov. Thornburgh is from a relatively low-tax state; Gov. Cuomo is from the nation's highest tax state.

What lessons can a beginning journalist draw from these excerpts? Look at how each journalist portrayed the people in the story. Although both stories acknowledge Cuomo's prominence, the *Times'* account casts the governor in the role of someone who is showing up those scoundrels in Washington. It helps that Cuomo is the governor of New York, home of *The New York Times*.

The *Journal's* account, on the other hand, strikes a more even-handed note, even comes across somewhat dryly. Cuomo rates an "asserted" and Thornburgh gets a "champion" in a story otherwise powered by relatively neutral verbs.

Both stories were written with the readers of the newspapers in mind. If New York is the highest-tax state in the nation and the deductibility of local taxes is in jeopardy, then what the New York governor says is of importance and interest to *News York Times'* readers. In fact, the story appears at the bottom of the first business page with a photograph, whereas the *Journal's* account appears on Page 14 and without a photograph. The *Journal's* readers are businesspeople from around the country, from low-tax states as well as high-tax states, and people who probably favor lower taxes period. Knowing that, the *Journal* reporter is not about to paint Cuomo as a David confronting Goliath. The *Times,* on the other hand, gives its readers an interesting story by adopting that stance. Conflict is newsworthy.

Both newspapers are considering the interests of their audiences. When a newspaper does that, it considers the makeup of its readership. What is the educational level of its readers? Where do they work (in a steel mill or for a defense contractor)? Where do they live (suburban area or urban area)? What is their racial makeup? What are their leisure time interests? Is religion important? Is church attendance high or low? What are their politics? What is the mix of all the preceding?

What journalists need to remember is that audiences play a major role in determining which stories are written and how. Stories are not merely laid down by journalists and then received with the same intensity or understanding by all readers. Readers bring to stories their prejudices and predispositions. What might appear positive to one reader could be negative to another. In a locale where hunting is popular, a newspaper will publish photographs of hunters and their kill. Not everyone in the newspaper's audience approves of those photographs; some people might oppose hunting and suggest that the newspaper is condoning a "wrong" practice by publishing the photographs. But the editor might reply that since hunting is important to many readers, he is responding to his audience. Curiously, though, the editor may never have skipped a year of publishing such photographs to see if the hunters really care as much about their absence as the nonhunters do about their presence.

Now that you have considered some nuances, it's time to discuss news values, starting with content. Let's discuss the content of one edition of a 25,000 circulation newspaper that publishes seven days a week. The newspaper is divided into four sections, which in itself makes a statement about what is news. Each section enables the editors to emphasize aspects of the community they think are newsworthy. Thus, the newspaper that begins a section with business news but buries sports in a section that leads off with arts is making a statement about its news values.

The bulk of Section 1 is devoted to what some people would call wire news, that is, nonlocal news. But an exception appears on Page One. It is a feature story about a local gunsmith who makes replicas of muzzleloaders. It is a human interest story, a typical feature story. Otherwise, the front page contains stories distributed by the Associated Press, the *Washington Post,* the *Los Angeles Times,* the *Philadelphia Inquirer* and Knight-Ridder Newspapers. Three of the stories focus on current events. In two instances, the events are elections; the third event is a demonstration in Moscow. All three stories are international.

The last two stories are not about specific recent events. One is a feature story on the demise of a sport called cornerball, which is played by the Amish and the Mennonites, and the other story tells about Congress's use of mailing privileges (franking). Neither the cornerball story nor the mail story is tied to a specific recent event and could just as easily have been published the day before or three days from today. So why are they newsworthy?

The cornerball story fits several categories on Eberhard's list. It has human interest and is about change and novelty. The mail story, despite the apparent lack of a current event, was current because it was an election year and candidates for Congress were announcing for office. The mail story represents an attempt to monitor the system. This is something the news media do.

Inside, a story details a meeting in the United States between the president of the United States and the chancellor of West Germany (soon to be unified with East Germany in a larger Germany). Another story announces

Figure 1.7 Front page of the Dayton Daily News, *February 28, 1990. Copyright © 1990 Dayton Newspapers, Inc.*

that the planned launch of a U.S. space shuttle has been delayed. One more story uses a recent controversy over cigarette smoking to focus on the first year of service by the Secretary of Health and Human Services. Similar in purpose to the mail story on Page One, this particular story recounts the secretary's first year in office and the problems he has had and makes the case that he has finally found a popular issue in condemning cigarettes. Twenty-five percent of one page is devoted to the weather forecasts—local, national and international. The weather is always of interest.

The second section, which is the local news section, contains a story, with photograph, about the owners of a local airport contesting a proposed development at the end of their runway. Controversy makes news, and this is all the juicier since one of the developers is also a state senator. The story outlines the concerns of the airport's owners and their suggested resolution. The story also reveals that the airport's owners have not contacted the developers about their concerns. The newspaper has become a mediator, publicly relaying messages between the squabbling parties.

Another story tells that an unidentified woman crawled out of an elevator stalled between floors and fell 20 feet to the bottom of the elevator shaft. She was in critical condition with a head injury. A third story is what is known as an advance. It announces that two municipalities' planning commissions are going to hold a joint work session to discuss proposed land use regulations. Consultants working on the regulations will be at the meeting, the story says, and the public is urged to attend and offer comments.

On the next two inside pages appear routine accident and police reports, a listing of municipal meetings for the week ahead and the milestone-type information—births, hospital admissions and discharges, deaths and funerals. (Some newspapers have started publishing the obituaries of pets.) Later on in this local section can be found state, business and entertainment news.

Section 3 carries the Dear Abby column, a profile of a YMCA director, and information for senior citizens. Inside is more information, most of it about library activities in the county.

Section 4 is the sports section. On this particular day, a Monday, most of its space is devoted to the results of Sunday's professional, collegiate and high school games and meets. Half of one page is given over to boxscores, other results and standings—all in minute type. This is the page for the truly devoted, who will read it in detail.

The last page of the paper will receive equal attention, but probably from a different segment of the audience. This page carries the television listings and reviews of shows on television that night.

Larger newspapers have more sections or divide the paper along different lines. Some newspapers devote an entire section to business, for example, and others give more space than one page to arts and entertainment.

A reporter covering an event that includes several topics must decide what is newsworthy and what is not. At the least, the reporter must select the one point of a story that is newsworthy enough to make the first paragraph.

Figure 1.8 A journalist covering a city council meeting takes advantage of a lull in the proceedings to begin writing his story on a portable computer. The story will be sent via telephone to the newspaper's main computer. Penn State photo by Dave Shelley.

One reporter, faced with four actions by a board of elected officials, had to choose from among routine appointments to advisory boards, an announcement by the township manager that construction of a new township building was on schedule, a vote on protecting well sites not just in the one municipality but across the region, and approval of plans to develop an industrial park, which had been reviewed by various advisory boards in public with no objections.

The reporter chose the appointments to advisory boards, but was redirected by his editor to rewrite the story and lead with the discussion on water. Why? Well, the newspaper's circulation area includes at least 65 municipal boards, all of which routinely appoint people to advisory boards. The appointments are of no interest outside the municipality. Water, on the other hand, cuts across municipal boundaries, and at this time it was a topic of concern to several municipalities in the newspaper's area. By highlighting water, the reporter was developing the story to have broader appeal. The water story would function as a unifier of several segments of the newspaper's audience.

Another time a reporter was assigned to cover a speech by Irene Natividad, the executive director of the National Women's Political Caucus, located in Washington, D.C. The topic of her speech was: "The political concerns and influence of women: emphasis on women of color." Among other things, Natividad spoke about how women had to become more involved at the grassroots political level. Under any other circumstance, that would have been the lead on the story. But this time Natividad was speaking on the eve of the announcement of a U.S. Supreme Court decision on abortion. During the question-and-answer session that followed her speech, she was asked to predict how the court would rule. She did, and that became the lead item in the story. The impending court decision made her insight newsworthy. (She was right, by the way.)

Another time student journalists were assigned to cover a talk by Mohamed Wahby, minister-counselor and director of the press and information bureau for the Egyptian embassy in Washington. His topic was "The peace process in the Middle East." His speech, while interesting, provided nothing new. After the speech, one enterprising student talked to Wahby for a few minutes and learned that the United States would soon get involved in an international conference on the Middle East. The conference would focus on direct talks between the warring groups in the Middle East. That became his lead. Five days later *The New York Times* front page included this headline: "U.S. to Seek Talks between Israelis and Local Arabs." The student journalist had scooped *The New York Times* because he had bothered to ask a few questions after a routine speech.

News is a construct put together by journalists. They aim to provide information they believe their readers and listeners should have or want to have. That information is usually timely and is pegged to current events. Sometimes news is what is said locally about something that will happen hundreds or thousands of miles away. Sometimes news is about local government or local problems.

Sometimes news is a human interest story about someone residing in the newspaper's circulation area. Sometimes news is a human interest story about a subculture not residing in the newspaper's circulation area. News is what journalists believe will interest their audiences. News is a disruption in the rhythm of a community, a state or a nation. News, in the words of historian Mitchell Stephens, is "what's on a society's mind."[15] News is what makes people talk.

Review Questions

What are some of the elements of news?

What do you consider newsworthy?

How does your view square with what appears in your campus newspaper or hometown newspaper?

How does the audience influence what is newsworthy?

What did Henry R. Luce of *Time* mean when he said, "Show me a man who thinks he's objective, and I'll show you a man who's deceiving himself."

Endnotes

1. Jean Otto, "The Meek Shall Not Inherit." Speech given at the University of Arizona, Tucson, November 11, 1988, at the presentation of the John Peter Zenger Award for Freedom of the Press and the People's Right to Know.

2. "There are three estates in Parliament but in the Reporters' Gallery yonder there sits a Fourth Estate more important far than they all. It is

not a figure of speech or witty saying; it is a literal fact very momentous to us in these times." From *Speaking of a Free Press,* published by the American Newspaper Publishers Association in 1987.

3. "The Fourth Estate ranks in importance equally with the three estates of the realm, the Lords Spiritual, the Lords Temporal and the Lords Common." *Speaking of a Free Press.*
4. *Speaking of a Free Press.*
5. Michael Schudson, *Discovering the News* (New York: Basic Books, 1978), 1
6. Thomas Connery, "Management Commitment and the Small Daily," *Newspaper Research Journal* 10, no. 4 (Summer/Fall 1989): 64.
7. Commission on Freedom of the Press, *A Free and Responsible Press* Chicago: University of Chicago Press, 1947.
8. Wallace B. Eberhard, " 'News Value' Treatments Are Far from Consistent among Newswriting Texts," *Journalism Educator,* 37, no. 1 (Spring 1982): 9–11, 50.
9. Albert R. Hunt, "Media Bias Is in Eye of the Beholder," *The Wall Street Journal,* July 23, 1985, 32. Reprinted by permission of *The Wall Street Journal,* Copyright © 1985, Dow Jones & Company, Inc., All Rights Reserved Worldwide.
10. James Brann, "A New Definition for News," *Nieman Reports* (Winter 1984): 51.
11. Herbert J. Gans, *Deciding What's News* (New York: Pantheon Books, 1979), 92.
12. Edward Epstein, *News from Nowhere: Television and the News.* (New York: Random House, 1973), 230.
13. David E. Rosenbaum, "Cuomo Takes Case to House," From *The New York Times,* July 18, 1985, D1. Copyright © 1985 by The New York Times Company. Reprinted by permission.
14. Jeffrey H. Birnbaum, "Cuomo, Others Plead with House Panel for State, Local Tax Break to Be Kept," *The Wall Street Journal,* July 18, 1985, 14. Reprinted by permission of *The Wall Street Journal,* Copyright © 1985, Dow Jones Company, Inc., All Rights Reserved Worldwide.
15. Mitchell Stephens, *A History of News.* (New York: Viking Penguin, 1988), 9.

Sources and Resources

Abel, Elie, ed. *What's News.* San Francisco: Institute for Contemporary Studies, 1981.
Bennett, W. Lance. *News: The Politics of Illusion.* New York: Longman, 1983.
Broder, David S. *Behind the Front Page.* New York: Simon and Schuster, 1987.

Chancellor, John. "A Portrait of the Press, Warts and All." NBC White Paper, June 15, 1985.

Chappell, Warren. *A Short History of the Printed Word*. Boston: Nonpareil Books, 1980. [Originally published: 1970].

Darnton, Robert. "Writing News and Telling Stories." *Daedalus* 104, no. 2, (Spring 1975): 175–94,

Dizard, Wilson P., Jr. *The Coming Information Age*. New York: Longman, 1982.

Eisenstein, Elizabeth L. *The Printing Press as an Agent of Change*. Cambridge: Cambridge University Press, 1979.

Epstein, Edward J. *News From Nowhere: Television and the News*. New York: Random House, 1973.

Fry, Don, ed. *Believing the News*. St. Petersburg, Fla.: Poynter Institute for Media Studies.

Hohenberg, John. *Free Press, Free People*. New York: Free Press, 1971.

Kielbowicz, Richard B. *News in the Mail: The Press, Post Office, and Public Information, 1700–1860s*. Westport, Conn.: Greenwood Press, 1989.

Manoff, Robert Karl, and Michael Schudson, eds. *Reading the News*. New York: Pantheon Books, 1987.

Miller, M. Mark, Michael W. Singletary, and Shu-Ling Chen. "The Roper Question and Television vs. Newspaper as Sources of News." *Journalism Quarterly* 65, no. 1, (Spring 1988): 12–19.

Newsom, Clark. "Special Sections Return Their Popularity." *Presstime,* (October 1982): 56–58.

Olson, Lyle D. "Technical Writing Methods Show Ways to Consider Audience." *Journalism Educator* 43, no. 2 (Summer 1989): 3–6, 76.

O'Mara, Richard. "The Tyranny of the Proximate." *The Quill* (June 1985): 30–33.

Reagan, Joey. "New Technologies and News Use: Adopters vs. Nonadopters." *Journalism Quarterly* 66, no. 4 (Winter 1989).

Rosenblum, Mort. *Reporting the World for America*. New York: Harper and Row, 1979.

Siebert, Fred S., Theodore Peterson, and Wilbur Schram. *Four Theories of the Press*. Urbana: University of Illinois Press, 1956.

Smith, Anthony. *Goodbye Gutenberg*. Oxford: Oxford University Press, 1980.

Sperber, A.M. *Murrow: His Life and Times*. New York: Freundlich Books, 1986.

Steiner, Linda. "The Role of Readers in Reporting Texts." *Journalism Quarterly,* 65, no. 3 (Fall 1988): 642–47.

Thornburg, Ron, ed. "Interest in Business News Hasn't Peaked, No Matter What Direction the Market Takes." *Editorially Speaking* 41, no. 10 (December 1987).

Tichenor, Phillip J., George A. Donohue, and Clarice N. Olien. *Community Conflict and the Press*. Beverly Hills, Calif.: Sage Publications, 1980.

Ungar, Sanford J. *The Papers and the Papers: An Account of the Legal and Political Battle over the Pentagon Papers*. New York: Dutton, 1972.

Chapter 2

The Elements of a
News Story

Chapter Objectives

In this chapter you will learn about the elements of a news story. You will learn that the first paragraph is called "the lead" and what its function is. You will learn about the time element, attribution and direct and indirect quotations (or paraphrases). You will also learn how those and other elements come together in a story.

Introduction

A good journalist strives to provide a factual, balanced, accurate, informative account of the news. The typical news story is designed to convey news quickly, clearly and unambiguously. The typical news story is not a great work of literature. Rather, it is prose with a purpose, its form dictated by function.

A Story's Elements

Before writing a news story, the beginning journalist should know the elements of a news story. Broken down, a news story usually comprises these elements: the lead, a time element, specific rather than general information, sources, attribution in direct and indirect quotations, and sentences and paragraphs.

The Lead

In the typical news story, the lead is the first paragraph. It is usually no more than one sentence. The lead concisely tells the reader or listener what the story is about. Eventually, you will see leads that are longer and leads that are subtle, but for now, focus on the basics. Here is a lead from a United Press International story:

> PRAGUE, Czechoslovakia (UPI)—A pipe bomb exploded during an election rally in a busy tourist area of the city Saturday, injuring 15 to 20 people, witnesses and the Czechoslovak News Agency said.

The Time Element

The time element tells when the news happened. Usually, it is confined to a day or a period in a day, such as Sunday or Sunday night or yesterday or yesterday afternoon. A more specific time may appear later.

Related to the time element is the tense of most of the verbs in a typical news story. Most of the verbs are past tense. Journalists can choose from a variety of tenses, all variations of present, past and future. But since by definition news is something that happened, past tense is the appropriate tense for most news stories.

In the following lead, the time element and past tense verbs are shown italic:

> WASHINGTON (UPI)—Retired Chief Justice Warren Burger, saying the law profession should "hang its head in shame," *criticized* advertising by lawyers *Friday* and *urged* an attorneys group to determine whether regulation is needed.

Specific Information

Specific information allows the reader and listener to know exactly what the story is about. Specific information includes names, ages, addresses, titles, number of votes. Rather than say a fire caused "much damage," a journalist will ask experts for their estimate of the damage and include that information in her story. Here are the first two paragraphs from a story on AIDS; the specific information is shown in italic:

> GENEVA (UPI)—Global AIDS cases reported to the World Health Organization rose by *8,973,* or *3.5 percent,* in May to a *total of 263,051,* the U.N. agency said Friday.
>
> The United States accounted for most of the increase with *6,309 cases* for a *total 132,436,* or *50.4 percent* of the world figure *as of May 31.*

Sources

The experts and other people providing information in a story are called sources. A story can have one source or many sources. Sources should have names, although sometimes sources have to be anonymous. Sources can also be documents and other publications, and when a journalist observes something and reports it, the journalist becomes a source. In the previous story, the World Health Organization is the source. In this story, it's an expert:

> ERROL, N.H. (UPI)—Observers watching the first pair of bald eagles to nest in New Hampshire in more than 40 years report sighting at least one eaglet, *a wildlife biologist* said Thursday.
>
> Chris Martin, *wildlife programs manager for the New Hampshire Audubon Society,* said it is possible that chicks are in the nest. He said observers, who check the nest near Umbaygog Lake several times a week, probably will be able to determine the exact number of eaglets by sometime next week.

Attribution

When a source is cited in a story, information is attributed to that source. Attribution lets the reader or listener know where information came from. Attribution is clearly marked for the reader or listener by an attribution tag. Two of the most typical attribution tags are "(person's name) said" or "according to (person's name or document)."

Attributed information appears as either a direct quotation or an indirect quotation. This is an example of a direct quotation with attribution tag:

> "They beat them with their fists," a duty nurse said of the Soviet soldiers who broke into the hospital. She refused to give her name. "I was afraid they would shoot me too."

As an indirect quotation, the nurse's exact words would be paraphrased, and where the first-person pronoun appears, the paraphrased statement would be shifted to a third-person pronoun:

> A duty nurse said Soviet soldiers broke into the hospital and beat patients with their fists. The nurse, who refused to give her name, said she was afraid the soldiers would also shoot her.

Journalists frequently call direct quotations *quotes,* and when a story contains some pithy direct quotation, people in newsrooms say, "That's a great quote."

One problem with direct quotations is the penchant of some journalists for using too many, thus relying on the subject of the news to "write" the story. Some journalists argue that a large number of direct quotations in a story shows people talking, and if the quotations are pithy, they can enliven a story. Others argue that people do not speak very precisely or concisely and that a journalist can paraphrase better. These same people argue that every time a journalist uses a quote he is not writing but transcribing. Use direct quotations sparingly. Use them when they make a point better than you can.

Some people are eminently quotable and to paraphrase them would be to deprive readers of delightful language. A modern example is Gen. H. Norman Schwarzkopf, who commanded a coalition of troops that drove Iraq out of Kuwait in 1991. Asked what he thought of Saddam Hussein, the leader of Iraq at the time, he said:

> As far as Saddam Hussein being a great military strategist, he is neither a strategist, nor is he schooled in the operational arts, nor is he a tactician nor is he a general, nor is he a soldier. Other than that, he's a great military man; I want you to know that.[1]

To paraphrase such a statement of irony would take away its flavor. Furthermore, the direct quotation says something about the speaker.

Journalists get into trouble when they misquote sources or quote sources out of context. Out-of-context problems arise when the careless journalist does not make clear the context in which something was said. For example, a journalist might ask a leading question such as this:

> *Journalist:* Madame Mayor, wouldn't you call this proposal sloppy?
> *Mayor:* Possibly.

That might translate into a story this way:

> The mayor said the proposal was "possibly sloppy."

But that would be unfair to the mayor because *sloppy* wasn't her word; it was the reporter's, who failed to note the context in which the word appeared. The problem also arises when a speaker qualifies her statements before giving a final assessment, an assessment that without the qualifications sounds stronger than the speaker intended.

Accuracy is a guiding principle for all ethical journalistic endeavors.

Sentences and Paragraphs

News stories are broken up into sentences and paragraphs. Simple sentences best convey the news, and the good journalist uses few complex and compound sentences. Sentence length varies, but typically sentences average around 17 words, and paragraphs are usually no longer than three sentences. Sometimes a paragraph consists of only one sentence, usually when the sentence expresses an unrelated idea, is atypically long, or is a great quote.

The following fire story contains many of the elements noted in this section.[2] It also demonstrates the typical structure common to basic news stories, the inverted pyramid. The inverted pyramid image suggests that the story moves from the most important information to the least important; the assumption is that the story can be cut (shortened) from the end, paragraph by paragraph. While the inverted pyramid is the most common structure of news stories, there are other structures and approaches (see later chapters).

In addition to Scheib's story, newspaper coverage of the fire included three photographs.

By Barbara Scheib
Staff Writer

*The writer's name at the beginning of the story is called the **byline**. A byline is not a required element.*

A quick-burning fire roared through the body and parts shop of D&M Chrysler Plymouth Inc. Sunday morning, destroying seven cars and reducing the concrete-block building to a blackened shell.

*The **lead** establishes this as a fire story. It tells generally what the fire did to whom and when. The **time element** is "Sunday morning."*

Fire officials are estimating the loss to the business at $800,000. The owners of the dealership, Daniel and Michael Faretta, had only $290,000 insurance on the building and its contents, according to City Fire Chief Reynold D. Santone.

*Numbers **attributed to sources** provide specific information for the reader. Note here and throughout that people are identified with titles. No name appears alone. Always identify people in a story as fully as possible.*

Among the cars crushed and burned in the blaze was a classic 1949 Buick convertible and a new van that was on a lift for repairs, the chief said. Information about the owners of the vehicles was not available.

*More **specific information** in the form of descriptions of the car. The information appears in an **indirect quote**.*

By mid-morning, the structure—which sits behind D&M's new-car dealership at 1549 Pleasant Valley Blvd.—looked more like it had been bombed than burned. The roof and pieces of several walls collapsed from the fire. More walls were knocked down on purpose so they would not fall on firefighters.

*Still more **specific information** in the form of an address. The reporter is also describing the result of the fire.*

The cause of the fire is still under investigation, but officials say they believe it was accidental. No one was injured.

*Most of the **paragraphs** in this story comprise one or two sentences.*

Santone said that firefighters were alerted at 7:15 a.m. By then, the building was already engulfed in flame. Assistant Fire Chief Gordon W. McConnell said he could see a tower of smoke from the vicinity of the fire as soon as he left Fire Station 1 on Washington Avenue. Six off-duty firefighters were called in as backup.
Santone said that all engine companies and equipment were called to the scene, only to find there was little they could do initially to effectively fight the fire

*Note not only the more specific time but also the **attribution**. After someone is identified by full name, subsequent references in print and broadcast are a matter of the medium's style. This newspaper uses last name only. Also note the additional detail and the nonsexist reference to the people fighting the fire. They are "firefighters," not "firemen."*

"The amount of heat generated was just unbelievable," he said. "When we got here there was no getting inside. There was just nothing we could do."

*This is the only **direct quotation** in the story, which is good, since some journalists over-rely on direct quotation.*

Figure 2.1 Major fires are part of the news diet of any newspaper or broadcast station. The Altoona (Pa.) Mirror *sent reporter Barbara Scheib and two photographers to cover this story. This photo by Michelle Bell is one of three that accompanied Ms. Scheib's story in* the Mirror, *February 12, 1990. Copyright © 1990* The Altoona Mirror.

He said the fire was out of control the first 45 minutes firefighters were there, then began to burn itself down.

The fire chief said the fire was particularly intense because of paints and other highly flammable materials stored in the building.

State Police Fire Marshal James Behe said this morning that the cause of the fire is under investigation but that the problem is centering on a gas-powered heater with an electric fan and fluorescent lights over the paint shop.

*Note the length of the **sentences** in this and the three subsequent paragraphs. The sentences range from 10 to 39 words for an average of 22, a little longer than usual.*

*Another **source** appears. This is the person who will ultimately determine the fire's cause, and the reporter will stay in touch with him until he announces the results of his investigation. At that time, the reporter will write a follow-up story.*

He said he has found no evidence to suggest that anyone entered the building or set the fire. All doors to the building were locked when firefighters arrived.

Santone said there were enough water and manpower to fight the fire. The Peoples Natural Gas Co. was called and asked to cut off gas service to the building until the flames were doused. Firefighters stayed on the scene until 3 p.m. cooling "hot spots" among the charred debris.

Firefighters were able to leave, when snow showers moved into the area and cooled things down.

Traffic on Pleasant Valley and Valley View boulevards was blocked for several hours to keep vehicles away from the scene. Blair County fire police were called in to direct cars away from the fire. Traffic was moving normally by 10:30 a.m.

Altoona police reported this morning that several cars ran over fire hoses at the fire scene. The department is warning drivers that it is a violation of the motor vehicle code to drive over a hose without permission from fire officials or police officers.

More specific information.

A little sidelight.

Writing the Lead

A famous play, *The Front Page,* is about a Chicago newspaper in 1928. The editor, Walter Burns, is watching his ace reporter, Hildy Johnson, write a story for the *Chicago Examiner*. The crux of the story is that the *Examiner* has captured a criminal.

Johnson begins this story this way:

> While hundreds of Sheriff Hartman's paid gun-
> men stalked through Chicago shooting innocent by-
> standers, spreading their reign of terror, Earl Williams
> was lurking less than 20 yards from the sheriff's office
> where . . .

The editor interrupts:

> *Walter:* That's *lousy!* Aren't you going to mention the
> Examiner? Don't we take *any* credit?

Figure 2.2 Rosalind Russell played a female version of ace reporter Hildy Johnson in the movie His Girl Friday *(1940), one of several film versions of Ben Hecht and Charles MacArthur's 1928 play,* The Front Page. *Copyright © Photofest, New York.*

Hildy: I'm putting that in the second paragraph.
Walter: Who the hell's going to read the second paragraph?

That is the first lesson beginning newswriters must learn: the importance of the first paragraph, the lead. The lead must be engaging enough so that readers and listeners will go on to the second paragraph (and find out what the *Examiner* did for law and order in Chicago one day more than six decades ago).

The lead is the one story element editors and reporters talk about most. The assumption is that if the lead is good, if it hooks the audience, the audience will want to know the rest of the story. And if the lead is not good enough, readers and listeners won't go on.

You may want to curse them for being so lazy, but busy audiences face many diversions. They may have obtained a summary of the news earlier in the day and may not want much more detailed information. Between working, commuting, childcare, community responsibilities, household chores, and hobbies, the public has little discretionary time to devote to news consumption. Editors and reporters assume that a good lead at the top of a well-written story can compete with the many other calls on the public's attention.

Essentially, the lead summarizes the story, although it could also accent a major point. The major point could be the murder of someone, a fatal accident, a sex scandal, foul weather (past or future), legislation vetoed, the veto overriden, the city council approving a ban on cruising.

The paragraphs that follow it amplify the lead by providing detail. Thus, if the lead says a person was killed in a one-car accident (*what*), the second paragraph would name the person who died (*who*). (A prominent person would be named in the lead.) The third paragraph would tell *how* the accident occurred. Subsequent paragraphs would provide detail in descending order of importance (the inverted pyramid structure).

Most news stories answer six questions, summed up in a poem by Rudyard Kipling:

I keep six honest serving-men
(They taught me all I knew);
Their names are What and Why and When
And How and Where and Who.[3]

Remember, it's the story, not the lead, that answers those questions. A lead that answered all six questions would be too long. A good lead focuses on the most interesting or newsworthy elements of the story, not all the elements. For example,

- *What* happened? Ten miners killed in a cave-in.
- *Who* did what? Mayor vetoes council decision.
- *Why* did something happen? The U.S. Senate, unhappy with an arms control agreement, rejected the treaty.

But don't sit around and try to figure out whether a story takes a *why* lead, a *what* lead or any other type of lead. Do not get engrossed in labels at the expense of substance. It is not important to categorize a story's lead; just write it, and write it well.

When covering an event, determine what action or statement would be of the most interest to readers or listeners and put that in the lead. Some

Figure 2.3 Newspaper and television reporters interview a district attorney (in car) near the home of a murder suspect. Copyright © Keith Nordstrom/The Sun Chronicle, Attleboro, Mass.

Figure 2.4 Journalists at a press conference, Chicago, 1990, where the Committee for Educational Rights announced the filing of a lawsuit against the state of Illinois for unequal allocation of education funds. Copyright © Catharine Reeve.

events contain more than one nugget of interest, but a reporter cannot lead with all of them. A reporter must decide.

Leads are brief, although they run longer than the average sentence. Brief leads are crafted by being specific enough to engage the audience but not overly detailed. For example, if three people were killed in an automobile accident, the lead would not include their names, but it would contain enough identifying information to help a reader decide whether to read more:

> Three New York City residents were killed last night
> near Cleveland when their car skidded on a patch of ice
> on Interstate 80 and went off the road.

A broadcast lead, on the other hand, might run two or three sentences and contain the main point at the end rather than at the beginning of a sentence or in the first sentence. In broadcasting, the aim is to advise listeners of what is coming and then to tell them. That makes it easier for them to grasp the news.

> An accident on Interstate 80 has claimed three lives. The accident occurred last night near Cleveland when the victims' car skidded on ice and went off the road. The dead were identified as . . .

As for subsequent paragraphs in the newspaper story, the second would list the victims by name, age, address, relationship to each other (if any), and remaining ones would give such information as the possible cause of the accident, police comments, and other details.

> Ohio Highway Patrol identified the victims as Joan T. Snyder, 34, the driver; her husband, John, 35, and their son Michael, 12. They resided in Greenwich Village.
>
> Police said a sudden drop in temperature after a rainstorm had left the road unexpectedly icy. Police had no other details on the accident.

Figure 2.5 Editors and reporters at their desks in the newsroom of The Sun Chronicle, *Attleboro, Mass. Copyright © Mark Stockwell.*

One piece of advice heard in the newsroom is, "Never write a lead you could have written before the event." This advice applies especially to planned events—meetings, speeches, demonstrations. For example, after the president has given the State of the Union address, the lead does not say that he spoke; it tells what he said. Governmental meetings fit this category also, for reporters usually have access to agendas and know what a particular group is planning to discuss.

Here are two leads about a planning commission meeting. Which one engages you?

The Centre Regional Planning Commission last night heard a summary of the third section of the Centre Region comprehensive plan from its author, planner Herbert Kauhl.	Over half of the 57,000 residents of the Centre Region are Penn State students, the Centre Regional Planning Commission learned last night.

The writer of the lead on the right saw something interesting in the plan and used it in her lead. She used it as a hook to engage her readers. After explaining the student population matter, she went on to report on other parts of the plan.

One of the most interesting yet overlooked elements in leads is *why*. Why was something done? It is not enough to say that a governmental body took a certain action; people want to know why. Compare these:

College Town Council voted last night to shut off the street lights on College Avenue from Atherton Street to High Street for a three-day trial period.	College Town will turn out some of its street lights on College Avenue for three days to see if lighting from Penn State provides enough illumination.

Two types of leads that are generally discouraged are quote leads and question leads. A quote lead is taboo because (being short) it has not established the context for the quote, thus making it difficult for readers to understand the quote. Also, people when speaking rarely phrase something in a way that the newswriter cannot paraphrase better. Question leads can frustrate readers who come to the news story looking for answers and who do not want to wade through a question to get them. As with everything else, there *are* exceptions and a reporter should not follow rules slavishly.

The Same Event, but Different Stories

No two reporters will cover the same event and write a story the same way. That should not bother anyone. No two meteorologists study their data and then come up with the same forecast. Thus, it is always interesting to compare stories about the same event to see how each journalist wrote the story. Here, from a newswriting class, are two stories based on watching a videotape of a civil case in small claims court. First, note that each story contains specific information—names, ages, addresses, amounts of money, make of car. Then note how each story develops. What does each writer choose to emphasize in the lead? How are the second paragraphs different? How are they similar? Which story handles the testimony of witnesses better? Which story does not identify the person being sued beyond his age and address? Did the writer of the shorter story omit information that should have been included?

Story 1

An Elm Grove woman won a breach-of-contract suit against a Yellow Springs man in Small Claims Court today.

Abby Wade, 26, of 425 Waupelani Drive, was awarded $300 from Arthur Longfellow, 31, of 314 Yellow Springs Road, by Judge Joseph A. Snyder because Longfellow reneged on an agreement to make repairs on a 1975 Volkswagen Bug that Wade had purchased from Longfellow in October 1987.

Story 2

A Yellow Springs man must pay an Elm Grove woman $300 because he reneged on an oral contract, a Small Claims judge ruled today.

Judge Joseph A. Snyder said, Abby Wade, 26, 425 Waupelani Drive, was awarded $300 to make repairs to her car, which Arthur Longfellow, 31, 314 Yellow Springs Road, had agreed to finish but did not.

Judge Snyder said that although Wade and Longfellow had no written statements or receipts from the sale, there had been an oral agreement that Longfellow would make the repairs Wade thought necessary. Longfellow broke that agreement, according to Snyder, when he did not make all the repairs Wade requested.

A witness for Wade said Wade had only $1,500 of the $1,800 Longfellow wanted for the car when she picked it up. Longfellow told Wade she could take the car and make a list of needed repairs, which he would make when he received the remaining $300.

Wade said that after she paid Longfellow the $300 he repaired the car's horn and installed seatbelts in the back seat but did not repair the car's brakes or gas gauge.

Longfellow lost a $1,500 countersuit he had filed for harassment and to recover parts and labor costs.

Longfellow sold Wade, a friend of a friend, a 1975 Volkswagen Bug for $1,800. Wade paid $1,500 and agreed to pay the balance when certain repairs, including the brakes and the gas gauge, were made.

Snyder said Longfellow and Wade had an oral contract, which Longfellow broke. Wade said she did not get anything in writing because Longfellow was a "friend of a friend" and she trusted him.

Snyder stressed the importance of always getting a contract or agreement in writing, even if it is made with a friend.

In court with Wade today were two friends who accompanied her to Longfellow's residence on separate occasions and testified that Longfellow agreed to complete the repairs.

Longfellow is the owner of Art's Repair Shop, 1015 Benner Pike.

Longfellow said he never agreed to make the repairs and is not responsible to repair Wade's car after she had been driving it for almost five months.

Longfellow lost his countersuit for $1,500 to compensate for minor repairs he did make on Wade's car which totaled $40 and for harassment.

Figure 2.6 Front page of the local news section, Reprinted from The Washington Post, *May 16, 1991. Copyright © 1991, The Washington Post. Reprinted with permission.*

Both stories have their virtues and their faults. In Story 1, the lead emphasizes who won the suit rather than who lost, which seems the best way to cover a court case in which two relatively unknown people are involved. Had the loser been well known, the emphasis in Story 2 might have been justified. The lead on Story 1, while not as specific as Story 2's lead, is smoother. Story 1 merely tells us that a breach of contract is involved; Story 2 says that but with more words ("because he reneged on an oral contract"). It also provides the amount of the settlement.

Story 1 provides more detail in the second paragraph, although the one-sentence paragraph is too long. Story 2, even though it is repeating something from the lead, has a shorter second paragraph. Story 2 also eventually gives additional information about Longfellow, information that enables the reader to understand that he repairs cars for a living. Story 2, though, provides more information than is needed. In effect, the writer of Story 2 gets into the minutiae of the case too early, which does not add to the story. The overall conciseness of Story 1 makes it the better of the two.

You now have an idea what the major elements of a news story are and how they come together in a basic story. The importance of the lead should never be forgotten. The next chapter talks about writing stories, and what pitfalls await the writer and how they can be avoided.

Review Questions

What is the first paragraph of a news story called?

What is its function?

In which paragraph does the time element of a news story usually appear?

Which element in a news story identifies a source of information?

Explain the difference between a direct quotation and an indirect quotation.

How would you describe the structure of a typical news story?

Endnotes

1. R.W. Apple, Jr. "Kuwait Is Retaken after 7 Months as Allies Destroy Main Iraqi Force." From *The New York Times*, February 28, 1991, 1, 9.

Copyright © 1991 by The New York Times Company. Reprinted by permission.

2. Barbara Scheib. "Fire Levels Auto Firm's Garage," *The Altoona Mirror,* February 12, 1990, 1–2. Copyright © 1990 by *The Altoona Mirror.*

3. Rudyard Kipling. From "The Elephant's Child," *Just So Stories,* (Garden City, N.Y.: The Country Life Press, 1902), 83.

Sources and Resources

Rowan, Katherine E. "New Examples Improve Understanding of Story Types." in *Journalism Educator* 44, no. 4 (Winter 1990): 26–30.

Chapter 3

The Fundamentals of Writing News

Chapter Objectives

In this chapter you will expand your knowledge of writing leads and developing news stories. You will study problem leads and leads that are clear, concise and interesting. Then you will learn about problems that occur in developing a story.

Introduction

No two people approach writing the same way. Reporters use various approaches, some opening a can of diet soda and then spilling words into the computer, others writing and revising a story one sentence and sip at a time. On deadline, the former is better.

Composing the Lead

Stories do not fall out of the sky or spring out of some electronic databank in a form suitable for publication. Journalists make stories by writing them. Based on the information they have acquired, the audience they seek to communicate with, and what they know of previous events, journalists write stories.

Remember, though, the ten steps outlined in the Prologue. Writing is not the first step; reporting is. Before journalists write, they gather information from a variety of sources and organize that information according to the requirements of the medium they are using (television, radio, newspaper, magazine). In the reporting process, journalist Paul Salsini says, reporters need to ask themselves several questions.[1]

He recommends that reporters ask themselves what the reader would want to know, who the story's characters are and which sources to talk to as well as what other research needs to be done. Salsini also advises asking

Figure 3.1 Reporter Mike Yaple of The Sun Chronicle, *Attleboro, Mass., conducts an interview by telephone and enters information directly into the computer. Copyright © Mark Stockwell.*

what is needed to make an interesting story, what does the story mean and, finally, what is the story? Some journalists go through this process by talking to someone else—another reporter or an editor.

Since writing reflects thinking, a journalist having a problem with a story should think more before writing. Questions complementary to Salsini's arise. What is the point of the event I just covered? That's the lead. What do I want to say? More important, what don't I need to say? (That question helps discover and thus avoid clutter.) What parts of the event are related? Keep related items together; unrelated items apart.

The first paragraph formed in the writer's mind should be the lead. In Salsini's list, What is the story? What's the point? Lisa Parker of the *Times Daily* in Florence, Alabama, told a Poynter Institute seminar that she writes down three words to get the gist of a story. That helps her get started

Figure 3.2 A writer and a television newscaster confer. Copyright © Catharine Reeve.

finding more words. As Don Fry, an associate director at Poynter, put it, "Words call up words." Journalism professor Carole Rich suggests answering these questions in 25 words or less.[2]

If you're stuck, try writing, "This is a story about a fire at an auto repair shop Sunday morning." That's a start, but since it is vague, you will need to add more. "This is a story about a fire that badly damaged an auto repair shop Sunday morning." That's getting better because you have now used a strong verb (*damaged*). Now work on specifics: "This is a story about a fire that badly damaged an auto repair shop Sunday morning and destroyed seven cars." A few more specifics and you have the lead:

> A quick-burning fire roared through the body and parts shop of D&M Chrysler Plymouth Inc. Sunday morning, destroying seven cars and reducing the concrete-block building to a blackened shell.

Writing a good lead is critical to writing the rest of the story. The lead, according to a study by journalism professor Beverly Pitts,[3] helps the writer realize a purpose and direction for the story. Writing the lead is a narrowing and focusing process for the journalist and, according to Pitts, can take up to one third of the time spent writing the entire story. Time spent writing a good lead is time well invested. Pitts calls the lead "a barometer by which to measure remaining parts of the story."

Pitts sees news stories as being written two or three sentences at a time, a micro approach rather than a macro approach. Journalists, she writes, "continually use memory, notes, analysis, planning, and rereading to propel them through the writing of paragraphs." What's been written, she says, helps journalists decide what to write next.

One critical element in the writing process is the writer's ability to recall in a general way parts of the event. General recall leads a writer back to his notes for detail, Pitts says. With recall so critical, then, a journalist must pay close attention when reporting a story.

Once the writing is done, Pitts notes, two kinds of editing take place—editing for revision and editing for polish. Stories are checked against leads, and if they are incompatible, revision of one or the other takes place. Stories are also checked for continuity and, of course, for mechanical problems.

Revision is discussed in Chapter 7. For now, let's focus on the writing of parts of the story and the problems encountered.

No-news Leads and News Judgment

The lead on a basic news story conveys some action or speaks about something specific. The lead that fails that test is known as a no-news lead. The assumption is that if there is no news in the lead, there is none in the story, so why should the reader bother to continue. Here are some no-news leads about the same event:

> The Society of Professional Journalists sponsored a program last night on "The Ins and Outs of Court Coverage," with keynote speaker Professor Norman Collins.

> Dr. Norman Collins spoke in detail at a meeting last night sponsored by the Society of Professional Journalists about law enforcement, court coverage and the mysteries that each of these duties entail.

> A Penn State assistant professor of journalism spoke last night to the Society of Professional Journalists about media court coverage.

> Last night in 169 Willard approximately 35 people were at a lecture concerning journalists' coverage of court cases.

> Covering the courts effectively and efficiently was the topic Thursday night in a speech by an assistant professor of journalism.

What was the point of the talk? Since you know that the person speaking was a journalism professor and that he was talking to a group of journalists (in this case, the student chapter of the Society of Professional

Journalists), telling what advice the speaker imparted to the students might make a good lead:

> Journalists covering a trial for the first time need to prepare by studying court procedures if they want to do a good job, a journalism professor advised journalism students last night.

That lead is more concrete than the preceding ones. The advice in Chapter 2 about never writing a lead you could have written before the event applies exactly to many no-news leads.

Action is important, but beware of generalities. The following leads are too general:

> The College Town Planning Commission Thursday voiced concern regarding the university moving many downtown offices back on campus.

> Elderly residents spoke out on the latest fair housing proposal at the College Town Council meeting Tuesday night.

The first lead would be better if it told what action the Planning Commission took regarding this problem rather than just saying it "voiced concern." It was not until the 14th paragraph that the writer of this story revealed what action the commission had proposed.

The lead on the council meeting could be improved by being specific about what the residents said. What did they "speak out" about?

> Elderly residents asked College Town Council last night to raise the age limit in the latest version of a fair housing proposal.

The lead must give the reader something to latch onto. Which one of the following leads contains news?

> Richard A. Hodel, operator of Hodel Industries Inc., addressed the College Town Council last night about the lack of public knowledge and the high cost of Pilsdon County's proposed solid waste plan.

> A local recycler told the College Town Council that residents are paying too much for the county's recycling program and that private recyclers could save residents money.

The lead in the left-hand column suggests something; the other lead says it. The right-hand lead, by the way, is an example of a "blind lead," which will be discussed shortly.

A lead may contain action, but still not provide explicit information:

> The College Town Planning Commission last night unanimously voted in favor of revision for the proposed YMCA.

This lead lacks interest. What are the revisions? Here is an improvement:

> The College Town Planning Commission last night endorsed the YMCA's plans for a day-care center in its new headquarters at Fairlawn Drive and Oak Road.

An excellent lead sometimes comes about because the writer has thought beyond the immediate story and emphasized larger events of which the story can be made a part. For example, an expert on the role of women in Nazi Germany spoke on a college campus one night. The expert, Professor Claudia Koonz, spoke about her research, but she also extrapolated from her research some observations about modern society. One student reporter, rather than leading with the behavior of people half a century ago, produced this timely lead:

> A political and social system that gives the power to men and leaves humanity to women is dangerous, an expert on women in Nazi Germany said last night.

The lead was timely because society, especially U.S. society, was focusing on the role of women; therefore, the reader would understand Koonz's insight.

When trying to think of what to lead with, remember that proposals for change make good leads; lead with the cure, not the disease.

Backing into Stories

Related to the no-news lead is the lead that backs into a story. This means that the writer, rather than putting the news up front, dilly-dallies around and meanders through the story paragraph after paragraph until finally telling the news almost by accident. Often a writer backs into a story when writing chronologically (they met, they took attendance, they talked, they voted) rather than getting right to the point (they voted; obviously they met, and presumably they talked before they voted). Here is an example of backing into a story:

> The pros and cons of entering into a contract with a television company to provide daily newscasts in the district's classrooms were discussed at length by the Philipsburg-Osceola Area School Board Monday night.
>
> Earlier this month the board had considered a three-year contract with Whittle Communications Satellite Education Network of Nashville, Tenn.
>
> Board members were in agreement with concern nationwide that today's public school students are not knowledgeable concerning daily news events.
>
> Joseph Mainello, school superintendent, said, "Students are not listening to news reports; we need to come up with a plan to correct this situation."
>
> Board members Raymond O'Brien and Michael Kochkodin were critical of what they saw as the disadvantages of the Whittle proposal. Members Howard Shaffer and Janice Walker expressed the view that even though the plan had some drawbacks, "let's give it a try."
>
> When the issue finally came to a vote, board president Robert Hoover, Russell Tice, Elizabeth Ferguson, O'Brien and Kochkodin were opposed to the Whittle plan. Voting in favor were Barbara Wilks, Ken Wood, Shaffer and Walker. The motion was defeated.

> The board plans to investigate other television sources of newscasts for the students.
>
> The board went into executive session . . .
>
> [The story continues for five more paragraphs on another matter.]

The copy editor, lacking the time to ask for a rewrite or to do a rewrite, headlined the story, "P-O Board Defeats Satellite News Plan," which at least gives the reader a sense of the news. But that does not excuse the reporter for having backed into the story.

This same principle applies to paragraphs within stories. Here is a paragraph in which the writer backs into the news:

> The commission heard arguments regarding the necessary dimensions in parking lots. John C. Haas, an architect, contended that a width of 14.5 feet is sufficient in one-way aisleways. However, zoning officer Herman Slaybaugh said 18-foot widths are necessary. At the request of the commission, Haas and Slaybaugh will attempt to reach a compromise over those measurements prior to the next town council meeting.

The news—the lead of the paragraph—is contained in the last sentence. A better way of starting the paragraph would have been to focus on the result first:

> The commission directed an architect and the zoning officer to attempt to reach a compromise in their disagreement over how wide one-way aisleways in parking lots should be. [Now explain the dispute and name the people.]

Backing into a story is not without virtue. It is a useful way of writing for broadcast because it allows listeners to grasp the context of the action before hearing about the action. The school board story, condensed, would make a better broadcast report than newspaper article:

The pros and cons of entering into a contract with a television company to provide daily newscasts in the district's classrooms were discussed at length by the Philipsburg-Osceola Area School Board Monday night.

Earlier this month the board had considered a three-year contract with Whittle Communications Satellite Education Network of Nashville, Tenn.

Board members were in agreement with concern nationwide that today's public school students are not knowledgeable concerning daily news events.

But when the debate was over, the Whittle proposal lost, five to four.

School superintendent Joseph Mainello told the board that "students are not listening to news reports; we need to come up with a plan to correct this situation."

With Whittle out of the picture, the board plans to investigate other television sources of newscasts for the students.

Blind Leads

You've been handed the current issue of the *New England Journal of Medicine* and asked to write a story about a study reported in the journal. The co-authors of the study are Dr. Jonathan L. Halperin of Mount Sinai Medical Center in New York City and Dr. David C. Anderson of Hennepin County Medical Center in Minneapolis. The study says that people with abnormal heartbeats can cut the risk of strokes in half by taking an aspirin a day. Strokes, which can be caused when abnormal heartbeats disrupt blood flow to the brain, are a problem that afflicts 75,000 Americans a year. You cannot get all that into your lead, so you must use general references rather than names as a way of reducing the length of your lead. Such a lead is called a blind lead.

This is Daniel Q. Haney's blind lead in the Associated Press story about the aspirin study:

An aspirin a day cuts in half the risk of strokes caused by abnormal heartbeats, devastating disruptions of blood flow to the brain that strike 75,000 Americans each year, a major new study concludes.

In this lead, the reader takes some things on faith and will wait until later in the story to learn more about the study and who conducted it.

For broadcast, the aspirin lead would be broken into shorter sentences and begin with the blind source:

> A major study today reports that aspirin can help reduce stroke. The study, published in *The New England Journal of Medicine,* found that an aspirin a day cuts in half the risk of strokes caused by abnormal heartbeats. Strokes occur when blood flow to the brain is disrupted. Affected are about 75,000 Americans a year.

A blind lead is one in which the main character or place in a story is identified generically rather than specifically. The usual practice, then, is to use the specific name in the second paragraph. A blind lead puts the emphasis not on the person but the result. Earlier, you saw these two leads:

> Richard A. Hodel, operator of Hodel Industries Inc., addressed the College Town Council last night about the lack of public knowledge and the high cost of Pilsdon County's proposed solid waste plan.

> A local recycler told the College Town Council that residents are paying too much for the county's recycling program and that private recyclers could save residents money.

The blind lead, on the right, puts the emphasis on what the person proposed rather than on him and describes him generically. The generic description is usually more useful to the reader, unless the person is well known.

Length of Lead

A good lead gets right to the point. A long lead discourages the reader because the point of the story is lost in the verbiage. Would you want to read this story?

The age-old problem of College Town parking intensified Tuesday night as Borough Council wrestled with a bigger issue of aesthetics vs. parking for 90 minutes before tabling the decision of whether to eliminate parking spaces for beautification purposes at the All's Quiet student apartment complex, 642 E. College Ave.

This writer was editorializing somewhat at the beginning of the story instead of telling the reader what happened. He had the right sense for alerting the listener but not for engaging the reader.

Here are the first two paragraphs of a story. The one on the left has too long a lead. The one on the right shows a version shortened by moving some information to the second paragraph.

Representatives of the Project Management Team last night said at the College Town Planning Commission's work session that the lack of enforcement and the weakness of current housing conversion laws have contributed to the deterioration of residential neighborhoods.

The representatives said the conversion of family homes to rental properties having three unrelated persons has led to property destruction, parking problems, noise and an exodus of families from the town's neighborhoods.

Representatives of the Project Management Team said last night that the lack of enforcement and the weakness of current housing conversion laws have contributed to the deterioration of residential neighborhoods.

The representatives told the Planning Commission at a work session that the conversion of family homes to rental properties having three unrelated persons has led to property destruction, parking problems, noise and an exodus of families from the town's neighborhoods.

The revised lead is eight words shorter than the original. The editor achieved that by moving some information to the second paragraph, information that he felt could be put off. A writer must decide what needs to be emphasized immediately and what can be deferred.

Dependent Clause Problems

A dependent clause is one that depends on the main clause for its meaning or context. Usually, it must appear somewhere in the middle or toward the end of a sentence; such placement is particularly important in a lead. Starting a story with a dependent clause is not normally a good idea because the dependent clause lacks context. The reader does not know what the clause modifies and therefore cannot grasp its significance. For example,

> *Defending allegations that the neighborhood action report "is trying to push students out of town,"* members of the neighborhood conservation action committee last night told the College Town Planning Commission the goal of the report is to preserve the family atmosphere of the neighborhoods.

That lead, because of its length, leaves everyone gasping, even without the dependent clause.

Even though the following lead is shorter, the dependent clause is still a problem because the reader has to wade through the time phrase without knowing to what it pertains:

> *For the first time in five years,* the Orange Grove United Way fund drive failed to reach its goal and the deadline will be extended two weeks, officials announced today.

Rewritten with the clause in its proper place, this lead works better:

> The Orange Grove United Way fund drive failed to reach its goal for the first time in five years, and the deadline will be extended two weeks, officials announced today.

Emphasis

Sometimes a writer picks the wrong verb for the main clause in a lead and thus subordinates the news. That is the case with this lead:

> Fire *broke out* in a College Town apartment this morning, killing three high school friends holding a party for a friend bound for the Air Force.

The main verb in any lead should also be the news verb, that is, convey the main action of the story. In this lead, the main action of the story is a fire *killing* three high school friends, not *breaking out*. The lead is improved by letting the main verb represent the action of the story:

> A fire in a College Town apartment this morning killed three high school friends holding a party for a friend bound for the Air Force.

One Issue per Lead

Similar to the lead with faulty emphasis is the lead that covers more than one issue. Such a lead is generally found in a story about a governmental meeting at which several items were voted on. For example:

> College Town City Council last night tabled the fair housing ordinance and authorized a study to examine alternatives for increasing parking.

Since the issues are not related, why yoke them? Instead, use the most interesting or pertinent issue from that meeting in the lead.

The Why Element

Putting unrelated issues into a lead deprives the writer of the opportunity to focus the reader's full attention on the main issue. A reporter can avoid this error simply by asking *why* before writing the lead. *Why* is often the missing element in news stories. Why did the City Council table the fair housing ordinance? Why did a town raise taxes? The reporter who asks this question and then answers it in writing will construct a better, more interesting story.

Figure 3.3 City council meeting. Copyright © Kenneth Martin/AMSTOCK.

Follow the Lead

The first paragraph of a news story is a promise to the reader. Subsequent paragraphs deliver on that promise. The first paragraph usually promises to tell the news—what happened in the last 24 hours. Subsequent paragraphs should fill out and further explain the action cited in the lead. Do not switch to another character or to a different topic, or take up history. Historical background can wait until at least the fifth paragraph. If the lead says people have been charged with a specific crime, the next paragraph ought to tell who they are.

If the lead says a fire badly damaged a car repair shop and destroyed some cars, the second paragraph should give a damage estimate. In the fire story presented in Chapter 2, the writer followed her lead:

> A quick-burning fire roared through the body and parts shop of D&M Chrysler Plymouth Inc. Sunday morning, destroying seven cars and reducing the concrete-block building to a blackened shell.
>
> Fire officials are estimating the loss to the business at $800,000. The owners of the dealership, Daniel and

Michael Faretta, had only $290,000 insurance on the
building and its contents, according to City Fire Chief
Reynold D. Santone.

In the following example the writer did not follow her lead
but detoured into the history of the story too soon. The controversy mentioned here had been going on for several months, and the newspaper had published several articles before this one, an account of the final
decision.

The great Spring Garden Township tree debate is
over—and the trees have lost.
Capping more than a year of discussion and controversy over the previously decided removal of hardwood
trees on Oakdale Drive, about 15 township residents
made a final attempt to save the trees at a township
meeting Wednesday night.
Several township officials and the developer of the
area where the trees will be removed told the residents
their efforts were too little and too late.
Widening the road as part of a 97-acre addition to
Wyndham Hills requires that more than 50 hardwood
trees be removed. Most of the oak trees on the street are
between 50 and 100 years old.

The first two paragraphs say "the trees have lost" and mention a
"township meeting Wednesday night." But details of the news—the final
decision—are lacking. Which governmental body met? Who were the
officials voting? How did each vote? Who were the protesting residents?
What did they say? This information did not appear until much later in the
story.
Although a summary of relevant past events can enhance a story
and even be essential for readers new to the story, this background should
be deferred to later paragraphs. The writer must first develop the news
lead.
The school board story examined earlier in the section "Backing
into Stories" also supplied history too soon—at least, too soon for a newspaper story rather than a broadcast. The tip-off is finding the phrase

"earlier this month" in the second paragraph, very close to the beginning of the story:

> The pros and cons of entering into a contract with a television company to provide daily newscasts in the district's classrooms were discussed at length by the Philipsburg-Osceola Area School board Monday night.
>
> *Earlier this month the board had considered a three-year contract with Whittle Communications Satellite Education Network of Nashville, Tenn.*
>
> Board members were in agreement with concern nationwide that today's public school students are not knowledgeable concerning daily news events.

To sum up, the leads of most newspaper stories convey recent news, and the stories should follow the leads by elaborating the news first and providing historical background farther down in the story.

Developing a Story

Some people argue that learning to write news stories is difficult because news stories are not "logical." They cite the inverted pyramid structure as evidence of illogical organization. Apart from the fact that this structure indeed makes sense to an editor who must lop off less important end paragraphs to fit stories into news holes, logic does play a part in newswriting if one keeps *purpose* in mind. Each newswriting rule has a purpose. If the writer understands this, writing will be easier.

Transition

Transition is both the glue that holds a story together and the bridge between unrelated issues in a story. Transition links sentences to each other and paragraphs to other paragraphs. Transition can be as simple as a repeated word or clause, or as complicated as a four- or five-paragraph anecdote. The longer the story, the more important transition becomes. Following is a two-paragraph story in which the repetition of one word glues the three sentences together:

> The chairman of the Orange Grove United Way fund drive announced today that the fund's deadline, originally set for today, will be extended two weeks in an attempt to reach its *goal*.
>
> The *goal* of $61,950 is short by approximately $2,000, according to H. W. Pearce. Pearce said this is the first time in five years the *goal* has not been met.

Here are two paragraphs that seem unrelated:

> The commission members agreed to evaluate such mixed zoning next year.
>
> "People like to have a place to get milk or bread two blocks away," commission member James B. Williams said, "but I'm not sure they want a place like that in their neighborhoods."

This is how the writer, in revising the story, linked the two paragraphs:

> The commission members agreed to evaluate such mixed zoning next year, *although one expressed skepticism about it.*
>
> "People like to have a place to get milk or bread two blocks away," commission member James B. Williams said, "but I'm not sure they want a place like that in their neighborhoods."

Now the quote makes sense in relation to the preceding paragraph.

A writer can signal a change in the topic with a short clause, as this student journalist did in an article about a speech on feminism:

> Pribram said that women in other societies play very different roles. U.S. society should stop using biology as an excuse for social discrimination, she said.
> *Turning to the subject of abortion,* Pribram said that biology threatens women's freedom. She said that groups supporting the outlawing of abortion argue that women's bodies have a "higher calling" and that women should not have the right to do what they want with their own body. Pribram argued that each woman's body should be a self-determined unit.

Single words such as *but* and *however* make for good transition, when what follows them contradicts or disagrees with what precedes them.

> In America, people should be able to choose their sexual life, *but* that is not the case, Rhonda Rivera, a specialist in gay and lesbian law, said.

Transition helps the reader and the good writer uses transition in that spirit.

Emphasis in a Sentence

Sentences can be divided into three parts—a beginning, a middle and an end. In print, the most important information—or the information worth emphasizing—should appear either at the beginning of the sentence or at the end. Generally, use the middle of the sentence for the attribution tag or for subordinate information. Use the beginning and end to highlight the important information in the sentence.

Sentence emphasis in broadcast follows a different pattern. Generally, sentences written for broadcast end with emphasis. The beginning of a broadcast sentence is used to warm up the listener.

Sentence and Paragraph Length

Sentence length should average about 17 words. Some people write sentences that go on forever. They write sentences as though they were drowning and coming up for air occasionally before plunging on to a new fact. Fortunately, writing does not have to be like drowning. Journalists should write short sentences. Each sentence should convey at most one or two facts.

Problem sentences are usually too long. But problem paragraphs are commonly too long or too short. If a writer comes to newswriting from a class in English composition, he or she has a tendency to write long paragraphs. Newspaper paragraphs tend to be short because the design editor wants some white space on the page. *Short* has unfortunately been translated to mean "one sentence." But a one-sentence paragraph can be as bad as an overlong one. A newspaper paragraph should be a collection of related sentences; when the sentences are not related, a one-sentence paragraph is legitimate. Remember, though, that ideas need paragraphs to be developed, so limit your use of one-sentence paragraphs.

Be Specific

In the changing news environment, the journalist comes across many new words daily and should be prepared to explain what they mean. Daniel Q. Haney of the Associated Press did not hesitate to explain that *strokes* are "devastating disruptions of blood flow to the brain" (see "Blind Leads" section). What is a *right-of-way*? What does an *arborist* do?

Similarly, budget stories cry out for specifics: How big is the budget? What is the tax increase, if any? What is the address of a store cited for health violations? The journalist should look it up. Better still, go to the store in person and check. Some journalists are very good at using revealing quotations and laying out the issues but not so good at supplying the important numbers and other details that go with the quotations and the issues.

Direct Quotations

Some believe that direct quotations raise the interest level of a news story or indicate authoritative sources. The more direct quotations, the merrier, they say. Others believe in using as few direct quotations as possible, and only when they're really good. (An exception would be dialogue, discussed in Chapter 10.) In their haste to use direct quotations, some writers abuse them.

One problem is repetition. First the writer paraphrases, then gives the same material in quotation marks:

> Such was the case for the Steelers, who lost their first WPIAL Section 2 game to visiting New Castle, 46-39, mostly *because they could not put the ball in the basket* and may even have had problems hitting the broad side of a barn.
> "We just did not put the ball in the hoop," said exasperated Steeler head coach Frank Sincek.

We know, coach. The writer just told us.

Another abuse of direct quotations arises when the quotation by itself insufficiently conveys meaning and the writer must insert information to make the meaning clear. Here is an example of the problem:

> "They (the Soviet solders) beat them (the patients) with their (the soldiers') fists," a duty nurse said.

When a writer needs parenthetical matter[4] to explain a quotation, the writer should paraphrase. In this particular example, the writer added the explanatory information outside the quotation marks:

> "They beat them with their fists," a duty nurse said *of the Soviet soldiers who broke into the hospital.*

(*Them* is clear from the paragraph preceding the quotation.)

In print, wherever possible, bury the attribution tag. Attribution tags can appear in three places: at the beginning of a direct or indirect quotation, in the middle, or at the end. Since the beginning and end of sentences are the strongest parts of the sentence, the best place to put the attribution tag is in the middle at a natural break. This usually works in sentences with clauses or in compound sentences. For example:

> "Except for a few minor items," Kurtz said, "the contractors feel we can move in on schedule."

When a direct quotation comprises two sentences, bury the attribution tag between the sentences.

> "I think that's a good idea," Nichols said. "We need more good ideas."

Broadcast writers lead into a direct quotation by putting the attribution tag at the beginning of a sentence. That alerts the listener.

Generally, do not invert attribution tags. The standard structure of English sentences is subject-verb. Thus, when a writer inverts the order to verb-subject, the reader is disconcerted. For example, write *Smith said* not *said Smith*.

Subsumption

All writing should be to the point. Sentences that meander will lose the attention of readers and listeners. To write concisely, use the best verb. The best verb is the one that subsumes all other verbs in a particular action. For instance, compare the verbs in the first paragraph with the verb in the rewrite shown after it:

> Winifred I. Jones *appeared* in court as a character witness for T.F. William. She *testified* that when he was a student in her Latin class, he was a model student.

> Winifred I. Jones, a character witness, *testified* that
> T.F. Williams was a model student in her Latin class.

If she testified, she had to have appeared. *Testified* subsumes *appeared*.

Strong Verbs

Always try to use strong verbs. Strong verbs denote action. The weakest verb is *is*. It does not denote action the way other verbs do.

Clichés

Clichés are words and phrases that have been used so frequently that they have become outdated or meaningless. Calling a football a "pigskin" and a football field a "gridiron" are but two of many examples. Look at clichés as second-hand prose. Do not use them. Use original language. Be unique.

Beginning newswriters need to find their own approaches to writing stories. Most teachers agree that devoting a lot of time to writing a good lead is a help in writing a good story. Eventually, journalists in all fields must write on deadline, and anything they can do to prepare themselves is of benefit.

Review Questions

What sort of a questions might a journalist ask to help herself get started writing a story?

What are some of the problem leads? Explain the problems.

What does "backing into a story" mean? What can a writer do to avoid it?

What is a "blind lead"?

What is transition, and who is responsible for making sure it appears in a story?

Discuss some of the problems that can occur with direct quotations.

How does a writer write to the point?

VOLUME 239 • NUMBER 166
58 pages
35 cents

The Boston Globe

SATURDAY, JUNE 15, 1991

SOX IN—DRYER
Saturday: *Partly sunny, high 80s*
Sunday: *Ditto*
High tide: *1:53 a.m., 2:25 p.m.*
Full report: *Page 24*

$2.5m pledged to put class through college

By Phyllis Coons
GLOBE STAFF

CAMBRIDGE – In the largest gift of its kind in Massachusetts, a Connecticut couple yesterday pledged $2.5 million to put 67 East Cambridge second graders through college.

The gift to the entire second-grade class of the Harrington School will provide motivational counseling, tutoring, mentoring and a summer school program through the next 10 years as well as free tuition for four years of college or vocational school.

Yesterday, as parents and teachers who had gathered at the school cried with joy, the future members of the class of 2001 talked all at once. "It's beyond the

whole world," said one. "Does college come after high school?" another asked.

Luis Maisonet thumped his friend John Braga on the back and said: "You know what this means? We get to go to college for free." Stephen Ren chimed in, saying he might become an engineer or a dentist, "maybe both."

George and Diane Weiss of Hartford, who have provided similar opportunities to children in Philadelphia and Hartford through their Say Yes to Education Foundation, chose to extend the program to Cambridge because of ties to the area.

George Weiss, a stockbroker, is a graduate of Brookline High School, and his wife earned a degree in education from Lesley College, which will run the

program here.

"It was always in our minds that we would work with Margaret McKenna as president of Lesley," said Diane Weiss. "It was just a question of when."

The Harrington School was chosen because many of the children come from disadvantaged homes and are at risk of failing, according to Albert H. Giroux Jr., a spokesman for the Cambridge schools. About 41 percent of the school's pupils come from lower-income families, 64 percent qualify for reduced-price or free lunches, 20 percent are in bilingual and English-as-a-second-language programs, and 25 percent are in special education.

"We have a special gift for you, a free college education."

GIFT, Page 20

Senate marathon yields a budget

Proposal totals $12.98b, toes no-new-taxes line

By Scot Lehigh and Peter J. Howe
GLOBE STAFF

After a 25½-hour session, the Senate yesterday passed a $12.98 billion budget that hews to Gov. Weld's adamant stand against any new taxes, but does not include a package of tax incentives for businesses that the administration and Senate Republicans had backed.

During the marathon debate, which left some senators wandering like zombies in search of coffee and others dozing at their desks, the Senate added only $39 million to the budget's bottom line, an amount the Senate Ways and Means Committee chairwoman, Patricia McGovern, said was the smallest addition in recent memory.

Senators also approved amendments to create a mandatory workfare program for welfare recipients and a 90-day residency requirement for welfare benefits. Other amendments struck out a portion of the Senate budget that would have allowed Sunday liquor sales and retail store openings on Memorial Day, July Fourth and Labor Da—

But the Democratic leadership narrowly turned away an attempt to add an 8 cent-per-gallon milk fee that would have aided dairy farmers, and more harshly rejected an amendment to add the package of business tax credits to the budget.

Attempts to raise revenues died with more of a whimper than a bang, as no roll-call vote was taken on an amendment to delay an income tax reduction, which was the only revenue-raising measure thought to have any chance of passage.

BUDGET, Page 23

7,200 at Digital face new layoffs

By Lawrence Edelman
GLOBE STAFF

With no upturn in its business in sight, computer giant Digital Equipment Corp. of Maynard said yesterday it will begin a new round of layoffs that could cut its work force by roughly 7,200, or 4 percent, in the next 12 months.

Digital, Massachusetts' second-largest employer, said the specific number and timing of layoffs had not been decided and would depend on whether sales rebound in the fiscal year that begins June 30. It could not say how many of its 29,000 Bay State employees may lose their jobs.

"There will be further work force reductions," said Dallas Kirk, Digital's director of public relations. If business conditions do not improve, the cuts "could be roughly the same size" as the 7,200 jobs Digital will have eliminated in the fiscal year that ends June 29, Kirk said.

DIGITAL, Page 17

Gyndie Jeremiah (left) and Jean Clemons cradle samples of their fledgling company's rag dolls, Raggs and Patches, which are gaining national attention.
GLOBE STAFF PHOTO / BARRY CHIN

Stitching up an identity

Dorchester mother-daughter team struggle to mass market their black rag dolls

By Peter S. Canellos
GLOBE STAFF

Jean Clemons of Dorchester had heard all about the studies that showed black children choosing white dolls over those their own color, and they made her angry.

She, after all, had cherished her own black rag doll, made by her mother, more than any other plaything during her Alabama childhood. And Clemons had made a black rag doll for her own daughter, Cyndie Jeremiah.

So when Jeremiah was pregnant for the first time two years ago, and visited 20 stores in a vain attempt to find a black rag doll to decorate the baby's room, she and

her mother decided to join with other family members to pool $50,000 and produce Raggs and Patches, which they say are the first widely produced black cousins to Raggedy Ann and Andy.

Now, as the dolls gain national attention through the new Spike Lee movie, "Jungle Fever," Clemons and Jeremiah are gearing up to bring their products – Raggs and Patches, along with planned Asian and Hispanic dolls, priced at $30 and up – to the mass marketplace.

Their task is daunting. Like many businesses trying to get established during a recession, they have been unable to obtain financing from a number of Boston banks. They have, however, been designated to receive technical and financial assistance from a new city program to

help small businesses and are hoping the city will help them obtain bank financing.

But their effort to put black, Asian and Hispanic creations into the doll carriages of America is motivated as much by a desire to promote equality as by a desire to make money.

As they see it, the studies of black children choosing white dolls, which were first performed in the 1960s and repeated in succeeding decades, underscore the importance of presenting black images in the marketplace and in the media.

"I was really upset to hear of the study, that black children thought white dolls were prettier," Clemons

DOLLS, Page 28

Kerry breaks party ranks to back China trade status

By John Aloysius Farrell
GLOBE STAFF

WASHINGTON – Sen. John Kerry said yesterday that he is breaking party ranks to support most-favored-nation trade status for China because he fears that a bill with tough restrictions proposed by Senate Democratic leaders could backfire and hurt the cause of Chinese reform.

The Massachusetts Democrat criticized President Bush's no-strings approach to China as unsatisfactory, but said he hoped to help forge a compromise.

If he and a handful of other Democrats, who were called to the White House last week for talks, can persuade Bush to soften his stance, they could defuse what is shaping up as a fierce partisan battle.

KERRY, Page 17

SEN. JOHN KERRY
"Looking for a middle course"

US regulators to weigh selling troubled N.H. banks

By Mitchell Zuckoff
and Peter G. Gosselin
GLOBE STAFF

In a move that demonstrates the depths of New England's banking troubles, federal regulators have called a meeting for next week to begin the process of selling off five of New Hampshire's biggest banks.

The meeting, scheduled for Mon-

day in Boston, appears to dim New Hampshire officials' hopes that the institutions could be propped up by an innovative mix of mergers, public assistance and private investment.

Most New Hampshire bank customers have little to worry about. Whether the banks are sold or propped up, services would not be disrupted, and customers' money is protected up to $100,000 per account

by federal deposit insurance.

But the meeting signals the likely arrival in New Hampshire of the bank closures and sales that have plagued Massachusetts and other New England states, capped by the January failure of Bank of New England.

It also appears to be a blow to efforts by Gov. Judd Gregg and the

BANKS, Page 20

Volcano stirs Filipino foes of US bases

By William Branigin
WASHINGTON POST

MANILA – Six new eruptions of Mount Pinatubo were recorded yesterday, including the strongest to date, as opponents of US military bases here sought to capitalize on fears that the volcanic eruption somehow could trigger nuclear weapons allegedly stored at the evacuated Clark Air Base.

The Philippine Institute of Volcanology and Seismology said the most violent eruption since Pinatubo came back to life this week was a blast at 3:20 p.m. that sent a column of ash more than 18½ miles into the air.

Early today, five more explosions shook the mountain, showering ash over a wide area.

The US Embassy, insisting yesterday that the nuclear fears are

VOLCANO, Page 17

Inside

REAL ESTATE: Desperate homeowners find an out

■ Penobscot's jumping again: Salmon symbolize the remarkable resurrection of a Maine river. Sports, Page 29.

■ Fenway fun: Clemens wins his ninth as Red Sox beat Angels, 9-4. Sports, Page 29.

■ Dame Peggy dead: Peggy Ashcroft (above), grande dame of British stage and screens around the world, has died at the age of 83. Appreciation by Kevin Kelly, Page 6; Obituary, Page 26.

FEATURES		CLASSIFIED	
Ask The Globe	16	Classified	37-48,58
Business	13	Autos	45
Comics	58,57	Help Wanted	45
Deaths	26,27	Real Estate	37
Editorials	18	Apartments	42
Horoscope	41	Comm'l/Ind'l	41
Living/Arts	6	Market Basket	47
Lottery	25	Yachts/Boats	31
Sports	29	Learning	28
TV/Radio	55		

© Globe Newspaper Co.

24642

0 947725

Figure 3.4 Page One of The Boston Globe, *June 15, 1991. Reprinted courtesy of* The Boston Globe.

Endnotes

1. Paul Salsini, "Reflections on the Richness of Reporting." From *The Coaches' Corner* 3, no. 1 (March 1988), 4–5. Reprinted by permission.
2. Carole Rich, "Tips for Finding Your Lead," *The Coaches' Corner* 4, no. 3 (September 1989), 9.
3. Beverly Pitts, "Model Provides Description of News Writing Process," *Journalism Educator,* 43, no. 1 (Spring 1989), 12–19, 59.
4. Brackets are the correct device for inserts in direct quotations, but according to *The Associated Press Stylebook* (1989): "They cannot be transmitted over newswires. Use parentheses. . . ."

Chapter 4

Language Skills

Chapter Objectives

In this chapter you will learn about sentence types and the problems that can arise within sentences. You will explore verb tenses and see how some stories use other than the past tense. You will also explore modification and punctuation.

Introduction

Language skills enable writers to build stories. Just as a good carpenter would not use a hammer to put in a screw, a good writer would not defy language conventions. Readers and listeners have certain expectations about language, even though they do not always follow the formal conventions of the language themselves. Unconventional writing usually means ineffective communication to a mass audience.

This chapter highlights some of the typical language skills beginning journalists need to understand. The chapter covers sentences, nouns, pronouns and verbs; modification problems and punctuation.

Sentences

Sentences and paragraphs should be seen as functional units of writing. Sentences convey a thought or describe an action; when combined with related sentences, they compose paragraphs. Generally, paragraphs stick to one topic. A change in topic is a signal to start a new paragraph, with the appropriate transition heralding the change.

Journalists have at their disposal four sentence types: simple, compound, complex, and compound-complex. A story built with a variety of sentence structures reads better than a story written using only one structure.

Simple

A simple sentence consists of subject and predicate. It usually expresses one idea or action. The preceding two sentences are simple sentences. Just because a sentence is simple does not mean it has to be short. Structure, not length, determines sentence type. Here is a simple sentence, the lead of a United Press International story. The predicate is italicized.

> Embattled St. Paul Fire Chief Steve Conroy *has received the support of his colleagues.*

Compound

A compound sentence consists of two related sentences joined by a conjunction. These *coordinating conjunctions* include *and, or, not, while, but, yet.* The following sentence from a United Press International story is a compound sentence.

> Lottery officials paid out a $1,000 winner within 25 minutes of the opening of the games,
>
> *and*
>
> officials said a $5,000 winner was reported in northern Minnesota in Warroad.

Actually, the subject of each sentence within the compound sentence is the same, *officials,* but the verbs are different. The following, from the same story, is another compound sentence, this one a direct quotation from a man who won $5,000 in the Minnesota State Lottery.

> "I opened them (the tickets) up
>
> *and*
>
> I could not believe it."

Complex

A complex sentence describes a major action and a subordinate action. A complex sentence enables a journalist to explain, clarify and qualify ideas within a story. This is a complex sentence broken apart to show the main sentence and the qualification:

> (*main*) Bruce Clarkson, 38, Brooklyn Park, bought one $1 ticket
>
> (*subordinate*)   when he stopped in a convenience store to buy pop.

The main clause by itself merely reports that Clarkson bought one ticket. The writer wanted to tell more about the purchase and did so in a subordinate clause. (A couple of sentences later he also revealed that Clarkson's $1 ticket won him $2.)

Here is another complex sentence, which contains a compound predicate in the subordinate clause:

> (*main*)   The lottery players included four women
>
> (*subordinate*)   who slipped out of a state government office near the State Capitol
>
> *and*
>
> bought several tickets, including two tickets for their boss.

Another example of a complex sentence follows. In this case, the subordinate clause begins the sentence, because the speaker wanted to limit the main point of his sentence.

> "If we can," Hutchinson said,
> "let's take the trip in the other direction."

Compound-Complex

As you can guess, a compound-complex sentence combines elements of compound and complex sentences. The compound aspect consists of two equal sentences joined by a conjunction. One or both of these sentences contain a subordinate clause, providing the complex aspect. Here is one such sentence from the *Atlanta Constitution*:

> (*main*)   Support for both programs was part of his campaign,
>
> *and*
>
> (*subordinate*)   although his position has not changed on these issues,
>
> (*main*)   Mr. Bush said he is not sure about the timing.

Such sentences tend to be long and are therefore infrequently used in written or oral news stories.

Parallel Construction

Sentence variety brings with it the possibility of unparallel construction within sentences. Sentences should be constructed much the way steps are constructed, with each riser the same as the one before and the one ahead. That way, the walker adjusts to one height and then proceeds up or down the steps with ease. If one step were nine inches high and the next six and the next eleven, the walker might stumble. Sentences that violate parallel construction can trip the reader.

Covering a speech on marital relations, a journalist wrote this sentence:

> Some unfair tactics are *humiliation* of a partner, *making* a partner feel guilty and *ignoring* a partner.

The italicized words should represent the same part of speech, but in this example the first one is a noun and the other two are verbals. This sentence can be repaired by changing the noun into a verbal (and dropping the preposition *of*), easier than converting the two verbals to nouns:

> Some unfair tactics are *humiliating* a partner, *making* a partner feel guilty and *ignoring* a partner.

The journalist needs to remember the sentence's beginning structure and, as long as it is a good one, follow it through to the end of the sentence. The writer of this sentence did not:

> The library director told the board that since January there has been an 11 percent increase in fiction borrowing, a 23 percent increase in circulation of children's books, and compact disc borrowing has increased by 21 percent.

What throws off the sentence is everything after *and*. The writer did not maintain parallel construction. Parallel, this is a better structure:

> The library director told the board that since January there has been an 11 percent increase in fiction borrowing, a 23 percent increase in the circulation of children's books, and a 21 percent increase in compact disc borrowing.

Agreement

The reader can also stumble when nouns and verbs or nouns and pronouns do not agree. Journalists must be alert for these problems so that they can avoid them or fix them during the revision process.

Nouns and Verbs

The noun attached to a verb is called the "subject," and the verb in a sentence must agree with the subject in both person and number. That's not as daunting as it sounds, since most verbs in the present tense have only two forms, one of which appears in five of the six persons. Here is a breakdown (also called conjugation) of the verb *to see*:

Person	Singular	Plural
First	I see	We see
Second	You see	You see
Third	He/she/it sees	They see

Only in the third-person singular does the verb change, adding an *s*. So getting the verb form right is a fairly easy thing to do in English. Sometimes, however, there is uncertainty about exactly what is the subject of a verb. Here are some common problem areas.

When a compound subject is connected by *neither-nor* or *either-or*, the noun closest to the verb determines agreement. In this example, that noun is plural:

> Neither the editor nor the two assistant editors know anything about page design.

When a collective noun stands for a unit, it takes a singular verb. When considered as individuals, it takes a plural verb.

> The jury *is* out.

> The jury *were* divided on the verdict.

Plural numbers treated as a unit take a singular verb:

> Fifty dollars is a lot of money to lose in a nickel-dime
> game of poker.

When using *number of,* determine if the stress is on *number* or on the noun following *of.* That reveals which noun affects the verb.

> The *number* of people in a football stadium on a Satur-
> day afternoon *is* usually high.
>
> A number of *people* in my neighborhood *are* opposed
> to the rezoning of the vacant lot.

Note that when the sentence begins with the definite article, *the,* the stress is on *number.* The indefinite article *a* signals a different stress.

Some words ending in *s* are not really plural and take a singular verb. They include *mathematics, semantics, phonetics, aesthetics.* Some, such as *acoustics,* go either way. Check the dictionary.

Also be alert for plural proper nouns that are really singular:

> Warner Brothers is a film studio.

And don't forget plural nouns from foreign languages, such as *criteria, data,* and *media,* that do not signify the plural by adding *s.* Usage gradually evolves in such cases, and often these nouns co-exist in English in singular and plural forms. Acceptance varies, however. Of the three nouns just mentioned, *data* is the most well established (though not unanimously) in both forms and, except in certain specialized fields, *media* the least so. The use of *media* as a singular noun is substandard in writing. Use *media* as a plural. *Medium* is the singular.

> The news media *are* not a monolith.

If you remember this example, you will remember to use *media* as a plural noun.

Nouns and Pronouns

Just as subjects and verbs must agree, so must related nouns and pronouns. It stands to reason that if a pronoun is taking the place of a noun, it must agree with that noun in person and number:

> *Dr. Jane Kerschner* called on the Congress to sup-
> port additional funding for AIDS research. *She* said
> the country would never find a cure at current funding
> levels.

The pronoun that begins the second sentence refers to the person in the first sentence. Since that speaker is third-person singular and female, the pronoun must agree. And it does.

Confusion arises when a writer erroneously uses a plural pronoun to refer to a singular noun. As you read the following example, keep in mind that a pronoun usually adheres to the closest noun in agreement. So even though the writer of the following example was not referring to *years,* that was the result.

> The United Way extended *its* annual drive today be-
> cause *it* failed to reach its goal of $61,950, according to
> chairman H.W. Pearce.
> This was the first time in five years that *they* failed to
> reach *their* total, Pearce said yesterday.

The writer really wanted to refer to *United Way* and did so correctly in the lead when he used *its.* But in the second paragraph, he linked the pronoun to the closest noun in agreement, *years,* and used *they* and *their.* Or perhaps he was thinking of Pearce and his United Way colleagues as individuals who failed to reach their fund-raising goal. In any case, the pronouns in the two paragraphs should match. Obviously, the reader will figure out what's going on, but good writing requires that the reader not be left to guess.

Journalists need to be extra alert in using pronouns because of the large number of attribution tags in most news stories and the desire for variety. Rather than repeat someone's name, a journalist will use the appropriate pronoun. Remember, when changing speakers, to make the change clear to the reader so that subsequent pronoun use will be clear.

Verbs

The key word in any sentence is the verb. The verb denotes the action of the sentence, an action that interests readers. Beginning journalists struggling with the lead on their stories are advised to find the verb that tells the story best and go on from there. The writer who focuses on the key verb of a news event will not only write good stories but be a good journalist too.

Tense

Many news stories are written in the past tense because most news has already occurred. Here is an example:

> With a four-piece Dixieland band playing and public television commentator Hodding Carter III marching along, about 250 demonstrators *rallied* Saturday outside The Atlanta Journal-Constitution building to protest the papers' acceptance of Editor Bill Kovach's resignation nine days ago.

Some news stories appear in the present tense, usually referred to as the "historical present." A common use of the present tense occurs when a journalist is citing a study. Since the study will say the same thing 24 hours later and even months later, the journalist uses the present tense both in the attribution tag and in the main verbs:

> U.S. manufacturers *are* optimistic about 1990 profits despite mixed views on the economy, *says* a survey by a Pittsburgh accounting firm.

Subsequent references to the survey appear in the present tense along the lines of the usage in the lead.

The present tense is sometimes used to describe future events. Here are the early paragraphs of a story about an upcoming event. Note that the writer mixes the future and present tenses.

> PHILADELPHIA (UPI)—As if Benjamin Franklin has not been studied, analyzed, written about, honored and quoted enough.
>
> This week some of the world's leading Franklin scholars *will spend* three days discussing their latest research on Franklin's life and achievements.
>
> The symposium, which *begins* April 17, *includes* lectures by 27 specialists in 18th century American literature, science, colonial history and art history. Lectures by Franklin biographers and editors *will take* place at several sites in Philadelphia and Delaware.
>
> Papers presented at the symposium *will be published* later in two volumes.

Sequence of Tenses

Journalistic writing deviates from more formal English in several ways. One of the more noticeable deviations occurs with the sequence of tenses.

The formal rule on sequence of tenses states that when a direct quotation is paraphrased, verbs are changed one degree, that is, from present to past. Journalists live by the paraphrase, and if they were to follow this rule, they would create inaccurate news stories, for by shifting tense, the journalist would be changing facts. Consider this example:

> "I'm not happy with the settlement. I feel they owe me more," the plaintiff said.

Following the rule on sequence of tenses would result in this paraphrase:

> The plaintiff said he *was* not happy with the settle-
> ment. He said he felt the company *owed* him more.

The paraphrased sentences suggest that the plaintiff is no longer unhappy and that the company does not now owe him more. To avoid the confusion, the writer should ignore the sequence–of–tenses rule:

> The plaintiff said he *is* not happy with the settlement.
> He said he feels the company *owes* him more.

Voice

Although verbs have two voices, active and passive, journalists should concentrate on using the active voice most of the time. Compare information conveyed in both voices.

> (*active*) California's strongest earthquake since the World Series temblor *triggered* rock slides, *broke* windows and *collapsed* a warehouse wall Wednesday.

> (*passive*) Rock slides *were triggered,* windows *were broken* and a warehouse wall *was collapsed* Wednesday in California's strongest earthquake since the World Series temblor.

The passive sentence plods along and hides the subject of the sentence until the middle. Thus, the reader does not learn until late in the sentence that part of California suffered another earthquake. This makes the sentence less effective and even confusing. But in the active sentence, the actor appears up front and the reader knows what is linked to the verb. Given that the passive voice not only hides the actor but enables a writer to drop the actor, it is amazing that journalists use as many passive voice verbs as they do.

After all, readers want to know *who* did something as well as *what* was done, and they want it stated clearly.

Strong Verbs

With so much emphasis placed on the verb, it stands to reason that the verb must be strong. Verbs that denote action are preferred to those that do not. One verb overused in newswriting is any form of *to be*. This verb is appropriate when it is linking a subject and its complement, which is the case here. But don't use it when a strong verb could be substituted. For example:

> Williams *is* to add three new aides to her congressional staff, a spokesperson said.

> Williams *plans* to add three new aides to her congressional staff, a spokesperson said.

The second sentence is better because of the strong verb.

Modification

The English language provides its users with a variety of ways of using words. Variety comes about through modification. Thus, we might have *cars,* which takes in every car in the world. But we can limit the meaning of the word by specifying *U.S. cars* or *red cars* or *cars built in Detroit.* All writers need to know how modification works, for if it is misused, the message is fogged. Fortunately, modification rules can be summed up in one principle: To be most effective, modifying words and phrases must appear as close as possible, and preferably next to, the word being modified.

Misplacement

Although the reader can usually divine the meaning of a sentence in which modification has been misplaced, the advice given earlier applies here:

Good writing does not require the reader to supply the meaning. So while the meaning of this miscast sentence is apparent, it still clunks and impedes understanding.

> The Pilsdon City Council Tuesday night tabled a recommendation to reduce parking at the Gateway Apartment Project, 642 E. University Drive, *in favor of more landscaping*.

The writer was not thinking carefully when she wrote the lead, nor was she paying attention during the revision process. Had she been, she would have realized that she had not made clear the trade-off of parking for landscaping, and she would have revised this way:

> The Pilsdon City Council Tuesday night tabled a recommendation to reduce parking *in favor of more landscaping* at the Gateway Apartment Project, 642 E. University Drive.

Here is another example of the problem, from a sign in the restroom of a doctor's office:[1]

> You may need a urine specimen for your appointment. Please check before emptying your bladder at the front desk.

To avoid indecent exposure and restore privacy:

> Please check at the front desk before emptying your bladder.

Another common modification problem is called a dangling modifier. In this circumstance, the modifier is not next to the word modified. Usually, what is being modified is the subject of the sentence. In this example, the problem occurs in the second sentence:

> Additionally, Hill Financial of Montgomery County lost $505 million last year. *After being declared insolvent,* Meridian Bancorp of Reading bought it last October.

What was declared insolvent? Was it Meridian Bancorp. Probably not, since in normal circumstances insolvent companies do not buy other companies. In this instance, a little rewriting rather than just moving the modifier will clarify the writer's intention:

> Additionally, Hill Financial of Montgomery County lost $505 million last year. *After being declared insolvent,* it was sold to Meridian Bancorp of Reading last October.

Other Faults

Journalists should know the difference between the articles *a* and *the*. *A* is an indefinite article and usually appears in a first reference to something. *The* is a definite article; it refers to something specific, something known, something mentioned earlier. The usual approach is to use *the* when referring to something already introduced. Thus, on first reference you would use *a proposal* and on subsequent references *the proposal*.

Generally, avoid possessive modifiers in first references. Here is an example:

> The Pilsdon City Council raised real estate and occupation taxes at *last night's* meeting.

Possessive modification suggests that a previous reference has appeared earlier in the story. Reading the preceding example, a reader might wonder on exactly which night of the week the meeting had taken place. Also, a possessive modifier usually works best when you are differentiating between two similar things, such as *last night's meeting* and *last week's meeting*. In such a case, both meetings would first be introduced and only then would a possessive modifier be used.

Types of Clauses

Clauses are among the important modifiers available to writers. All clauses are either *essential* or *non-essential*. An essential clause is needed to complete the meaning of a sentence. A non-essential clause can be dropped without doing serious damage to the meaning of the sentence. A non-essential clause is usually additional amplification and is always set off by commas. But it is the function, not the punctuation, that makes a clause non-essential.

> (*essential*)   A group *that supports state Sen. Jim Ramstad* started a committee Monday to encourage him to run for Congress in Minnesota's 3rd District.

> (*non-essential*)   Sundeen, *a retired Burlington Northern depot agent who turned 64 Monday,* said he got the $5,000 winner in about the middle of the $20 worth of tickets.

Here are the first sentences without their clauses:

> A group started a committee Monday to encourage him to run for Congress in Minnesota's 3rd District.

> Sundeen said he got the $5,000 winner in about the middle of the $20 worth of tickets.

The identification of the group urging someone to run for Congress is essential. But it does not matter if Sundeen is retired and from what; that has nothing to do with where he found his winning lottery ticket.

Under the rubric of essential/non-essential, English grammar offers a variety of clauses.

A *relative clause* shows a relation and is introduced by a relative pronoun, such as *who, which, what, that.* Here are examples of essential and non-essential relative clauses:

> (*non-essential*) "Sales are exceeding our expectations," said George Andersen, *who heads the Minnesota State Lottery.*

> (*essential*) The lottery players included four women *who slipped out of a state government office near the State Capitol and bought several tickets, including two tickets for their boss.*

Adverbial clauses modify verbs, verbals and adjectives. This adverbial clause modifies the verb *opened*:

> The 3rd District seat opened *when Republican Rep. Bill Frenzel announced he would not seek reelection.*

Another modifier is the *verb phrase,* which begins with a verbal:

> "Each day that our temperatures rise into the 60s or 70s with high wind conditions and low humidity will be dangerous until significant greening occurs," the governor said in a statement *prepared yesterday but not released until this morning.*

No matter what their labels, modifiers function best when set as close as possible to the word or phrase they modify. That is the major principle of modification.

Punctuation

Punctuation, far from being something invented by ninth-grade English teachers to harass pupils, is really a set of symbols that define the relations between words. Punctuation helps journalists make their meaning clear.

Comma

The most abused of the punctuation marks is the comma. Usually the problem is one of omission. Writers seldom forget the period that ends a sentence, and if they have misused an apostrophe, it is because they have used one where it was not necessary. But the comma suffers from not being used when it is needed.

One underused but necessary comma is the comma in apposition. Writers remember the first comma but forget the second. If they remembered that commas usually appear in pairs, they would not have the problem. Here is an *Atlanta Constitution* sentence with two phrases in apposition. Note the correct use of the commas around the phrases.

> Arnold Rosenfeld, *editor of the Austin (Texas) American-Statesman,* has been appointed editor of The Atlanta Journal-Constitution, Jay Smith, *publisher,* announced Tuesday.

A similar case is when a writer uses a long title as the subject of a sentence and puts a name in apposition. The idea of using a title instead of a name as the subject of a sentence has journalistic merit, since the reader may not recognize the name but understands the title. This is correctly punctuated:

> The superintendent of Valley Stream Schools, Mary F. Picciano, announced today . . .

In a different context, someone's title might function as a modifier to the person's name. In that case, no commas.

> Defense Secretary Dick Cheney revealed today . . .

Attribution tags are separated from direct and indirect quotations by a comma or, depending on placement, commas. These examples show the correct punctuation:

"Bill Kovach will grace the Nieman program, as he has and will continue to grace journalism," *Nieman curator Howard Simons said in a statement.* "We are lucky, pleased and proud to have him."

Nieman curator Howard Simons said in a statement, "Bill Kovach will grace the Nieman program, as he has and will continue to grace journalism. We are lucky, pleased and proud to have him."

"Bill Kovach will grace the Nieman program, as he has and will continue to grace journalism. We are lucky, pleased and proud to have him," *Nieman curator Howard Simons said in a statement.*

Another candidate for city manager, *the mayor said,* might have different credentials but not fit the city's current needs.

Boschwitz raised $1,809,589 from private contributors in 1989 of which 74.5 percent came from nonresidents, *according to figures from the Federal Election Commission that were published in the New York Times Monday.*

According to figures from the Federal Election Commission that were published in the New York Times Monday, Boschwitz raised $1,809,589 from private contributors in 1989 of which 74.5 percent came from nonresidents.

Non-essential clauses, which were discussed earlier in this chapter, are set off by commas. The preceding sentence is an example.

Commas, by the way, always go inside quotation marks in news copy.

Semicolon

The semicolon is seldom overused; like the comma, it suffers because it is seldom used when it should be. The semicolon replaces the coordinating conjunction in a compound sentence. Since compound sentences can be long, journalists seldom use them, which might explain the underuse of the semicolon in newswriting. For those rare times when a compound sentence appears in news copy, here is the correct use of the semicolon.

> "Homelessness isn't the problem," Quinn said; "what causes it is the problem."

Hyphen

The hyphen connects words to create compound modifiers:

> During the season Broten became the North Stars' *all-time* leading scorer.

> The *19-year-old* Modano is a candidate for the Calder Trophy that goes to the NHL's top rookie.

> Bellows had his best season, leading all NHL left wings with 55 goals and finishing second in points with a *career-high* 99 points.

The hyphen is used in broadcast copy between letters when the letters are to be read individually. Hyphens are also used in various number combinations and number-letter combinations. These examples come from an Associated Press broadcast wire:

> "Dark Shadows" was a popular daytime series several years ago on *A-B-C*. The new prime-time series will be on *N-B-C*.

> The *N-R-C* staff has proposed that *G-P-U* Nuclear Corporation be assessed a *50-thousand* dollar fine.

> Chief journalist Rich Beth says the *A-Four* Skyhawk attack jet crashed just off the base near the end of the runway about 10:45 a.m.

> Nineteen-year-old Mike Messick of Middletown won the title yesterday for his *12-hundred-85* pound steer, named Simon.

Dash

The dash sets off a phrase or word the writer wants emphasized.

> Each year the United States sends Israel about $3 billion in military and other support—about $700 for each Israeli.

Apostrophe

The apostrophe indicates possession or the omission of a letter in a contraction. Both usages appear here:

> PHILADELPHIA (UPI)—As if Benjamin Franklin *hasn't* been studied, analyzed, written about, honored and quoted enough.
> This week some of the *world's* leading Franklin scholars will spend three days discussing their latest research on *Franklin's* life and achievements.

Some writers have problems with *its*, which is possessive, and *it's*, which is the contraction of *it is*. Here are some correct examples:

> *It's* (it is) going to be a beautiful day.

> The United Way extended *its* annual drive today because it failed to reach *its* goal of $61,950, according to chairman H. W. Pearce.

Quotation Marks

Quotation marks appear around the exact words of a speaker or the exact words taken from a document. In addition, journalists attribute the words to the person or document. To do otherwise is to plagiarize (see Chapter 12).

Parentheses and Brackets

Parentheses are seldom used in journalistic writing and then only in routine and standardized ways. For example, they are used to add explanatory material to proper names: *The Sharon* (Mass.) *Advocate.*

Sometimes a writer feels the need to insert an explanatory word in a direct quotation to make the quotation clear. The writer encloses the insert in parentheses:

> Gathers, 23, was "sacrificed on the altar of (college) basketball," the suit charges.

Many editors and writers believe that if the quotation cannot stand without the insert, it should be paraphrased. Parenthetical inserts break the flow of a quotation and should be used sparingly, if at all. Parenthetical inserts confuse the readers because the readers do not know who inserted the words—the speaker or the reporter.

Brackets are the correct device for inserts in direct quotations, but mechanical limitations for years have kept them out of newspapers. *The Associated Press Stylebook* (1989) states brackets "cannot be transmitted over newswires. Use parentheses. . . ."

Period

The period appears in abbreviations and ellipses, and signals the end of a declarative sentence. Journalists struggling to find an ending for a story may complain to an unsympathetic editor that they do not know how to end the story. The editor may reply: "With a period."

Review Questions

What is a sentence?

Identify from stories in an available newspaper the following sentence types: simple, compound, complex, compound-complex.

Explain the two types of agreement problems most common in
  writing.
What is the difference between active and passive voice, and which is
  preferred in newswriting?
Describe a typical modification problem.
What is the difference between an essential and a non-essential clause?
What is the comma in apposition and how is it misused?
What is the difference between a hyphen and a dash?

Endnote

1. Reported in *The Editorial Eye* 13, no. 10 (October 1990). Published by
   Editorial Experts Inc., Alexandria, Va.

Sources and Resources

Berner, R. Thomas. *Language Skills for Journalists.* 2nd ed. Boston: Houghton
  Mifflin, 1984.
Cook, Claire Kehrwald. *Line by Line: How to Edit Your Own Copy.* Boston:
  Houghton Mifflin, 1985.

Chapter 5

Reporting

Chapter Objectives

In this chapter you will learn about what drives a reporter and how reporters determine what a story is. You will learn about the process of reporting, including originating the story and doing background work. You will also get some idea about the biases that can affect reporting.

Introduction

News stories are based on facts gathered by reporters. Journalists do not make things up out of thin air. No journalist can fashion a news story without gathering relevant information, getting details, finding examples and then planning the story. The factual base of news stories is what distinguishes them from fiction.

Norman Mailer won one of journalism's highest honors, a Pulitzer Prize, for his book *Armies of the Night* (1968). Subsequently, he wrote a book about the Apollo space program and in it discussed the accolades he had received for his journalistic work. Writing about himself in the third person, he says:

> He thought it was the superb irony of his professional life, for he knew he was not even a good journalist and possibly could not hold a top job if he had to turn in a story every day. He had known such journalists, and

Figure 5.1 Norman Mailer concedes defeat in the Democratic primary election for mayor, New York City, June 18, 1969. At a news conference a month earlier Mailer commented on his receipt of the Pulitzer Prize for Armies of the Night *and rebuked the press for inadequate coverage of his mayoral campaign. Copyright © AP/Wide World Photos.*

their work was demanding. They had first of all to have enormous curiosity, and therefore be unable to rest until they found out the secret behind even the smallest event.[1]

Editors throughout the country were asked a few years ago what they sought in beginning reporters. Language and writing skills were high on everyone's list. But then, in the article describing the survey of the editors, the author included some of the editors' comments that had not found their way onto the official list. One editor said that what he wanted in a reporter was someone who took a different route to work every day. In other words, a curious person.

Good editors also like reporters who don't hang around the office waiting for the phone to ring. Curious reporters are usually out of the office digging up news. They may use the phone to schedule interviews or to check a fact. But usually they get out on the street and feel life, just like the cop walking the neighborhood beat. Inexperienced reporters sometimes try to write about matters they have not seen. A reporter assigned to write a story about a particular traffic problem should go to the scene of the problem. See it firsthand. There is no substitute for being there.

It is true that many news stories originate from the police blotter, or from town council and school board meetings, or from planning commission and zoning board meetings. It is true that many news stories come from a reporter's beat or specialty, from labor, medicine, education, sports, the legal system, business, science, religion or politics. But what really underlies every successful story is curiosity. Good reporters want to know everything. They won't take no for an answer. They search everywhere. They are never satisfied. They know that little stories lead to big stories.

A good reporter goes beyond the routine information from the beat to see if there's a better story. For example, Vanessa Winans of the *York* (Pa.) *Daily Record* once read on the police blotter that the bookkeeper for the York YMCA, Judy Reed, was robbed while taking the Y's money to the bank for deposit. Winans could have written a four-paragraph story from the information the police gave her. But instead she called Mrs. Reed and got a better story. To find her, Winans had to dial several phone numbers because the police did not have Mrs. Reed's home address or her husband's name, which would have made finding her phone number easier. One of the questions Winans asked the victim: What went through your mind as you were struggling with the robber? Another Winans story (see Box 5.1)—this one about an attempted theft—also resulted from the reporter's approach of following up routine news to get a better story.

Stories grow from other stories. A few years ago, Gary Rummler of the *Milwaukee Journal* wrote a series on teenagers who were dealing with abuse. After the series appeared, Rummler received phone calls from adults who had suffered abuse as children. His curiosity whetted, Rummler inter-

Robbery Victim Goes Down Fighting

YMCA bookkeeper struggles with thief who took cash, checks

By Vanessa Winans

Judy Reed did not give up without a fight when she was robbed while on the way to make a bank deposit in the rain Monday.

Mrs. Reed, the bookkeeper for the York YMCA, was walking in the 100 block of west Market Street at 10:15 a.m. when she saw a man pass her, she said Monday night. She saw him stop at a parking lot, turn, and wait for her to pass.

Moments later, she felt a pull at the white satchel that contained the YMCA's weekend receipts—$1,100 in cash and $2,300 in checks, she said.

Tightening her grip on the satchel, the 5-foot, 51-year-old woman whirled to face the much-taller robber. She said she tried to jab the man with the point of her umbrella, but at the moment of truth, it blew inside out. So she tried to hang on to the satchel.

I was tugging and he was tugging," she recalled. "Eventually, he was stronger, and he pulled it out of my hand. I fell down and started yelling, 'Police! Police!' "

Her attacker said nothing as they struggled.

The man, who did not show her a weapon, ran north through the Columbia Gas Co. parking lot, city police reported. Police had not caught the thief Monday night.

The robber was black, about 5 feet 8 inches to 5 feet 10 inches tall, wearing dark or neutral clothes, in his 20s, with a thin to medium build and close-cropped hair, Mrs. Reed said.

The woman said she tried to fight the man because the idea of being robbed angered her.

"I was just mad," she said. "I wasn't going to give in to him completely."

In retrospect, she was glad she fought, despite her bruised left hip and left elbow and three broken fingernails. She takes classes at the YMCA and considers herself fit. But if another robber had a gun or knife, she wouldn't argue again, she said.

Box 5.1 Curiosity paid off for Vanessa Winans, a staff writer for the York (Pa.) Daily Record, *when she pursued routine police blotter information and obtained these stories, dated August 21, 1990, and December 3, 1990. Copyright © 1990 by the* York Daily Record. *All rights reserved.*

Continued

Norman L. Walters, YMCA president, said the deposit robbery was the YMCA's first.

YMCA officials plan to change the way employees take deposits to the bank, Mr. Walters said. The money taken Monday was insured and the checks were all marked for deposit.

"You would guard against that in the evening or the early morning, but you'd think at that time of day, you'd be safe," he said. "It's supposedly the safest corridor to the bank we've got."

Mrs. Reed, who has walked the route for the 22 months she has been the YMCA's bookkeeper, said the attack upset her.

"I get shaky when I think about."

Woman Chases Off Would-be Thief from Car

by Vanessa Winans

Wendy Gable never expected it to happen to her.

The 25-year-old York woman left the Pinc Panther's nightclub at 11:30 p.m. Saturday, planning to go to another bar, she said Sunday.

As she approached her car, parked a short distance from the Loucks Road club's parking lot, she saw her 1990 Isuzu Amigo's interior light shining. A few steps closer to the car, she could see a man sitting inside.

"I walked around to the side of the car, and he was sitting there," she recalled. "I said, 'What the hell are you doing in my car?'"

For a moment, the two stared at one another. Then he got out of the Amigo, ran to another car and drove away without turning on his car's headlights.

Gable chased him for a few blocks, then gave up. Driving quickly, the man weaved his 1970s-model two-door, cream-colored car in and out of traffic.

"I decided it wasn't worth getting myself in a wreck," she said. "I wasn't going to chase some maniac around."

The man got into her car by unsnapping the convertible top at the car's rear. He was described as white, 5-foot-9, 180 pounds, with acne and a light complexion, and brown hair, according to the complaint Gable filed with the York city police. The report also said he wore a black T-shirt, jeans and a brown leather coat.

On Sunday, Gable remained angry at the would-be thief, especially when she looked at the damage to the glove box

Continued

and stereo, which he did not take as he ran.

"You save up all your money to buy a nice vehicle and to have somebody ruin it so quick . . . ," she said. "It's real shame that somebody has to live their life like that."

Gable said the attempted theft has made her reconsider where to park, where to keep a spare key and other aspects of car ownership she hadn't examined. She's sorry she has to do so.

"York is such a nice place," the California native said. "I just never thought anybody would do this to me."

viewed several adults, talked to an expert or two, read three books, and then wrote a six-part series.

The curious reporter has a perspective that goes beyond the community. The reporter is able to compare and contrast local issues with issues elsewhere. Some of that can be done merely by accessing other newspapers' electronic libraries and searching for stories on the same or related issues. Such stories provide the reporter with sources to call or visit (as the budget allows).

In Florida, some editors at the *Orlando Sentinel* wanted to know the impact of the state's early release program for prisoners. The program was designed to ease overcrowding in prisons but instead, the *Sentinel* discovered, it recycled criminals, some of whom graduated to a higher level of criminal activity. Not even state corrections officials were aware of the immensity of the problem.

At the *Philadelphia Inquirer,* Donald L. Barlett and James B. Steele got similar results after they thoroughly investigated a federal tax reform law to see just what the law really did (see Box 5.2). For their efforts, they won a Pulitzer Prize for national reporting.

A reporter new to an area was impressed by how efficiently the local transportation system operated during a heavy snowstorm. Curious about its efficiency in those circumstances, he checked with the transportation authority, drivers, passengers, meteorologists, and other interested parties and produced a 350-word story. It was a nice news feature

Figure 5.2 James B. Steele, right, addresses co-workers after it was announced that he and Donald L. Barlett, left, had won the 1989 Pulitzer Prize for national reporting. Copyright © AP/Wide World Photos.

that kept the public informed. And it came about because someone was curious.

At one newspaper, reporters on beats are required to meet with other beat reporters to informally discuss what is going on. The reporter in one municipality revealed that plans for a new shopping center had hit a snag because the shopping center had not been designed with public transit in mind. So the regional transportation authority intervened informally and got the municipality to make some changes.

How could that planning mistake be avoided in the future? The transportation beat reporter interviewed the authority's manager and learned that he was preparing legislation requiring authority review of all plans in those municipalities using the regional bus system. The transpor-

Knight-Ridder's 1989 Pulitzer Prize Winners

When the Tax Reform Act of 1986 was passed, press coverage and speeches heralded the bill as a blow to special-interest groups and a victory for the middle-class Americans. But when Donald L. Barlett and James B. Steele, Inquirer investigative reporters who have worked as a team since 1971, began analyzing the new law, they found the bill wasn't such a blow to special-interest groups after all.

Barlett and Steele found hundreds of mysterious tax breaks for specific individuals and corporations. The exemptions were written in obscure language and gave no clue as to the targeted recipients or the ultimate cost to taxpayers.

In September 1986, the Senate Finance Committee released a list of 650 recipients of so-called transition rules that exempted certain businesses, projects and individuals from complying with specific provisions of the new law.

Congressional tax-writing committees and their staffs refused to provide any information, insisting that the identities of the beneficiaries of the preferen-tial tax provisions had to be kept secret.

Barlett and Steele were determined to find out who benefited from the exemptions and how they got them passed.

The search for answers sent the reporters crisscrossing the country interviewing people in more than two dozen states and the Virgin Islands. They collected and searched through thousands of pages of documents from state and federal courts and local, state and federal agencies.

"We relied on public records—Securities and Exchange Commission documents, corporation records, court papers, bankruptcy proceedings, financial disclosure records of the House and Senate and one of the newest and most valuable tools a reporter can have these days— electronic databases," said Steele. "It was a laborious, painstaking process but was absolutely essential to getting to the root of this story."

The Philadelphia Newspapers library pitched in with 11 of its 13 librarians conducting more than 700 searches of five databases.

Box 5.2 This story about the Pulitzer Prize–winning reporters Donald J. Barlett and James B. Steele appeared in Knight-Ridder News, *Summer 1989. Reprinted with permission of* Knight-Ridder News.

Continued

Over 15 months of research, Barlett and Steele began to put the pieces together. "It was a complex issue that had to be made readable," said Barlett. "We had to write in terms that readers could understand and relate to in their own lives."

The result was a seven-part, 40,000-word series, published in the *Inquirer* April 10–16. The articles exposed those who, by law, had been excused from paying taxes.

Recipients included White House dinner guests, members of *Forbes* magazine's list of the 400 wealthiest Americans, major campaign contributors and personal and business friends of congressmen.

Reaction to the series was quick and explosive. The *Inquirer* was flooded with letters and calls from angry readers.

Newspapers across the country carried the series, touching off a wave of outrage wherever the articles appeared. The public outcry reached Washington, prompting 51 members of Congress to co-sponsor a bill demanding the secrecy surrounding special tax breaks come to an end.

The publication *Tax Notes* observed that the series had members of Congress running scared. An Arthur Andersen & Co. publication quoted a congressional aide as saying, "The committee is operating under new 'Philadelphia rules.' "

When the technical corrections to the 1986 tax law were passed, the effects of the "Philadelphia rules" were evident. Not a single new tailor-made tax law was included.

Tax Notes reported that "aides attributed much of the strict scrutiny to a series published last spring by the *Philadelphia Inquirer.*"

"It was one of the most rewarding projects we've ever done," said Steele. "This is a case where a newspaper had a positive effect on public policy."

The Pulitzer is the second for the team of Barlett and Steele, who have received virtually every major national journalism award for their investigative reporting. The first, for national reporting in 1975, was for the series "Auditing the IRS."

They are the authors of two books. *Empire: The Life, Legend and Madness of Howard Hughes* in 1979 and *Forevermore: Nuclear Waste in America* in 1985.

Barlett, 52, was born in Dubois, Pa. He attended Pennsylvania State University and served three years as a special agent with the United States Army Counter Intelligence Corps. He began his journalism career in 1956 as a gen-

Continued

eral assignment reporter at the *Reading* (Pa.) *Times,* later holding a similar position at the *Akron Beacon Journal.* He began working as an investigative reporter at *The* (Cleveland) *Plain Dealer* in 1965. Barlett, married with a son, joined the *Philadelphia Inquirer* in 1970.

Steele, 46, was born in Hutchinson, Kan. He graduated from the University of Missouri and began his journalism career at the *Kansas City Times,* covering labor, politics and urban affairs. Steele, married with a daughter, also joined the *Inquirer* in 1970.

tation manager that felt money and time could be saved if the authority were involved early in the process. The transportation reporter wrote a story, using the shopping center as her example of why the regionwide legislation was needed.

Remember the story in Chapter 1 about journalists covering a speech by the minister-counselor and director of the press and information bureau for the Egyptian embassy in Washington? In that circumstance, a curious journalism student came up with a scoop because he interviewed the minister after a fairly routine speech. Among those scooped were the other members of the class who left at the end of the speech or during the question-and-answer period. They hadn't been curious or persistent, and because of that they had missed getting a very interesting story.

Local government tends to be a major source of stories for reporters. But lazy reporters write nothing beyond the bare facts that they glean from the town council meeting or the police blotter. They do not look for a larger story. They aren't curious. Good reporters, on the other hand, see each meeting and each blotter item as an opportunity to pursue information further and write a unique story (see Box 5.3). They look for trends. They maintain good files. They ask questions. They are curious.

Good reporting includes getting specific information. Nothing raises an editor's eyebrows more than to read an account of a city council meeting and see a direct quotation attributed to "a member of the audience." Wasn't the reporter curious enough to find out the speaker's name and address and other particulars?

Background Yourself, then Break the News before the Meeting; Watch for Trends

By Kathleen O'Dell

It rarely occurred to me to tell a cub reporter how to cover a meeting—until now. After I compiled my list of tips, I was surprised to note how much there is to consider before and during a meeting if the job doesn't come to you instinctively.

Here's what I would tell my reporters:

• Do your homework. Meeting coverage seems to be 60 percent background work and 40 percent actual meeting work. If it's possible, find out before the meeting what is expected to happen, and background yourself on those points. If you can't get hold of an agenda in advance, talk to someone on the board or the listed speakers. Attend the study sessions that often are scheduled days before the regular meetings of school boards and city councils. Those meetings are where decisions begin to take shape and issues are raised.

• Break the news before the meeting. The days before a meeting offer a good chance to run stories exploring issues that are expected to be raised at the session. You thus will be keeping your readers ahead of the story—not behind it. This has additional reader value: It lets those who might be interested in an issue know more about it and decide whether they want to attend the meeting.

• Background yourself on the names, personalities and special interests of the board members or meeting principals. If you don't have the time to do this beforehand, ask some trustworthy person at the meeting to help you identify the people. And be sure you get the names correctly.

• Be sure your quotes are correct. If you miss part of a quote during the meeting, pull the speaker aside later. When you're writing your story, you'll be glad you've done this.

• Don't rely on your memory to get answers or quotes or correct name spellings after the meeting. Jot down questions as they occur; keep a running list in the front of your notebook during the meeting.

Box 5.3   Kathleen O'Dell's tips for writing better meeting stories appeared in Editorially Speaking, *a magazine within* The Gannetteer *39, no. 1 (January/February 1985). Reprinted with permission of Gannett Co., Inc.*

Continued

- Immediately alert your city editor by phone or messenger if something unusual or unexpected happens at the meeting. That will allow him or her to plan for the space if needed, to send a photographer or to assign a reporter at the office to prepare background on the surprise issue, because you won't have time to do the backgrounding.
- If possible, arrive at the meeting early. This will allow you to keep an eye on the board. By showing up half an hour early at a school board meeting one year, we discovered that members were having casual, but unannounced, closed executive sessions. Arriving early also gives you time to interview people about meeting issues. It's a good time to get quotes if you must leave the meeting early to make a deadline.
- Always staff important meetings with a photographer or bring a camera yourself.
- Read agendas and meetings handouts carefully, and as much before the meeting as possible. Buried in one school board financial handout in Springfield this year was a line item authorizing purchase of a car radar detector. Reporters found out that the superintendent had asked for the "fuzz-buster" for use on school trips—and his vacation to Mexico.
- Get details, such as the number of people attending, any protest signs that were displayed, applause, heckling and any gestures or mannerisms the speakers made that you can include in your story to add life to it.
- Always keep in mind this question: "How will this affect the readers?" It will prompt you to ask the most important questions for the story and help you write the lead as well as the rest of the story.
- Watch for trends that develop over weeks or months of meetings with the city council, county commission and so on. After 10 meetings, you may realize that a particular councilman is building a powerful alliance with some group or other council members. It may become obvious that a board is spending an unusual amount of money on vehicle repairs or computer purchases. Some stories don't happen at meetings but do stem from such tidbits that you can pick up there.
- If you decide not to attend a meeting, cover yourself. Arrange for a trustworthy person at the meeting to alert you dur-

Continued

ing it if something important happens, and always talk to the person after the meeting to check on what happened.

Kathleen O'Dell of Gannett's Springfield (Mo.) Newspapers has been involved in meeting coverage as both a reporter and a city editor—and she has the added perspective of having returned to reporting at her request after having worked the city desk.

O'Dell, 30, has been with the Springfield Newspapers since 1977 as a copy editor, reporter, columnist, special-projects writer and city editor. She also worked 18 months at USA Today as a national reporter and later editorial writer.

Some reporters who cover meetings believe their job is that of recording secretary. It is not. Questions may arise during a meeting that should be answered in a story. For example, during a planning commission meeting the members of the commission express concern that the local university, which is leasing off-campus space, may suddenly stop doing so and thus create economic problems in the town. Even though no one on the planning commission gave details on how much space was being leased and how much rent the university was paying, that information should have been in the story the next morning.

Where would it come from? After the meeting, the reporter could check with the planning commission chair or the staff planner. Either one might have a good idea. If they don't, call the university's spokesperson. If that bombs, call the university official who oversees leases. If that fails, call a real estate agent who leases to the university. The agent might give you a figure. Make sure the source for the figures is clear in the story.

The same curiosity should drive a reporter to verify all claims in a story. If A says something about B, call B for a comment. If B contradicts A, call A back. On a larger scale, Jean Ward and Kathleen A. Hansen offer advice on verification, advice they link to the traditional tests of evidence.[2] In addition, they urge reporters to make sure information is internally and externally consistent. Is information from different sources used in a story consistent? Does information derived from one source agree with that from other sources? When dealing with different pieces of information, Ward and Hansen urge, compare the pieces for quality. Not all sources are equally reliable and forthcoming, and the reporter who believes he has written a balanced story merely by quoting all sides of an issue could be wrong. A reporter has to evaluate all sources for knowledge and credibility. What is the source's reputation? A congenital liar is useless. Ward and Hansen also suggest that the reporter ensure that the information has been provided in its true context and that any statistics be validly derived. That means checking the original document. Also, does the information have one unmistakable meaning? Is it recent? Is it relevant?

A reporter must interview not only the people who speak up the most or the loudest, but also the people who are silent. Beware of people who claim to represent a segment of the community and who sound as though they might. Check with other people in the community to see if the spokesperson is self-appointed or really representative.

In researching stories, reporters need to appreciate that their best sources may not be the people at the top but the people at the middle level. People at the top feel the need to hoard and guard information, for they believe that to share it is to diminish their power and authority. A reporter who relies on such people will be their servant, which is not a good position for a journalist to be in.

Reporters also need to cultivate sources on their beat. Talk to people without interviewing them. Develop rapport. Every conversation does not need to result in a story. The reporter whose every contact with someone results in a story will give the source the feeling that the reporter is "using" the source. Cultivate sources the way you would a garden. Do a little work every day but do not try to harvest crops every day.

News stories begin with background work. Not doing background work is akin to starting a novel in the middle. Sources appreciate a reporter who has done some background work. A good reporter checks the clip files so she knows something about the story and can fine-tune her questions. Approaching a source with too broad a question could result in a rebuff. One beginning journalist found himself losing an interview with the administrator of a hospital because his first question was, "Tell me everything you know about the open meetings law." Granted, the interview had to do with whether the hospital's board came under the law, but the question was the reporter's way of finding out what the law was. He should have read the law and background clips in order to have specific

Figure 5.3 Reporter, right, conducts on-the-street interview. Copyright © Kenneth Martin/AMSTOCK.

questions ready for the interview. Remember, specific questions usually beget specific answers. (The next chapter discusses what to do when they don't.)

Stories can be found in many places. Curious reporters listen during conversations at social events. They read specialized journals. Meetings, of course, generate follow-up story ideas. Journalists also ask themselves what might interest readers and what readers need to know. The classified advertising section of a newspaper, especially the legal advertisements, yields tips on stories. It never hurts when bumping into someone you see only occasionally to greet him or her with a "What's new?" and then to stand back and listen. Try that in a beauty shop or barber shop. Both businesses traffic in information.

News releases also offer story ideas. The announcement that a company has a new CEO (chief executive officer) may mean the previous one was fired. Is the company having problems? Or the fact that there is a new

CEO may suggest a news feature or a personality profile. A news release announcing shorter hours at the local library could lead an inquisitive reporter to find out what is behind the change. Perhaps a change in state funding caused a shortfall in the library's budget and forced the cutback. The taxpayers and library patrons need to know about this.

Then there is investigative reporting. Andrew Schneider of the *Pittsburgh Press* once gave a talk entitled, "Eight Steps toward Successful Investigative Reporting,"[3] and while this chapter focuses on the more basic reporting concepts, Schneider's ideas can still be applied. A story, he said, starts with an idea. Step two is research and identification of sources. In steps three, four and five, determine the scope and timeline of the story and develop a budget. Step six is figuring out the objectives, and step seven is preparing the story. (Step eight is layout, which is beyond the scope of this book.)

Schneider says that the reporter is the best source for a story idea, since a reporter exploring her own idea will be doing something she wants to do. But, he notes, ideas also come from editors and fellow reporters. Schneider cautions, though, that a reporter seldom embarks on an investigative piece on company time without first consulting with her immediate editor.

With an idea in mind, a reporter next does some research and identifies sources. The reporter wants to make sure she is not going over old ground. She is looking for a fresh approach. Then she wants to know what and who her sources are going to be and where the desired information can be found.

Now the reporter must determine the scope of her story. "In your initial planning," Schneider says, "you've got to know where you're going." The problem Schneider is warning against is the one of a reporter picking a topic that is too wide in scope. Such stories become unwieldy. If the reporter lacks a hypothesis, she will have difficulty doing research and determining the scope of her story.

Narrowing a general area like "the city jail" to specific questions like "Are they starving the prisoners?" is an essential step in shaping good news stories, according to Frank Caperton, managing editor of the *Indianapolis News* (see Box 5.4).

At some newspapers, the timeline, as Schneider calls it, does matter. Some reporters have been turned loose and allowed to do research for an

Finding the Story in an Idea and
Other Advice to Journalism Students

By Frank Caperton

I want to start by telling you a story, I think many of us learn by stories. It comes from my own experience.

When I was a graduate student at Columbia I took a short seminar in feature writing. As the day for the first meeting approached we were all really looking forward to it with a great deal of anticipation because the professor was an adjunct member of the faculty. His name was Robinson and he was a freelance writer who had written fiction, non-fiction and poetry. He had been published in the *New Yorker* and other national magazines and had been an articles editor at the *New Yorker*. So he was somebody pretty hot.

We all got to this room where we were going to have this first meeting early. He was about five minutes late and he did not make a great impression. He was so quiet and diffident. He walked to the front of the room and apologized for being late and for breaking off our small talk.

And he said, "Well, you can't talk about feature writing unless you have a story idea. It's 9:15, I'd like to see you back here at one o'clock and we'll talk about your story ideas." Suppressing our glee, we filed out of the room and really had a great time that morning.

We thought, what a cinch. We've got a seminar on feature writing and we get a whole morning just to come up with one story idea. So, we all drank cokes and coffee and talked about sports or whatever we wanted to talk about, had lunch, and at 1:00 we filed back in.

This professor came back and it was amazing how undiffident he was that afternoon. He looked down the room and he said, "You sir, what's your story idea?" This poor soul said, "Well, I'm going to do a story on the city jail." The professor said, "Oh, what a great area, but what is your story? What is it about the city jail that makes it a story? Are they abusing prisoners? Are there homosexual rapes? Are they ripping off money on the food bill

Box 5.4   Knowing the difference between an "area" and a story is the subject of this speech by Frank Caperton, managing editor of the Indianapolis News, *at the Roy W. Howard Public Affairs Reporting Seminar, Bloomington, Indiana, September 3–4, 1988. Reprinted with permission of the author.*

Continued

and starving them? What is the story?"

He went all around the room. There were 15 of us and it turned out that there were 15 areas, and not a single story idea. For the next few days we learned how to do a rough outline of a story, how to write a summary of what the story was about.

I have subsequently come to believe that the whole purpose of those days was to teach us the difference between an area and a story. It is not a problem only for student journalists.

Early in my career in Macon, Georgia, we had a very small staff, a medium-size paper, about 50,000 circulation, maybe eight reporters assigned to the city desk, I remember this reporter's byline disappeared from the paper for a week or ten days. With eight reporters on the city desk you notice things like that when they're not on vacation.

So, I went to the city editor and asked, "What is Sue working on?" The city editor said, "Oh, she's doing a series on welfare." I said, "Well, that's a great area. What is the idea?" And he said, "Well, she's interested in welfare. She thinks it would be a great series." We discussed it for another ten minutes and it was clear there was no story idea. But I gave

them three or four more days to come up with one and they did not. So, she went back to writing other stories. I suspect that, as she was a young reporter, it was really beyond her at that point.

It happens on the big newspapers. I was an assistant city editor on the *Miami Herald* and there was a reporter there who didn't know the difference between an area and a story, and was not about to learn. When he took on a story, he investigated everything around it. He would discuss with the city editor the publication date and what he had. All week long my stomach would hurt because I would know that at about 6:30 or 7:00 on Friday night he was going to dump an absolute mess on my desk. And that somewhere in that mess there was a story. Between 7:00 Friday night and sometime Saturday I had to rewrite that and purge it of material that was not a story. So, know the difference between an area and a story.

What we're really talking about is what is it about this that is a story. Once you have decided that, the marvelous thing that does for you is you know who you need to interview, what documents you might need, you begin to have some idea of how to lessen the universe of things you might research. Your statement and your list of sources may

Continued

change as you interview and research, but having it makes your
life a lot simpler. It also makes it a
lot more likely that your editor is
going to give you the time. Almost always we'll ask a reporter
to do a feasibility memo, write
down what the story is about,
what information is needed.
And it's remarkable how some
reporters lose interest when
they're asked to be specific. If
you'll be specific you'll get more
time than a lot of other people on
the staff.

I once hired someone to be a
court reporter whose career was
to be a court reporter on a big
newspaper. She had taken semi-
nars on court reporting and legal
affairs. She had great clips. About
six months after she came to work

for us her copy started getting
lifeless and dull. This went on for
a few weeks and I called her in and
we talked about it. She said, "All
of these murder trials are just
alike. Each one is just another
murder trial." And I talked to her
about how I thought she was
poorly focused, that she had gotten wrapped up learning court
language and focusing on the system. She had lost contact with the
particular, with the individuals
caught up in the system. She was
seeing everything alike.

She made a good effort and
what was probably for her a good
decision, she became a lawyer.
So, if you want to stay alive in this
business and keep your sense of
enthusiasm for it, you really have
to care about the particular.

extended period before starting to write, although this is less likely to occur
at smaller news outlets. Editors need to know how long a reporter might
be researching a story so that they can deploy other newsroom resources
accordingly. Good stories take time, and editors know that and will allow
for it.

When it comes to a budget for a story, editors need to know what
kind of travel the reporter is planning. This dovetails with the earlier step
of identifying sources. Some sources may be in the state capital or in
Washington, D.C. Will Freedom of Information requests need to be filed?
Will an attorney be needed to help in the process?

The objectives stage encompasses many of the preceding stages.
Schneider says reporters need to know what it is they want to write or

photograph, what has been done before, who are possible sources, what are the ground rules (for instance, will your editors allow off-the-record interviews?), how long will it take, and how many people are involved and how much will it cost?

Story preparation caps the reporter's work. This is where the effort of the reporter's research pays off. Schneider warns that writing a story about something being wrong is not of much use if the story does not include some information on how the wrong could be righted.

Ward and Hansen note the amount of back and forth that occurs between a reporter's sources on a particular story.[4] The process they describe emphasizes that what a reporter learns in an interview may lead her to a library source, and a source subsequently found in the library may lead the reporter back to the person interviewed. The Ward-Hansen model begins with developing the right questions and ends with the selection and synthesis of the information gathered, a process that results in the story.

Another approach comes from Robert I. Berkman, the author of *Find It Fast: How to Uncover Expert Information on Any Subject,* a book that every reporter should have. Berkman describes how to define the goal of a search, locate the basic sources, obtain the technical sources, talk to experts, redirect focus (as needed) and get expert review.[5]

All manner of biases can affect the work of journalists. S. Holly Stocking and Paget H. Gross have compiled a list of problem areas that journalists and journalism students need to be aware of.[6] They note, among other things, that journalists should not rely entirely on eyewitnesses, because eyewitnesses are often unreliable. They warn against making too much of a compelling anecdote that contradicts scientifically collected statistics. They caution against a reporter's predisposition leading him to seek only those sources that confirm the story the reporter believes exists. And they advise journalists to be careful about false correlations.

Citing earlier research, Stocking and Gross warn about problems with eyewitnesses. "Observations can vary and err as a function of a variety of factors such as prejudice, temporary expectations, the types of details being observed, and stress," they write. Several years ago, clerks from stores that had been robbed picked the robber from a lineup. The news media had a field day because the person identified was a Catholic priest. So confident were the police of their eyewitnesses that they never checked the priest's alibi. Six months later, the real robber confessed. Not surprisingly to specialists, the robber and the priest didn't even come close to looking alike. The eyewitnesses were unreliable for a variety of reasons, among them stress. When you're looking down the barrel of a pistol, you are not focusing on the person holding the gun but on the gun itself.

Stocking and Gross say people fail to appreciate the validity of statistical information against the randomness of a compelling anecdote. Journalists, they say, need to be cautious that the anecdote they use fits the statistical information. People tend to generalize from anecdotes even when the anecdotes and the statistics disagree. If the anecdote does not fit, don't use it.

When seeking out sources to test a theory against, journalists need to be cautious that they do not discount sources that refute the theory. Nothing is wrong with a journalist's researching a story from a particular viewpoint or hypothesis, but the journalist needs to work as hard at disproving the hypothesis as at proving it. Some journalists, Stocking and Gross note, will discount as "shoddy" the sources that contradict their hypotheses.

As suggested earlier, sources need to be evaluated for their biases. A group of Republicans will most likely respond more positively to a speech by a Republican president than by a Democratic one. Generalizing Republicans' response to the population as a whole would fail to take into account the biased nature of the source.

Correlation problems occur when, for example, a characteristic and an event are spuriously associated. Stocking and Gross cite the example of pairing long hair and presence at demonstrations; once that correlation is made, journalists covering a demonstration may overestimate the number of long-haired people present. A reporter could also associate a long-haired person with certain political leanings and then assume all long-haired people have the same politics.

Reporting requires journalists to be aware of many facets, both of themselves and their sources. Good reporters are curious; they want to know everything. They examine many sources. The next chapter continues to examine the techniques reporters use as well as some of the sources.

Review Questions

What are some of the routine sources of news?

What can beat reporters do to ensure they keep others informed?

List 10 pieces of advice Kathleen O'Dell gives to reporters.

Recount some of Ward and Hansen's advice on the verification of information.

What would an editor mean if she told a reporter to "cultivate a source"?

What is background work?

Endnotes

1. Norman Mailer, *Of a Fire on the Moon* (Boston: Little, Brown), 16. Copyright © 1969, 1970 by Norman Mailer.
2. Jean Ward and Kathleen A. Hansen, *Search Strategies in Mass Communication* (New York: Longman, 1987), 35.
3. Andrew Schneider, "Eight Steps toward Successful Investigative Reporting." Speech given at the Roy W. Howard Public Affairs Reporting Seminar, Bloomington, Ind., September 3–4, 1988.
4. Ward and Hansen, *Search Strategies in Mass Communication,* 5.
5. Robert I. Berkman, *Find It Fast: How to Uncover Expert Information on Any Subject* (New York: Harper and Row, 1987), 245.
6. S. Holly Stocking and Paget H. Gross, "Understanding Errors, Biases That Can Affect Journalists." *Journalism Educator* 43, no. 1 (Spring 1989), 4–11. Although not all of these are detailed here, the biases the authors cite are the eyewitness fallacy, underutilization of statistics, confirmation bias, misperceptions of risk, sample errors and biases, misunderstanding of regression, hindsight bias, illusory correlation and fundamental attribution error.

Sources and Resources

Caperton, Frank. "Finding the Story in an Idea and Other Advice to Journalism Students." Speech given at the Roy W. Howard Public Affairs Reporting Seminar, Bloomington, Ind., September 3–4, 1988.

Kessler, Lauren, and Duncan McDonald. *Uncovering the News.* Belmont, Calif.: Wadsworth, 1987.

Lefton, Lester A. *Psychology.* 3rd ed. Boston: Allyn and Bacon, 1985.

O'Dell, Kathleen. "Background Yourself, Then Break the News before the Meeting; Watch for Trends." *Editorially Speaking* 39, no. 1 (January/February 1985).

Ruth, Marcia. "Specialized Reporting: Newspapers Respond to Varied Information Needs by Assigning Good Reporters to Hone in on Business, Science, Religion and Other Fields." *Presstime* (December 1985), 6–9.

Chapter 6

Gathering Information

Chapter Objectives

In this chapter you will learn about the major sources of information. You will learn how to conduct research and interviews, and how to use observation as a reporting tool. You will also learn about the value of documents, including electronic databases, and something about the practical side of note taking.

Introduction

News comes from a variety of sources, and reporters mine those sources using a variety of techniques. Three major sources of information are in interviews with individuals, observation and documents.

Interviews

Interviews can range from a quick question after a town council meeting to a scheduled rendezvous. Whatever the level, a reporter needs to be prepared. Preparation can include thinking about the questions that need to be asked, and consulting the newspaper's library or electronic database for background on the person to be interviewed.

Often, the best interviews are conducted in person rather than over the telephone. The in-person interview gives a reporter a chance to meet the subject face to face and to observe the subject as the subject responds to particular questions in his or her own environment. The telephone is a wonderful interviewing tool, but it does not substitute for being there.

The face-to-face interview suggests a greater commitment on the part of the source and the journalist, and it gives the journalist the opportunity to try several approaches to getting an answer. The face-to-face interview sometimes means the journalist goes to the source's office, which provides the opportunity for a journalist to learn something by chance.

Interviews also provide reporters with the possibility of getting some useful direct quotations. Interviews allow people to tell the story in their own words, which can sometimes be better than the reporter's. Interviews allow reporters to gather anecdotes, which enable them to put abstract ideas into human terms. Interviews allow reporters the opportunity to get the subject of the interview to reveal himself.

Figure 6.1 President Ronald Reagan speaking to reporters at a press conference in the Oval Office of the White House, August 1985. Copyright © AP/Wide World Photos.

Never go to an interview without having done as much research as possible about the person and the subject matter. Granted, the purpose of the interview is to learn something, but in many cases, reporters who have done their homework use interviews to confirm what they already know.

Furthermore, a source will have a difficult time toying with the facts if the reporter has prepared in advance. And how does the source know this? By the questions asked. The questions are evidence that a reporter has prepared herself. And if that is not enough, if a source answers a question in a way that is inconsistent with the reporter's research, the reporter can always say, "According to what I've read . . ." and go on to correct the record.

In preparing for an interview, a reporter will come up with a series of questions. An unskilled interviewer makes the mistake of asking only prepared questions rather than picking up cues that may lead to different questions. As Tad Bartimus of the Associated Press puts it, listen for the unexpected opening and pursue it. "Toss your own script out the window," she writes, "and follow the trail your subject is blazing for you."[1]

Be careful not to interrupt someone in the middle of an answer. That could sidetrack the person and destroy the response. If, during an answer, a good question comes up, jot it down in the margin of your notepad, highlight it, and get back to it later.

Related to this advice is the saying "dumb is smart." Do not assume anything. If the subject of an interview starts to explain something you think you already understand, do not say, "Oh, I know what you mean. Here's my next question." Let the person explain, because the person may end up saying something you do not know.

Frequently, the best questions in an interview come after the formal interview is over and the reporter has put the notebook away. During the chit-chat that follows, the reporter may ask a question that catches the source off guard and results in a candid answer. The master of this was a television detective Lieutenant Columbo. Played by Peter Falk, Columbo was adept at seemingly having ended an interview and, on his way out the door, turning around and catching the suspect unaware with "Just one more question, if you don't mind."

If at all possible, conduct more than one interview, especially when you do not know the subject. Stranger-to-stranger does not make for the best of interview conditions. Once the interview subject knows the reporter, he or she will probably be more relaxed and provide a better interview next time. This is especially crucial in profiles, where a reporter is trying to capture the essence of someone. If more than one interview is impossible, a reporter would do well to begin the interview with casual conversation just to set the subject at ease. Remember, most people are not adept at dealing with the news media.

The reporter should begin the interview by stating its purpose. "I'm writing a story on the parking situation in town, Mayor Bailey, and I want to get your feelings on the matter." This is a focusing statement, both for you and for the mayor. It functions just like a headline on a story.

The reporter sets the tone for the interview, and the wrong tone at the outset can destroy the interview. For that reason, do not ask hard-hitting questions first. Starting off with soft questions not only relaxes the interview subject but also allows the reporter to establish a set of answers against which later answers can be compared. It is the same approach an attorney uses in court when questioning a hostile witness.

When the tough questions need to be asked, the reporter should make every effort not to antagonize the subject by acting as though the questions originated with the reporter. The reporter is not an advocate for a particular cause and should not sound like one. When tough questions need to be asked, the reporter can deflect antagonism by casting them in a way that does not offend the subject. In other words, do not put the subject of an interview on the defensive.

For example, you are interviewing a controversial local politician who has not cooperated with the news media and in fact has been hostile. Furthermore, she does not like your newspaper because your editor has criticized her in editorials. So the politician thinks you're "out to get her." You need to preface the touchy questions in a way that makes someone else the source of the questions:

> Mayor Bailey, let me play devil's advocate on this parking issue. I want to outline some different approaches to solving the parking problem and see what you think of them.

With this approach, the mayor's position is being challenged, but not by you. The mayor may react negatively, but not toward you. If that approach does not work, wait a few questions and then come back:

>Mayor Bailey, some people would say that the better way to solve the parking problem is not by building a new garage but by instituting a park-and-ride program. How do you feel about that?

What the reporter is trying to do is distance herself from the parking issue. The reporter is trying to get a variety of views on the issue, including the mayor's, but the reporter should not imply through her questions how she feels about the issue.

Most questions should be cast as neutrally as possible. Remember some of the comments in the last chapter about reporter bias? Imagine this leading question:

>Tell us about the terrible parking situation in your city, Mayor Bailey.

That question presumes the parking situation is terrible. It may be, but let the mayor tell you that. You have done your homework and you know the facts.

>"Mayor Bailey, how would you describe the parking situation?"
>"Not bad."
>"But, Mayor, people are complaining that there's no place to park."
>"It's their imagination."
>"But, Mayor, I checked with the police department the other day and they tell me that they've issued 50 percent more tickets for illegal parking this year than for the same period last year."
>"Fifty percent?"
>"Yes."
>"That sounds pretty bad to me."

The tone of questions needs to vary. If all your questions are neutral, the person being interviewed will be given a platform to say anything. As the previous example shows, when a neutral question elicits an answer that does not square with the facts, the reporter can change the tone of the questions. Jane Evinger suggests avoiding questions that can be answered with yes or no and, when they cannot be avoided, following up with "Can you elaborate on that?" or "Why did you say that?"[2]

In another approach, the reporter keeps repeating "Why?" after every answer. You see, answers are like the descending rings to hell in Dante's *Inferno,* and if you keep asking "Why?" the subject of the interview will keep digging deeper to answer the question. A variation of "Why?" is "Why's that?" The repetition approach is helpful because people often answer questions superficially. They are not trying to deceive; they believe they have answered the question. When a reporter keeps asking "Why?" the person being questioned works a little harder on the answer and a better answer usually results. The repeated "Why?" suggests that the reporter is looking for a precise answer. The source appreciates that. After all, imprecision reflects badly on the source.

Make sure that the subject of an interview labels fact, opinion and second-hand observation. Mayor Bailey may say that the police have issued 25 percent more parking tickets this year, and while that sounds like a fact, the reporter should confirm the figure with the police. Just as a matter of routine, a reporter should attempt to verify all facts.

Make sure you understand the answer to a question, and if you don't tell the subject of the interview so. The person should be willing to recast the answer so that it is clear to you. If it is not clear to you, you will not be able to explain it well in your story. Furthermore, if you get an answer that does not seem to fit, ask how the answer relates to the situation being discussed. This can be done agreeably simply by saying, "I do not see how that fits. Would you tie it in for me, please?"

During the interview, if at all possible, don't tip your hand. Do not tell anyone your interview schedule. Let the subjects of interviews infer where you have been and where you are going, but never confirm unless you need to challenge a statement. For example, a banker once said to a reporter during an interview, "Well, you will see this in the court documents anyway." The reporter did not let on that he had not thought of looking at the court documents, but you can be sure that he was in the courthouse at 8 a.m. the next day. By acting dumb, he was led to a gold mine.

A reporter can lead the subject of an interview in more ways than one. Neutral questions, of course, are one way of avoiding this problem. Reporters must also be aware of other signals they send, signals that could be misinterpreted by the subject of an interview. For example, reporters should be consistent in their note taking. Do not convey to someone that what he is saying is not important by suddenly stopping the note-taking process. Even if you are writing down trivia, write them down. Besides, they may turn out later not to be trivia.

Also, reporters can use various cues to keep the subject of an interview talking. Saying "uh-huh" or "OK" or nodding your head encourages the person being interviewed to keep talking. Broadcast journalists frequently nod their heads to keep someone talking and thus reduce the need to cut into an interview to keep it going.

Another effective approach is silence. Most people abhor a verbal vacuum and will keep talking to fill it. Let them talk. Who knows what they will say?

Finally, the dress code. Bartimus says "Appropriate dress is desirable." On the same page as her article "Skillful Interviewing" is a picture of her in blue jeans and a plaid shirt, sleeves rolled up two turns, talking to a former Montana sheriff similarly dressed. A mountain range provides a distant backdrop.

Figure 6.2 Tad Bartimus of the Associated Press, left, interviews a former Montana sheriff. Associated Press photo. Published with permission.

But if that backdrop had been the skyline of Manhattan, and Bartimus had been talking to a business person dressed in a suit and sitting behind an impressive desk in a posh office, Bartimus would have dressed accordingly.

Many good tips on interviewing are provided in Jane Evinger's article "Dirty Tricks Teach Interview Pitfalls" (see Box 6.1).

Observation

As an excellent example of the power of observation in newswriting, here is the beginning of the first of seven stories on people who were discharged from mental asylums under the guise of social reform. The series was written by Donald C. Drake and published in the *Philadelphia Inquirer*.[3]

> Dawn was just beginning to brighten the eastern sky. It was a sunrise that went unnoticed by the man asleep on the steam grate opposite Rittenhouse Square, folded up between a concrete trash receptacle and a newspaper vending machine.
>
> An electric digital display in a nearby bank window gave the time: 5:54.
>
> The sleeping man was wearing baggy corduroy pants, a wool hat, a shirt and a dirty blanket worn over his shoulders like a shawl.
>
> His eyes still closed, the man reached into his open shirt to scratch at the lice, as he had been doing all night. A bread truck roared by on Walnut Street, followed a few minutes later by a milk truck. Then it was quiet again.
>
> The sidewalk, which in two hours would be crowded with people hurrying to their jobs, was deserted now. The only signs of life were the man and a lone car that waited obediently at an empty intersection for the light to change.
>
> The man started to stir and, still without opening his eyes, pushed himself up to a sitting position, leaning back against the concrete trash receptacle. Joggers began to appear across the street, resolutely circling the park, too intent on their exercise to notice the solitary man.

Dirty Tricks Teach Interview Pitfalls

By Jane Evinger

Because experience is often the best teacher, advanced print reporting students at the University of Hawaii-Manoa unknowingly take part in a "booby-trapped" interview early every semester. The interview subject is primed by the instructor to play "dirty tricks" so the session purposely becomes a reporter's nightmare.

Students are given about a week to prepare for the interview. They review the interviewee's resume and newspaper clippings and study the interviewee's area of expertise. But nothing can really prepare them for what lies ahead.

The class is small, 12 to 15 students, but to ensure total participation, each student is required to ask at least one question, but is limited to no more than three questions during the 90-minute interview.

The most difficult part of setting up the exercise is finding a suitable person to be interviewed. It must be someone whose background is interesting enough to provide students with material for questions, who is able to think fast and who is willing to play "dirty tricks" for a good cause.

Interview subjects have included the assistant city editor of Honolulu's highest-rated late-evening newscast, the top administrative assistant to Honolulu's outspoken city prosecutor and the author of 11 published books, both novels and non-fiction.

In advance of the interviews, interviewees are sent a list of possible "dirty tricks" to pull if the occasion arises and are encouraged to use "dirty tricks" of their own. The list includes:

1. Denounce the press in general—"never get quotes right" or "you people are only interested in bad news and in getting people."

2. Turn the question around and interview the interviewer—"What do you think?" or "What would you do?" This is fun; some students will bite and answer several questions before the light dawns.

3. Go off the record, either before or after answering the question, to see what students will do.

Box 6.1   This article by Jane Evinger provides many good interviewing tips for beginning journalists. It originally appeared in Journalism Educator *39, no. 4 (Winter 1984): 28–29. Reprinted with permission of the author.*

Continued

4. At some point, deliberately misstate a fact everyone should know, such as "Vice President Howard Baker said" or "As the 49th state, Hawaii is . . ."

5. Be hostile to someone— "That's a stupid question." "You didn't do your homework or you would know the answer to that question." "That's none of your business" (a response that is particularly effective if it deals with something that is a matter of public record).

6. Wander wildly off the track. Students often are too polite to try to bring an interviewee back to the question.

7. If there is an opportunity, answer only "Yes" or "No" and see if you get a follow-up question.

8. Instead of answering a question, refer the interviewer to some difficult-to-obtain or time-consuming source—"I refer you to my book X, in which I discuss that question thoroughly."

9. Be inconsistent—say one thing at one point in the interview and another, contradictory, thing at some other point to see if anyone catches it.

10. Talk jargon to see if anyone is sharp enough to insist on plain English for the "average" reader.

11. Answer a question with a folksy but inappropriate anecdote. If possible, make it a very appealing anecdote so the questioner will be tempted to use it.

12. Ask to see the stories before they are published.

13. Mumble or speak softly so the interviewer will be forced to ask that the answer be repeated.

14. Answer a question, then say "Now, I want you to quote that, it's important. But don't use me as the source—that would get me in a lot of trouble and I'll deny it. Just say the quote came from a knowledgeable source or something like that."

15. Defame someone—call a lawyer an "ambulance chaser" or a doctor a "quack."

Most students initially appear bewildered during the interview, but at some point they realize what is going on, and become so involved with the game that they feel slighted if they don't get a chance to field a difficult answer.

However, a few students may not realize they have been victims of a set-up and must be enlightened at the conclusion of

Continued

the interview. It is stressed that the interviewee was asked to act nasty and recalcitrant so that students could experience and later discuss some of the problems they may face during future interviews.

The interview is videotaped with two cameras, so when it is replayed during the next class period, students can see themselves and the subject. Often, in seeing themselves, they realize they have been so busy taking notes that the interviewee was forced to talk to the top of their heads, or that in trying to maintain eye contact and rapport, they have nodded assent through out their stint as the questioner.

During the discussion, many ways of handling interviewing problems often come up:

1. Trying to convince interviewees who denounce the press that the reporter is accurate and trustworthy, or letting the interviewees vent their hostility, in hopes of then proceeding calmly with the interview.

2. Answering inquisitive interviewee's questions in hopes of creating rapport or saying "I'm sure our readers are much more interested in your opinion on that."

3. Explaining the need for attribution to interviewees who try to go off the record and urging that the material be placed on the record for the sake of credibility, or returning to the material later with related questions in hopes of getting the information on the record, or flatly refusing to accept off-the-record information.

4. Correcting misstated facts or asking for clarification.

5. Telling hostile interviewees about the sources checked before the question was asked or explaining why the answer to the question is necessary.

6. Allowing wandering interviewees to ramble in hopes it will lead to something useful or bringing them gently back to the question by saying "That's interesting, but . . . ."

7. Phrasing questions so that they cannot be answered "Yes" or "No" or asking "Could you elaborate?" or "Why do you say that?"

8. Pleading deadline pressures or asking for a summary of interviewee's views when they refer reporters to other sources.

9. Seeking clarification or stating the inconsistency to self-contradicting interviewees.

Continued

10. Asking jargon-speaking interviewees for definitions or explanations understandable to lay readers.
11. Expressing interest in the inappropriate anecdote, but asking how it relates to the subject, or whether interviewees have a more appropriate anecdote.
12. Refusing to allow sources to see stories before publication because this violates a newspaper's policy, but, if policy permits, agreeing to check major points by telephone.
13. Asking mumbling or soft-spoken interviewees to speak more clearly, explaining that "This is such interesting information that I want to be sure I get it all."
14. Pressing sources who refuse to be identified for on-the-record attribution and, if that fails, testing just how far the identification can go beyond "knowledgeable source."
15. Pointing out the defamatory material to interviewees who defame someone and asking for documentation.

Students, once over their initial discomfort, have found the exercise valuable. They realize it is less painful to experience interview problems in the classroom than to face them for the first time when they gather material for course projects or, later, on the job.

It took a long time, maybe 15 or 20 minutes, for the man to wake up fully, but by 6:15 his eyes were open wide, staring down the elegant street that had been his home for three years. At first he did nothing but sit, stare and scratch.

Another day was beginning for Jim Logue Crawford, 69, former mental hospital patient.

How did Drake capture that vignette? Do you think he awoke at 7 a.m. and went to his office, then walked to Rittenhouse Square, found Jim Crawford and interviewed him? Or was he in Rittenhouse Square observing the man when Crawford awoke?

Drake was in Rittenhouse Square on his 18-month tracking of re-leased mental patients in Philadelphia. He wanted to know how they lived, and so he observed them. It is part of Drake's approach to be, in his words, "more than a facts and figure reporter."

Reporters should use observation in all manner of stories, from the most basic to the most extensive. Take a fire, for example. Is the account of a fire all facts and figures? Well, it can be. Somewhere the time of the alarm is recorded and the number of trucks and firefighters dispatched is known. It is often not hard to find the owners of the property. The insurance company, among others, can give an estimate of the damage. Those are facts and figures, and should be reported. But what about the reporter's observations? They are valid also and can be made part of the story. In the following excerpts from the fire story first discussed in Chapter 2, the reporter's observations are italicized:

A *quick-burning* fire roared through the body and parts shop of D&M Chrysler Plymouth Inc. Sunday morning, destroying seven cars and *reducing the concrete-block building to a blackened shell.*

Fire officials are estimating the loss to the business at $800,000. The owners of the dealership, Daniel and Michael Faretta, had only $290,000 insurance on the building and its contents, according to City Fire Chief Reynold D. Santone.

Among the cars crushed and burned in the blaze was a classic 1949 Buick convertible and a new van that was on a lift for repairs, the chief said. Information about the owners of the vehicles was not available.

By mid-morning, the structure—which sits behind D&M's new-car dealership at 1549 Pleasant Valley Blvd.—*looked more like it had been bombed than burned. The roof and pieces of several walls collapsed from the fire. More walls were knocked down on purpose so they would not fall on firefighters. . . .*

Santone said there were enough water and manpower to fight the fire. *The Peoples Natural Gas Co. was called and asked to cut off gas service to the building until the flames were doused. Firefighters stayed on the scene until 3 p.m. cooling "hot spots" among the charred debris.*

Firefighters were able to leave when snow showers moved into the area and cooled things down.

*Traffic on Pleasant Valley and Valley View boulevards
was blocked for several hours to keep vehicles away from the
scene. Blair County fire police were called in to direct cars away
from the fire. Traffic was moving normally by 10:30 a.m. . . .*

Good reporters include in their notes not only what they heard and read, but also what they saw. Larry Campbell of the *Anchorage Daily News* says that he draws heavily on observation: "If my assignment takes me to a classroom," the education reporter writes, "I might sense the aroma of wet snowpants dumped in the wardrobe after recess or see a boy in a red striped shirt rhythmically kicking a buddy's chair in front of him. Are the walls bare, or are they a cacophony of construction paper Thanksgiving turkeys or Halloween pumpkins? I might watch the Chatty Cathys, sitting next to each other and always chirping and giggling in each other's ears." [4]

Recording observations requires a reporter to function more like a vacuum cleaner than an editor. Throw out your biases, your stereotypes, your predispositions. Keep an open mind. Rather than making a judgment that an observation is not worth recording, include it in your notes. Later, especially when working with a writing coach, the reporter may discover the telling observation that unifies the story.

What should a reporter observe?

New journalist Tom Wolfe would say, pay attention to people's status life. Look at their furniture, how they decorate their house, what color scheme they used.

Others suggest reporting body language. In one memorable campaign, two opponents sat next to each other during a candidates' night. One was running a dirty campaign. Throughout the night, the other, a woman, sat with legs crossed and knees pointing almost at a right angle away from her opponent. It was clear she did not like the person.

Also report physical characteristics. You do not have to say someone is big. You might say that when the person sits, he fills a chair with no room to spare. Look for touching. Some people touch others unconsciously. Other people abhor touching and recoil if touched. Touching can also suggest intimacy between two people, an intimacy they may be trying to keep private. Look for the way people interact, how something is said rather than what is said.

How people dress is worth observing. But with any observation, do not make judgments; merely report. Let the reader make the judgments.

Let the reader decide if the person with a green shirt and red tie and argyle socks and gray suit is flamboyantly dressed. Also remember that your observations are exactly that—yours—and that any event comes with multiple perspectives. The observations of others are worth getting because they can reinforce yours or help fill out the picture you are trying to draw.

Observation requires the reporter to behave like a fly on the wall— unnoticed and unobtrusive. Do not annoy anyone. Just watch. Take it all in, and then use it to be more than a facts and figures reporter.

Documents

Documents are a great source of information. A valuable document can be something as simple as a one-page addendum to an annual budget or a non-profit group's income report to the federal government. A document, assuming it is not a forgery, is proof of something. It may prove a past action, or it may suggest a future action. Journalists love documents.

One of the most basic of all documents is the telephone book. There a reporter can find a name, an address, verify a spelling, check an area or zip code, locate a business. Another useful directory is a city directory or street list in which residents of the town are listed block by block. Such a directory tells who lives side by side and who lives across the street. It usually gives the phone number of each person and also has a cross-listing that allows a reporter to locate someone by address or alphabetically. One reporter covered a fire in a town 40 miles away by telephone merely by finding people who lived near the scene of the fire, calling them and interviewing them.

Still another standard document is the map. Good maps are divided into grids and list street names and grid coordinates. Some maps show physical characteristics, such as forests and mountains and the highways and byways. Roads are designated by ownership and responsibility, so a map is useful for figuring out if a particular road is a U.S. route, a state route or a local road.

Government offices are repositories of documents. On the local level are planning and zoning documents, official correspondence, contracts, the results of health and code inspections, and so on. Courthouses offer, in addition to court decisions, copies of wills and deeds, and listings of property ownership and the assessed value of property. Many legal transactions must be recorded with some office in the courthouse, and with the possible exception of sealed court decisions or court actions regarding juveniles, these transactions are available for public consumption.

One immediate source of documents is the newspaper's library. A good newspaper, even a small one, attempts to have on hand certain local documents that are referred to from time to time. Within this category are the newspaper's own clip files, probably slowly being converted to electronic form.

Whether print or electronic, the newspaper's library is a good starting point for research on any story. The reporter can glean from the library whether the story has already been done or what related stories might have been done locally. If the reporter has access to a national electronic database, he or she may check other newspapers to see what they have done on a particular subject. A newspaper subscribing to Vu/Text provides a reporter with access to more than 60 U.S. newspapers, five news and business wires, eight business publications, five magazines, some Canadian sources, and miscellaneous information about ships and recipes.[5] Add the Nexis and Dialog databases to that, and the reporter can access an additional 650 full-text news, business, government and international services and a legal database called Lexis.

Journalists, of course, need to use the electronic databases in creative ways. Scott Armstrong argues that if journalists had made a systematic search of Nexis and Dialog, they would have reported the Iran-Contra scandal thoroughly.[6] Database searches, Armstrong argues, would have given journalists knowledge of what others had done, and thus the journalists could have built on each other's work. Instead, many worked in the dark and did not pursue some stories that a database search would have suggested were worth pursuing.

Various telephone companies provide gateway services, meaning that dialing one phone number gives a reporter an opportunity to branch into a variety of databases. One of the first database and gateway services was CompuServe, whose offerings include electronic mail, public weather reports, news files, stock quotes, travel services, electronic shopping and electronic forums.

The federal government provides various databases. Some are available for a fee; others are free, except for the long-distance phone call to access them. A useful voice and video database is the Media Resource

Center and the Videotape Referral Service, which are operated by the Scientists' Institute for Public Information. Reporters can get a list of possible sources, which the center gleans from its own computer database, and also videotapes that can be used to illustrate news stories on television. As more and more information is developed electronically, more databases will arise. Not all of them will be economical, and newspapers will undoubtedly hire a librarian to do the searching for a reporter to keep costs down.

Good reporters, by the way, are not lulled into believing that what they retrieve from an electronic database is gospel. The information in many databases is only as good as the sources it was derived from.

A library that is a repository for state and federal documents—known as a Federal Depository Library—is an excellent place to do research, especially if the topic is national and the reporter is adapting it to the local situation. Such a library holds copies of congressional hearings, which offer not only a great deal of background but also the names of people the reporter can call. Market and corporate information is probably available in such a library. Also available are thousands of reference books, magazines and reviews. And while a particular book may not focus directly on the issue being researched, its index and bibliography might allow the reporter to find more specific sources.

One of the best resources in any library is the librarian himself. Librarians are experts at finding information or knowing how to find information.

Note Taking

Taking accurate notes is a critical part of good reporting. The best reporting effort in the world can be undermined by inaccurate or illegible notes.

The computer and the photocopying machine have reduced the chance for error, simply because no human hand intercedes in the note-taking process. But when covering a meeting or interviewing someone, a reporter relies on a notebook and a pencil.

Note taking is an individual art, and as long as the notes are clear and accurate when the reporter sits down to write, the particular approach to taking notes does not matter. One reporter's methods may not work for another.

Unless you have learned shorthand, you will need to make up your own. Look for words that readily lend themselves to abbreviation or a short form and develop a standardized shorthand. For example:

Shorthand	Meaning
/w	with
acc	according to
thru	through
&	and
devel	develop
devels	developers
b4	before
hier	higher
hi	high
1/2	one-half
rec	recommendation
gov	government
fed	federal
demo	demonstration
rel	related
bus	business
orig	original
alt	alternate
pt	point
st	state
pop	population
est	estimate

So if someone said, "We need an estimate of the state and federal populations before we can make a recommendation on development," the reporter's shorthand might produce, "we need est st-fed pops b4 we can make rec on devel."

Each reporting situation presents unique opportunities for shorthand. For example, a reporter usually abbreviates the names of speakers at a meeting, being careful not to shorten anyone's name to a single letter so that the reporter might confuse the person with someone else whose last name begins with the same letter.

Also make sure a question ends with a question mark. That may sound silly, unless you realize that note taking is not the art of writing down every word, but usually just the key words of an interview or meeting.

Verbatim note taking has its drawbacks. It is more important for a reporter to understand what is being said than to write down every word. Not everything said is worth recording. Listen for stage directions and rhetorical throat clearing that really mean nothing, except as facilitators in a meeting. If the chairman of a meeting says, "OK, what do we do next?" why write it down? And if someone says, "Let's do parking," why write it down until everyone has spoken and the group has decided what to discuss next?

Rhetorical throat clearing may be worth paying attention to, but not at first sound. Rhetorical throat clearing is words and phrases with which a speaker begins a statement while groping mentally for the right words to make the salient point she wants to make. For example:

> "*After careful thought and in my considered opinion,* I say
> we do not raise taxes."

The salient point is the speaker's statement not to raise taxes. That's what the reporter must get into his notes. The throat clearing just alerted him to the coming point.

Elsewhere in a notepad are check marks. They indicate items in the notebook that after the meeting the reporter had to check on to clarify a fact or a statement. Such checking is essential and professional. It enables a journalist to write an accurate story and also to develop credibility with sources. Some journalists might use a question mark to signal an ambiguous line in the notes, but a question mark could be read as indicating a question. The check mark says "check."

Some other tricks come to mind. One journalist uses a grid when covering some multiple-speaker events as a way of cataloging the positions of various speakers. For example, in covering a candidate's night, she set up a grid with the names of the six candidates across the top and the issues, as they arose, down the left-hand side. She still took thorough notes, but she also used the grid to develop an instant summary of where the candidates stood on the issues. The grid became a story-organizing device, since she could organize her story by lumping together the candidates who agreed on certain issues. It also enabled her to contrast statements and positions.

One favorite notebook is a 6 × 9 pad with a rule down the center. The center rule enables reporters, such as sportswriters, to use the halves of the page to record actions by the opposing teams. For a football game, a sportswriter can write down the left-hand side for one team's offensive drive and then switch to the other half after a score or a punt or a fumble and record the other team's actions there. The sportswriter can use the blank space opposite her notes to put asterisks to signify key plays that she wants to get into her story. Such an approach doubles as an outline and enables the writer to begin writing as the game is ending.

Some beginning journalists use tape recorders for the most routine events. A tape is useful as a backup in a long interview and can be played back to check a quote or a fact. But a tape recorder is not infallible, and it alone should never replace a notebook and several sharp pencils or fresh pens.

One of the country's best non-fiction writers, Tracy Kidder, seldom uses a tape recorder. He does not like them because the tapes must be transcribed, because he finds recorders unwieldy and because they miss subtleties. "Also," Kidder once said, "a tape recorder tends to make me lazy, so I might stop taking notes and miss a lot."[7]

Gathering information requires journalists to explore a variety of sources and use a variety of techniques. The best stories come from the best research.

Review Questions

What advantage does a face-to-face interview have over a telephone interview?

In what sequence should questions be asked, if some of the questions are confrontational and others are friendly?

How should a reporter dress for an interview?

What is the message behind Donald Drake's statement to be "more than a facts and figure reporter"?

What does Larry Campbell draw on when he is reporting?

What are some of the other aspects a reporter can observe?
What is a document?
List 10 places in your community where documents can be found.
How reliable is an electronic database?
How can a reporter guard against publishing inaccurate information?
Why does Tracy Kidder seldom use a tape recorder?

Endnotes

1. Tad Bartimus, "Skillful Interviewing," *AP World,* (Spring 1989), 9–11.
2. Jane Evinger, "Dirty Tricks Teach Interview Pitfalls," *Journalism Educator* 39, no. 4 (Winter 1984).
3. "The Forsaken: How America Has Abandoned Thousands in the Name of Social Progress," by Donald C. Drake, July 18, 1982, 1. Reprinted by permission of *The Philadelphia Inquirer.*
4. Larry Campbell, "The Vital Links: Good Reporting/Good Writing." From *The Coaches' Corner,* 3, no. 1, (March 1988), 1–2. Reprinted by permission.
5. All information on what is available in electronic databases is current as of January 1, 1990.
6. Scott Armstrong, "Iran-Contra: Was the Press Any Match for All the President's Men?" *Columbia Journalism Review,* (May/June 1990), 27–35.
7. Michael Schumacher, "How Tracy Kidder Writes His Books," *Writer's Digest,* (November 1990), 33.

Sources and Resources

Aumente, Jerome. "New PCs Revolutionize the Newsroom." *Washington Journalism Review* (April 1989): 39–40, 42.

Biagi, Shirley. *Interviews That Work: A Practical Guide for Journalists.* Belmont, Calif.: Wadsworth, 1986.

Cates, Jo. "What reporters and Editors Should Know about Databases." *Style* (Summer 1989): 20–22.

Endres, Frederic F. "Daily Newspaper Utilization of Computer Data Bases." *Newspaper Research Journal* 7, no. 1 (Fall 1985): 29–35.

Evinger, Jane. "Dirty Tricks Teach Interview Pitfalls." *Journalism Educator* 39, no. 4 (Winter 1984): 28–29.

Johnson, Dirk. "Part of Reporting Is Simply a Matter of Asking Questions." *The Coaches' Corner* 3, no. 1 (March 1988), 1, 3.

Johnson, James W. "If You Take Super Notes, Skip This." *The Quill* (May 1990): 29–31.

Keir, Gerry, Maxwell McCombs, and Donald L. Shaw. *Advanced Reporting: Beyond News Events.* New York: Longman, 1986.

McManus, Kevin. "The, uh, Quotation Quandary." *Columbia Journalism Review* (May/June 1990): 54–56.

Metzler, Ken. *Creative Interviewing: The Writer's Guide to Gathering Information by Asking Questions.* 2nd ed. Englewood Cliffs, N.J.: Prentice Hall, 1989.

Ullmann, John, and Jan Colbert, eds. *The Reporter's Handbook: An Investigator's Guide to Documents and Techniques.* 2nd ed. New York: St. Martin's Press, 1990.

Veronis, Christine Reid. "More Journalism Students Get Experience Gathering Data by Computer." *Presstime* (March 1989): 50.

Ward, Jean, Kathleen A. Hansen, and Douglas M. McLeod. "Electronic Library Effects on News Reporting Protocols." *Journalism Quarterly* 65, no. 4 (Winter 1988): 845–52.

Webb, Craig. "Government Databases: Reporters from Everywhere Can 'Visit' Federal Agencies by Tapping Uncle Sam's Growing Number of Information Banks." *Presstime* (April 1989): 18–20.

Chapter 7

Vision and Revision

Chapter Objectives

In this chapter you will be introduced to the concepts of visualizing stories before writing them and revising them once they are written. You will learn about various problems in writing stories and how to fix those problems. You will also see how rewriting improves writing.

Introduction

The journalist should think about what the story is before beginning to write. Planning a story includes note taking, organizing notes, listing people to be interviewed, researching background, and talking with co-workers about the story.

After writing the initial draft, the writer should edit the work, difficult as that is to do objectively. Copy should be tightened, facts and spelling checked, and the story reread to ensure it makes sense as a whole.

Thinking as Part of Writing

A stereotype of the journalist has a reporter rushing from the scene of a fire to a newsroom, racing over to his desk and immediately beginning to type out the story. The suggestion is that the story is originating as the reporter types.

But that is not where a story really starts. The reporter is able to begin writing immediately because on her way back from the fire, or other event, she has thought about the story—that is, she has done her analysis aforethought. She may also continue the process of thinking while revising the initial draft of the story, especially if she is not working on deadline. Even on deadline, a writer can make structural changes on the computer much more easily than in the days of cut-and-paste editing.

In envisioning a story, a journalist must first do her homework. She also needs to be prepared for the unexpected. The story once written, revision takes over. The journalist checks her work against expectations and then rewrites as needed.

Vision

Stories do not leap into a journalist's mind from a prefabricated mold. A journalist does not reach into some file and pull out a School Board Form and shape a school board meeting story according to the form. A journalist has to see what part of the meeting or event is news and then write the story. Seeing a story is linked with having good news sense, knowing what is going on in the local community and knowing what is important to readers or listeners. Beginning journalists can compensate for inexperience by doing extensive background work.

But for those stories based on events of the moment, seeing the story requires the journalist to marshal all of his senses. Part of seeing stories involves making a checklist of people you may want to talk to, something like a prebriefing. Writing the story, then, is a debriefing. Part of seeing stories involves analyzing what information has been gathered and then putting it into context for the reader. Recall the lead-writing advice given in earlier chapters. The reporter needs to ask, "What's my story?"

Most governmental bodies distribute meeting agendas before the actual meetings take place. Using these, a journalist can see what items might be major, then read clips or interview people for background in advance of the meeting so that he understands the issues. It is easier for the reporter to write on deadline when he understands what he's writing about.

A broadcast journalist might dispatch a videographer to get visuals that show the issue. If the issue is traffic problems in a residential area, the videographer has to shoot video when the problem occurs, which may not be when the governmental body is discussing it.

Other planned events also lend themselves to this kind of homework. The most likely news peg for a Memorial Day service at the local cemetery will be the remarks of the invited speaker. Knowing the history of Memorial Day celebrations and getting background on the speaker are two helpful ways of seeing what the story might be.

But planning ahead should not blind the reporter to unexpected and newsworthy things that come up at an event. The agendas of some governmental bodies include open time for non-agenda items. These open-ended segments are ripe for unexpected news, and the good journalist who has done his homework can process the unexpected much more easily.

Seeing an event unfold also enables a journalist to evaluate what is significant and what is not to the people involved. The journalist can star his notes from this viewpoint for quick reference later as he writes. This marking of notes can include determining what angle will make a good lead and what might neatly end the story.

A journalist should also talk about a story before writing it. Part of that process occurs before the journalist covers an event; it occurs as the journalist researches the topic and plans for covering the story. The process continues as the journalist drives back from an event or, better still, it can take place with an editor. Talking to an editor allows a reporter to "test" the story. The editor may detect problems with the emphasis or the proposed organization. A journalist who starts to write on deadline without having given any thought to the story ahead will need more time later to repair the damage.

When not under deadline pressure, the journalist can also talk with other reporters about the story and problems related to it. Writers' support groups have been effective vehicles in improving writing in newspapers. Writing is not the solitary act it was once presumed to be.

Seeing a story, then, is part of the process of writing. Journalists who take the time to do background work and to analyze their research to establish what the story is will find writing the story that much easier.

Revision

The best writing is rewriting. Extensive rewriting on deadline is impossible, but rewriting is a valuable exercise for beginners, even though the time demands seem overwhelming. Seeing how a lead can be better crafted or how a change in the order of paragraphs aids story flow helps the beginner on the next story. Rewriting defines the quality of good writing.

One benefit of putting words on paper is that it allows the writer to examine the words and learn. But the ego can get in the way. The first thing any good writer does is learn to critically evaluate his own work.

Every story deserves a gut reaction from the writer. How does the writer feel about the story? What does the writer like and what does he not like about the story? In other words, is the writer comfortable with the work? No matter how modest a story, did it live up to its intention? The answers to these questions can provide a preliminary guide in fixing the story. Following are some other areas to consider.

Emphasis

The writer needs to ask if the story's emphasis or concept is the right one. In effect, the writer must ensure that the angle in the story focuses on the news the reader needs. Here is an example of a story with the wrong emphasis:

> The Cardiff Area Senior Citizens Advisory Commission yesterday elected a new chairperson.
> The commission elected as chair Helen Konstas, who represents Patton Township. Mildred T. Lipkis, who represents College Town, was elected vice-chairperson.
> Konstas said her immediate concern was paying the rent for the Senior Citizens Center in College Town. The $34,000 annual rent has been funded by a Community Development Block grant from College Town. But College Town cut that in half when the federal government reduced its community grant. . . .

2

Another way Pennsylvanians may cast their ballot is through the absentee method. If you are t~~emporarily~~ ~~living some place~~ else where on Election Day and know it soon enough~~,~~ you may vote via an absentee ballot. ~~Technically, absentee ballots are for people temporarily not residing in their home precinct--such as military personnel--but I know of people who are out of town on business around election time and exercise their franchise by obtaining an absentee ballot.~~

Still a third way some Pennsylvanians vote is to go to their county courthouse no later than a week before the election and cast their ballots then. The ballots on put in the appropriate precinct boxes and counted with all the others. (Is this legal option?)

So Election Day is but one of three opportunities we provide. And if the weather's bad or a voter is busy or forgetful on election day, we have a low turnout.

Would we improve the turnout of registered voters if we provided a more convenient way of voting? What if everyone voted by mail? Would voting by mail increase the number of registered voters voting?

Here's how voting by mail would work:

Approximately six weeks before the election, the county board of elections would send a postcard to each registered voter. Registered voters would be defined as ~~some~~ those who just

Figure 7.1 The author's editing of his own op-ed essay.

What is the emphasis problem? Primarily, it has to do with the story's focus and lead. Telling the reader that the commission elected a new chairperson does not say much. More important is that the new chairperson must find a solution to the rent problem. Given the original story, the copy desk might write this mundane headline:

Seniors commission
elects new officers

But the assignment editor cuts the story off before it reaches a copy editor and asks the reporter for a rewrite, putting the emphasis on the rent issue. Thanks to having the story in a computer file, the reporter easily rewrites the first two paragraphs and moves some information in a matter of minutes. This was her new approach:

> The new chairperson of the Cardiff Area Senior Citizens Advisory Commission said yesterday her immediate concern is paying the rent for the Senior Center.
> Commission chair Helen Konstas said she is worried about where the money for rent is going to come from next year. The $34,000 annual rent has been funded by a Community Development Block grant from College Town. . . .

How would that story fare with the headline writer? Probably something like this:

New senior officer
sees rent shortfall

This is not sensationalism. The reporter must write something that will interest the reader and something the reader should know. After all, the reader, as a taxpayer, may have to make up the shortfall. A routine change of commission officers is nothing for the reader to be concerned about, but when the new chair voices concerns, the reader wants, and needs, to know.

Let's examine another story. In this case, a man pleads guilty to burglary and theft. He admits to stealing his landlady's television set and selling it to a detective. This could be a routine one-paragraph story, something like this:

> Jackson E. Bridgette III, 23, of the first block of East South Street, York, pleaded guilty to burglary and theft Monday. He was sentenced to four to 23 months in the county jail, court costs and restitution. Police had arrested Bridgette for stealing a television set from his landlady.

Sometimes, though, the information available to a reporter provides potential beyond the bare-bones police blotter story. This is such a story. And so the reporter fleshes it out:

> A York man picked the wrong person—an off-duty city police detective—as the potential buyer of a pocket-size television set he had stolen the previous day.
>
> Jackson E. Bridgette III, 23, of the first block of East South Street, pleaded guilty to burglary and theft Monday as a result of the incident.
>
> Senior Judge James E. Buckingham of York County Common Pleas Court sentenced him to four to 23 months in county jail and payment of court costs plus restitution.
>
> Bridgette has been in jail on the charges since March 30 in lieu of $10,000 bail.
>
> Detective Scott E. Rohrbaugh said he was inside a York restaurant March 14 when Bridgette approached him, stating he recalled having seen him at a York bowling center.
>
> Unaware of Rohrbaugh's profession, Bridgette offered to sell him the small TV set for $30. The detective countered with a $20 offer that was accepted, and the stolen merchandise was turned over to the law enforcement officer.

Rohrbaugh said Bridgette told him he was moving and had other items to sell if he was interested.

Two days later, Connie Lara, the TV set's owner, appeared at the restaurant, where Bridgette worked, and confronted him about taking the set from her bedroom.

Rohrbaugh returned the set to Lara and took a complaint about the theft. Lara told the officer she had rented a third-floor bedroom to Bridgette at 26 E. Jackson St.

On March 13, she left her apartment, locking both doors to her bedroom. When she returned nine hours later, one bedroom door had been forced open and the TV set, which had been on a dresser, was missing.[1]

What's the most interesting aspect of that story? The writer seemed to put greater emphasis on the outcome of the criminal's plea than on the fateful nature of his act. But isn't the better story about selling the television set to an off-duty police officer? Revised with that in mind, here is yet another version:

A York man picked the wrong person—an off-duty city police detective—as the buyer of a pocket-size television set he had stolen the previous day from his landlady.

Det. Scott E. Rohrbaugh said he was seated inside a York restaurant on March 14 when Jackson E. Bridgette III, 23, of the first block of East South Street, York, approached him and said he recalled having seen him at a York bowling center.

Unaware of Det. Rohrbaugh's profession, he offered to sell him a small television set for $30. The detective countered with $20, which was accepted, and the stolen merchandise was turned over to the law enforcement officer.

Det. Rohrbaugh testified later that Bridgette told him he was moving and had other items to sell.

Two days later, though, the set's owner, Connie Lara, confronted Bridgette at the restaurant where he worked and accused him of having taken the television set from her bedroom.

Lara said that on March 13 she had left her apartment, locking both doors to her bedroom. When she returned nine hours later, one bedroom door had been forced open and the television set was missing.

Lara told police that she had rented a third-floor bedroom to Bridgette at 26 E. Jackson St., York. Police arrested Bridgette.

On Monday, Bridgette pleaded guilty to burglary and theft. Senior Judge James E. Buckingham of York County Common Pleas Court sentenced him to four to 23 months in county jail, payment of court costs and restitution.

Bridgette has been in jail in lieu of $10,000 bail since March 30.

That draft sets up the story but requires the reader to read nearly to the end to learn what happened to Bridgette. Casual readers might not want to read to the end, so give them the essence of the story in the opening paragraph. If they want to read more, they can; if the opening paragraph tells them enough, they can move on to other stories in the paper.

A York man picked the wrong person—an off-duty city police detective—as the buyer of a pocket-size television set he had stolen the previous day from his landlady. *Now he's serving time for his mistake.*

Police and court records provided this account:

Det. Scott E. Rohrbaugh said he was seated inside a York restaurant on March 14 when Jackson E. Bridgette III, 23, of the first block of East South Street, York, approached him and said he recalled having seen him at a York bowling center.

Unaware of Det. Rohrbaugh's profession, he offered to sell him a small television set for $30. The detective countered with $20, which was accepted, and the stolen merchandise was turned over to the law enforcement officer.

Det. Rohrbaugh testified later that Bridgette told him he was moving and had other items to sell.

Two days later, though, the set's owner, Connie Lara, confronted Bridgette at the restaurant where he worked and accused him of having taken the television set from her bedroom.

Lara said that on March 13 she had left her apartment,
locking both doors to her bedroom. When she returned
nine hours later, one bedroom door had been forced
open and the television set was missing.

Lara told police that she had rented a third-floor bedroom to Bridgette at 26 E. Jackson St., York. Police
arrested Bridgette.

On Monday, Bridgette pleaded guilty to burglary and
theft. Senior Judge James E. Buckingham of York
County Common Pleas Court sentenced him to four to
23 months in county jail, payment of court costs and
restitution.

Bridgette has been in jail in lieu of $10,000 bail since
March 30.

The two-sentence lead neatly summarizes the story for the casual
reader but still leaves enough unexplained for the reader looking for a good
story. The final version also acquired a new second paragraph. In rereading
an earlier version of the story, you will discover that it lacks attribution
in some places. Rather than attribute everywhere, the rewriter came up
with a catch-all attribution sentence. The structure of the final version is
not an inverted pyramid but instead an hourglass, a structure discussed in
Chapter 8.

Structure

The structure of a story reveals how a story is put together. A story can
have a structure that works or a structure that doesn't work. Structural
problems cover a variety of problems in the overall organization of the
story. Such problems can include backing into a story or not developing a
lead. In the following example, both the lead and structure present problems and will need to be fixed as part of a structural redesign:

Patton Township Supervisors last night authorized
the submission of the Liquid Fuels Tax grant application
for two road projects in the township.

The supervisors recommended that work on a portion of Meeks Lane, at the intersection of Skytop Lane,

and the upper portion of Julian Pike be recommended for funding by a Centre County Liquid Fuels Tax grant.

The Meeks Lane proposal, according to Township Manager Thomas S. Kurtz, includes the acquisition of property owned by Louis Glantz, Port Matilda. Glantz has an agreement with the township to sell the property for $10,000, Kurtz said. The property would be used to widen the curve at the intersection of Meeks and Skytop lanes, he said.

The cost of the Meeks Lane project is estimated at $24,000, Kurtz said. The total cost of the project, including the land acquisition, is $34,000, he said.

The Julian Pike proposal, estimated at $20,000, would include road resurfacing and the replacement of guard rails.

The supervisors requested that both projects be recommended after they were not able to agree on a single project.

"Both are facilities for commuting traffic from other municipalities," chairperson Philip I. Park said.

Supervisor Elliot Abrams said, "The likelihood of saving someone's life would be greater on Julian Pike."

However, Supervisor Victor L. Dupuis said that priority should be given to the Meeks Lane project since traffic is expected to increase on that road.

"Guard rails increase speed," Dupuis said. "You feel you have that protection. I'd just as soon keep as much traffic off Julian Pike as possible."

In other matters . . .

As you read beyond the lead, you realize that the lead reflects a routine decision, but the body of the story suggests otherwise. Furthermore, the early paragraphs of the story give background on the projects rather than giving a flavor of the discussion that preceded the decision. How much detail on the projects does the reader need to understand the debate?

The following lead establishes that the story is about an other than routine decision:

Unable to agree on a single project, the Patton Township Supervisors last night agreed to seek state money for two.

Now the reader has some flavor of the discussion behind the decision and wants to know something about the projects. Here is the second paragraph:

> The supervisors were torn between widening a curve on Meeks Lane and resurfacing the Julian Pike as well as replacing guard rails.

Compare that with the second paragraph of the original, which suggest specifically what was going to be done. So now the reader has a flavor of the debate and knows what the projects are. The writer needs to flesh out the debate more:

> Unable to agree on a single project, the Patton Township Supervisors last night agreed to seek state money for two.
>
> The supervisors were torn between widening a curve on Meeks Lane and resurfacing the Julian Pike as well as replacing guard rails.
>
> "Both are facilities for commuting traffic from other municipalities," chairperson Philip I. Park said.
>
> Supervisor Elliot Abrams said, "The likelihood of saving someone's life would be greater on Julian Pike."
>
> However, Supervisor Victor L. Dupuis said that priority should be given to the Meeks Lane project since traffic is expected to increase on that road.
>
> "Guard rails increase speed," Dupuis said. "You feel you have that protection. I'd just as soon keep as much traffic off Julian Pike as possible."
>
> The Meeks Lane proposal, according to Township Manager Thomas S. Kurtz, includes the acquisition of property owned by Louis Glantz, Port Matilda. Glantz has an agreement with the township to sell the property for $10,000, Kurtz said. The property would be used to widen the curve at the intersection of Meeks and Skytop lanes, he said.
>
> The cost of the Meeks Lane project is estimated at $24,000, Kurtz said. The total cost of the project, including the land acquisition, is $34,000, he added.

The Julian Pike proposal, estimated at $20,000, would include road resurfacing and the replacement of guard rails.

In other matters . . .

Other Checkpoints

As part of revision, a journalist must also examine direct quotations, the ending, spelling, grammar, style and other details. The journalist must also tighten copy.

TIGHTENING COPY. The beauty of the written word is that it can be economically presented to readers. Readers do not have a lot of time to devote to a wordy story. Tightly edited stories use space wisely and make room for more stories.

It is not uncommon, especially when writing under the pressure of deadline, to produce a flabby sentence, a sentence that can easily be tightened by the reporter who takes a minute to check her copy. Here is an example:

A college graduate, he went to UCLA, where he earned a B.A. degree in theater.

The sentence contains two verbs, *went* and *earned*. What the writer needs to find is the right verb. Which one verb can carry that sentence? Try this:

He earned a B.A. degree in theater from UCLA.

It stands to reason that if he earned the degree from UCLA, he had to have attended UCLA. Thus, *earned* is the key verb, the one that subsumes all other actions.

Some phrases fatten sentences rather than help them, such as *it is/there is/there are*. Consider this flabby sentence:

> Judge Charles C. Griffiths *therefore* said *it was* the dogs
> *who* caused the accident *and* not Phillips.

Rewritten:

> Judge Charles C. Griffiths said the dogs, not Phillips,
> caused the accident.

Look for the opportunity to collapse two sentences into one, but do not collapse two sentences if the result is long. Here are two sentences that can be combined. As you read them, consider why.

> Abbey said a task team is already being assembled.
> The team will consist of three managers and three employees.

Given the shortness of the first sentence, why not immediately say who is assembling the task team and describe its make-up and finish with one sentence?

> Abbey said he is assembling a task team of three managers and three employees.

The overall five-word reduction may seem minimal, but consider not only the quantitative change but the qualitative gain. The new sentence is smoother because it has been recast in the active voice and is more direct.

Deadline editing challenges the writer to look for other areas of wordiness. Reduce *on the grounds that* to *because* and *in the intervening time* to *since*. Also remove unnecessary particles from verbs, such as *continue on,* *follow after, miss out, ponder over, slow down, slow up, cancel out, revert back, raise up, slim down, head up, check out.* Also watch for the problem with modifiers. *Game-winning run* equals *winning run* and *three separate buildings* equals *three buildings*.

Other examples of wordiness:

Wordy	*Tightened*
gave approval	approved
make a visit	visit
hold a meeting	meet
get in contact with	contact
get under way	begin, start
express different views	differ
made two attacks	attacked twice
caught many by surprise	surprised many
held a rally	rallied

PLACEMENT OF ATTRIBUTION TAG. Also check on the placement of the attribution tag. Normally, the attribution tag works better in the middle of a direct quotation than at the beginning or the end. It should go at or near the beginning of a sentence if necessary to signal a new speaker. From a story about a meeting on building a domed football stadium next to the Georgia World Congress Center (GWCC) comes an example of burying the attribution tag and getting maximum use out of the direct quotation:[2]

> Several council members said after the meeting that they agreed to give ground because of the dome's potential for improving life in the Lightning and Vine City communities, near the GWCC.
> "Very little changed at all in the last-minute talks," said Councilman Jabari Simama, whose district abuts the dome site. "I remain committed to the project, but what we saw last week was little more than political theater."

Later on, a new speaker appears at the front of an indirect quotation:

> GWCC Executive Director Daniel A. Graveline said interviews with prospective dome architects will likely begin in July, and an architect could be hired almost immediately thereafter. Actual design will probably take nine to 10 months, he said, adding that earth could start turning with site preparation this fall and construction would likely begin by spring.

CHALLENGE DIRECT QUOTATIONS. A journalist should also challenge the direct quotations she does use. Many direct quotations are not worth using, especially when they are incoherent, bombastic or foggy. Here is a sentence from a library board meeting that contains an abominable partial quotation:

> However, the board decided against this move and Jensen added that the library should open at the regular time with the "implementation of a system that requires a rotation of employees every third year to work the library while the others attend the annual function."

Got that? Of course not. The writer owes it to the reader not to use such unclear language. A paraphrase is in order:

> . . . Jensen added that the library should open at the regular time after a rotation system is put into effect. Such a system would allow employees to attend the annual function.

VERIFY, VERIFY, VERIFY. Deadline is too late to check arithmetic in a story. No reporter should walk away from a news event without having checked the numbers.

The arithmetic is not the only information a journalist should check. Also verify names, addresses and titles. Don't shy away from using a dictionary. The more certain you are about the spelling of a word, the more certainly you need to check. Also look over copy for typographical errors. Was the *not* of *not guilty* turned into *now*?

THE ENDING. The standard news story does not have an ending. As an editor once said to a cub who claimed to be struggling trying to find an ending for his story, "Newspaper stories don't have endings; they just stop." In reviewing the story the writer should make sure that the story stops on a clear note rather than an ambiguous one and has not raised an issue it has not resolved. Given that the standard news story peters out, endings are not normally a problem. In Chapter 9, where other story types are discussed, endings take on more significance and are discussed in greater detail.

Work with the Copy Desk

A final step in the revision process is copy editing, which is done by someone else. Give the desk time to edit the story. The copy editor must make sure the story works at two levels. Do the parts of the story fit to make a complete story? Are the mechanical parts in shape? Is the grammar standard? And then the copy editor must write a headline. A good headline sells a story. All of that takes time. Good copy editors are the friends of good writers and will strive to improve someone's prose when given enough time. First the writer does what he can to revise the story, and then he gives the copy editor enough time to do her work.

After the copy editor's work is done, it wouldn't hurt if the copy editor and the journalist found some time to discuss the changes the copy editor made to the story. Ideally, discussion occurs as the changes are being made. But another side of the discussion is a form of debriefing, of the copy editor just talking in general about the editing of a particular story. Such debriefing enables the journalist to learn something about editing and more about writing.

Revising a story is part of writing a story. In revising, a journalist makes sure the story lives up to its intention. She ensures the emphasis is

correct and that the story flows smoothly. Even on deadline, any revising that a journalist can do will help a story. And revising stories when not on deadline helps the writer hone her skills for the next time.

Review Questions

When does writing begin?

What can a journalist do to help himself see a story?

What role can an editor play in helping a journalist see a story?

How does emphasis in a story match news values?

Why should a writer want to tighten her writing?

Endnotes

1. Dean Wise, "Man Uses Wrong Channels to Get Rid of Stolen TV." From the *York Daily Record,* July 10, 1990, B1. Copyright © 1990 by the *York Daily Record.* Reprinted by permission.
2. Jim Newton and A. L. May, "It's on Go: Council OKs Georgia Dome," *Atlanta Constitution,* June 6, 1989, A01. Copyright © 1989 by Atlanta Newspapers Inc. Reprinted by permission.

Sources and Resources

Berner, R. Thomas. *The Process of Editing.* Boston: Allyn and Bacon, 1991.

Coulson, David C., and Cecilie Gaziano. "How Journalists at Two Newspapers View Good Writing and Writing Coaches." *Journalism Quarterly* 66, no. 2 (Summer 1989): 435–440.

Fry, Don. "How to Form a Writers Group" *The Quill,* (March 1988): 25–27.

Figure 7.2 (facing page) The Wall Street Journal copy desk in the 1940s (top) and today. The typical horseshoe copy desk and copy editor's green eyeshade have been replaced by conferences at computer terminals and the glare of VDT screens. Copyright © AP/World Wide Photos. Bottom photo by Neil Selkirk.

Guruswamy, Krishnan. "Writing Coaches—What Do Staff Writers at the St. Petersburg Times Think about Them?" Paper developed at the newspaper management program of the Poynter Institute for Media Studies, St. Petersburg, Fla., 1984.

Laakaniemi, Ray. "An Analysis of Writing Coach Programs on American Daily Newspapers." *Journalism Quarterly,* 64, no. 2-3 (Summer/Autumn 1987): 569–575.

Rich, Carole. "Coaching in the Newsroom and the Classroom." Paper distributed at the Poynter Institute for Media Studies, St. Petersburg, Fla., 1989.

Scanlan, Christopher, ed. *How I Wrote the Story.* 2d ed. Providence, R.I.: Providence Journal Company, 1986.

Wolf, Rita, and Tommy Thomason. "Writing Coaches: Their Strategies for Improving Writing." *Newspaper Research Journal* 7, no. 3 (Spring 1986): 43–49.

Chapter 8

Building on the Fundamentals

Chapter Objectives

In this chapter you will learn about some of the different organization schemes that journalists use instead of the inverted pyramid. You will learn about creative lead writing and the use of anecdotes in place of the standard lead. You will also learn about endings that do more than just stop.

Introduction

The inverted pyramid stands as the paragon of news story organization. But in reality it has remained useful only for certain types of deadline stories but otherwise not fitting for an audience that can—and does—get its news summaries from radio and television. Besides, journalism professor John H. Boyer argues, the inverted pyramid is not the way human beings talk to each other.[1]

Looking for Atmosphere

Newspapers want to make the reader care and feel, and want to show people in action, according to Donald M. Murray, a news writing coach who was formerly a journalist and English professor.[2] A story that might normally follow the inverted pyramid pattern now takes a new form on its way to the reader.

Among the various forms Murray has seen are "narrative, problem-solution, chronological account, biographical profile, all sorts of traditional rhetorical forms, and some that have not been studied and named." He points to the increasing use of anecdotes, which were once common only to magazines. And he makes the case that more newspaper stories attempt to show rather than tell, which is a way for the reader to feel the atmosphere of an event and to see the people in action. Furthermore, stories have endings instead of just petering out.

But some believe that newspapers have published too many stories that are not compelling and that are also irrelevant. So the underlying message is, when straying from the traditional a reporter should still focus on the main point of the story. An anecdote that does not lead into the main point is useless. A chronological account that "hides" the story's main point (see, for example, Box 8.1) does not serve the reader. When applying the advice given here, stay on track.

Leads

Not every story that crosses a reporter's desk is made of doom and gloom. Some stories are light or humorous. These stories let us step back from the seriousness of life to enjoy a moment of mirth.

In 1972, the government of China gave two pandas to the United States. Named Hsing-Hsing and Ling-Ling, they were placed in the National Zoo in Washington, D.C., and then people waited for them to mate. As an Associated Press story 11 years later put it, "The couple's courtship has been scrutinized, their behavior analyzed, their failures televised."

And while it is true that getting captive pandas to mate is a challenge, this story took on a less serious tone. Here was the stuff of soap operas. A couple. An audience. Sex. Finally, the couple consummated their relationship. Imagine the typical lead:

> Two pandas given to the United States by China 11 years ago have finally mated, National Zoo officials announced today.

Wasps Swarm Boy in Wheelchair

HIGHLAND CITY—Ten-year-old Ryan Smith, who suffers from muscular dystrophy, accidentally steered his electric wheelchair into a foot-deep wasps' nest Tuesday afternoon.

The wheels lodged in the nest, and Ryan was too weak to swat the wasps that attacked. His father was stung 35 times trying to rescue him.

"They were swarming all around him. . . . He was screaming for me to come help him," said the father, Bruce Smith. "I can't imagine what he went through in the 5 to 10 minutes before I was able to jerk him out."

Ryan, who weighs only 44 pounds, had about a dozen stings on his tongue alone. His other stings were too numerous to count. Ryan's father covered the boy with a comforter and rushed him to the family's pool a few hundred feet away.

Highland City paramedics answered a 911 call at the home. Ryan was taken to Lakeland Regional Medical Center and then flown by helicopter to St. Joseph's Hospital in Tampa.

As the wasps' venom coursed through his body, he recited vocabulary words, multiplication tables and worried about whether his accident would postpone the family's vacation.

His family isn't thinking much about the vacation right now. Ryan died early Wednesday.

Box 8.1   This Associated Press story is a chronological account that "hides" the news. The writer attempted to build drama but instead achieved melodrama by not mentioning until the last paragraph that the boy stung by wasps had died. Adding to the confusion is the use of the present tense in the lead, which suggests that the boy is still alive. Reprinted with permission of Associated Press.

But that did not appear, because an Associated Press writer demonstrated some imagination. This is the actual lead:

> Hsing-Hsing and Ling-Ling have finally done their thing-thing.

The rest of the story is a straightforward account of what happened, quotes and all, along with background and history. The writer was smart enough not to continue the tone of the lead lest the copy desk give him a fling-fling.

Would you like to know how to figure out the quality of the French red in the bottle without paying to open the bottle and sipping the wine or taking some expert's word for it? An economist at Princeton University came up with a formula he contended did just that. This was breaking news.

> A Princeton economist says he has devised a formula
> for predicting the quality of French red wines.

But the nature of this news demands different treatment, and Peter Passell of *The New York Times* chose a more intriguing way to lure the reader into his story.[3]

> Calculate the winter rain and the harvest rain (in millimeters). Add summer heat in the vineyard (in degrees centigrade). Subtract 12.145. And what do you have? A very, very passionate argument over wine.

Now isn't that better than *who, why, what, when, where and how*? Of course. It engages. What makes it work is the use of the second person (*you*). The reader is invited into the story.

Likewise, the reader is hooked by a story by Lauralee Jones of the *York Daily Record.*[4] Assigned to do a story on where letters addressed to Santa Claus go, Jones realized that young people reading the story would discover that the letters do not go to the North Pole but to the local post office, which answers them. So even before her byline appears, Jones placed the following:

> WARNING: *Parents, the subject matter in this story may not be suitable for children.*
>
> By Lauralee Jones
> *Daily Record Staff Writer*
>
> Sorry to disillusion you, folks, but Santa Claus isn't getting his mail . . . .

By imitating the warning labels on movies, videos, records, cigarette packages and alcohol containers, Jones caught the readers' attention immediately.

Stories

At some point, the standard definition of what constitutes a lead begins to blur. In the traditional news story, the first paragraph tends to be the theme or focusing statement for the story to follow. Everything that follows amplifies the first paragraph. Consider this story excerpt:

> The vice president of a Minneapolis advertising agency yesterday concluded his 18-day national ride as a hobo on trains to dramatize the plight of the homeless.
>
> Todd Waters, who lives in St. Paul with his wife, Dori, called his train trip from New York City to Los Angeles the "Penny Route" because he got people to pledge a penny for each of the 3,082 miles he traveled. The money will help the homeless throughout the United States, Waters said.
>
> During his travels as a hobo, Waters stopped at shelters for the homeless in cities along the way. He asked that donations be sent directly to shelters in New York, Buffalo, Cleveland, Detroit, Chicago, Kansas City, Phoenix and Los Angeles. Aside from the $2,000 earmarked for a shelter in Minneapolis, Waters said he has no idea how much money has been collected to date, but he thinks the response has been good.
>
> Waters said he chose to ride the trains to illustrate that there are thousands of homeless who do. "I wanted to show that it's not only top to bottom," he said. "It's coast to coast."
>
> Waters, who has been riding the rails for 11 years as a hobby, said the number of homeless riders has increased a thousandfold. And the riders don't fit the movie image of the stogie-smoking, happy-go-lucky hobo. They are, instead, women, children, mental patients and the "new poor" who have been uprooted by an economic bulldozer.
>
> "The only people out riding are those who are desperate," Waters said. "You don't run into a lot of hobos." . . .

That's a fairly straightforward account of Waters' arrival in Los Angeles. But when Theresa Walker of the *Los Angeles Times* wrote the story, she tried to capture the atmosphere of what it was like riding the trains.[5] She wanted to show Todd Waters in action. She observed Waters and reported her observations. Her opening paragraph establishes an atmosphere rather than telling the story. The reader must read through the fourth paragraph to get what might appear earlier in the traditionally structured story.

> Todd Waters, haggard and hungry from not eating for two days, peered warily out the Southern Pacific boxcar in Colton on Thursday morning, eyeing the yard for a railroad detective. None in sight, he quickly sprinted to safety.
>
> He looked like any other transient.
>
> But unlike his fellow travelers, Waters was at the end of the line. His arrival was the culmination of the "Penny Route," an 18-day trip from New York City to Los Angeles that he used to dramatize the plight of the nation's growing number of homeless individuals by seeking a penny pledge for each of the 3,082 miles he traveled.
>
> Waters is vice president of a Minneapolis advertising agency. He lives comfortably in St. Paul with his wife, Dori. He does not have to ride the trains. But he wanted to illustrate that there are thousands who do. . . .

The story was written on deadline. The event occurred Thursday morning, and the story appeared in Friday morning's paper.

Even meetings, which some consider reportable only in the inverted pyramid form, offer the writer an opportunity to use his imagination. Consider this lead on a meeting story:

> The College Town Commission for Pedestrian and Traffic Safety last night rejected a businessman's request to change the left-turn restriction at the intersection of Railroad Avenue and North Atherton Street.
>
> Thomas Smith, 943 Red Gate Road, said he does not believe the number of accidents caused by left turns at the intersection is enough to justify the economic hard-

ship that the 10 a.m. to 7 p.m. restriction causes his business. Smith said the restriction forces the customers of his business, Unlimited Rent-Alls, 140 N. Atherton St., to travel six blocks through three busy intersections to reach the area they could reach in seconds through a left turn from Railroad Avenue.

A journalist covering the meeting first went to Smith's place of business and followed the circuitous route a driver had to take because of the restriction. Then instead of writing the preceding lead, which does not explain the problem very well, he produced this:

Unlimited Rent-Alls is located at the corner of Railroad Avenue and North Atherton Street in College Town. But a customer leaving the business and wanting to go north on North Atherton may not just turn left. Instead, the customer must drive one block west to Barnard Street, two blocks south to West Beaver Avenue, one block east to Atherton, and then two blocks north to arrive at the spot he'd be at if he were just allowed to make a left turn.

In the words of Thomas Smith, part-owner of Unlimited Rent-Alls, "The drivers have to travel through three high traffic accident areas to make a left turn" onto North Atherton Street. Smith's customers have to take the long way because the City forbids left turns between 10 a.m. and 7 p.m. Monday through Friday.

Last night Smith appeared before the Commission for Pedestrian and Traffic Safety in an effort to get the left-turn restriction modified. Smith argued that the left-turn restriction was causing an economic hardship on his customers and that some of the businesses on Railroad Avenue are losing customers.

"The consensus of the business owners on Railroad Avenue is that 3:30 p.m. to 5:30 p.m. is the proper time for no left turns," Smith told the commission. That's the only time left turns should be restricted, he said, asking that the commission modify the current restriction.

But the consensus of the commission was to not recommend that City Council change the present restriction.

[Three more paragraphs explain the commission's reasoning behind standing pat.]

The second account is a variation of Murray's problem-solution form. In this instance, the readers first needed to understand the problem before they could appreciate the commission's recommendation not to modify the restriction. Furthermore, the second account is more like the way one neighbor might tell the story to another.

How do you write a story about a group of people protesting in front of a restaurant where they believe drug trafficking has taken place? Since it was not the kind of protest that attracted police and arrests, the usual lead about how many protesters were arrested was not appropriate. Cindy Stauffer of the *Lancaster* (Pa.) *New Era* chose the atmosphere approach:[6]

> The group of children and adults stood silently, hands raised, fingers pointing.
> Some of the youngsters held up signs reading "Down with Dope, Up with Hope" and "No More Drug Dealers on Our Streets."
> Across the street, at La Rosa Restaurant, people clustered at a door to see what was going on, only to encounter the accusing stare of the city's newest anti-drug group and the bright lights of a TV crew and a camera that recorded the scene.
> Curiosity dissolved into anger for some at the restaurant at South Duke and Locust streets as it dawned on them they were the target of a group that has attempted to make drug dealers unwelcome in the southeastern section of the city.
> A man opened the door and shouted, "Get that light out of here!"
> After a few minutes, the TV crew shut off its light.
> The 30 protesters didn't budge.
> "We're letting people in the neighborhood know we know there's drugs in this neighborhood," said Tom Hyson, a city school board member and a leader of the group.
> The march was the latest effort of Demonstrate Against Drug Dealers, an anti-drug group formed almost two months ago. . . .

Another story structure that some journalists use has been named the hourglass by Roy Peter Clark, an expert on the newswriting process and an associate director and dean of the faculty at the Poynter Institute for Media Studies. It has, he notes, three parts: the top, which tells the story quickly; the turn, a transitional sentence or paragraph, and the narrative, a chronological retelling of events. Here is an hourglass-structured story. Note the non-traditional two-sentence lead.

> The hands of a Blair County man were amputated in an industrial accident Friday at Appletown Papers Inc. in Roaring Spring. Undamaged parts of his right hand were then used by a surgical team at Allegheny General in Pittsburgh to reattach his left hand during an 18-hour operation.
>
> The man, Daniel Harshberger, 25, of Martinsburg, was listed in guarded condition Saturday evening at Allegheny General. Dr. Glen Buterbaugh, an orthopedic surgeon and head of the 25-member team that performed the surgery, said Harshberger is awake, alert and doing well.
>
> [The basic story has been told and now the writer turns to a more detailed and chronological telling.]
>
> Company officials and emergency and hospital personnel told this story:
>
> Both of Harshberger's hands were amputated at 2:15 p.m. Friday when they were caught in a machine that presses excess water out of pulp during a paper-making process. The accident severed each hand in two places— the thumb and the palm and the fingers and palm on each hand.
>
> Emergency personnel packed the severed hands, and Johnstown Memorial Hospital's Life Flight helicopter transported Harshberger to Allegheny General.
>
> At Allegheny, Buterbaugh said doctors determined that they could reattach the left thumb and palm to the left wrist and three fingers and palm from the right hand to the left hand. The four left fingers and the right little finger were too badly damaged to be reattached, he said.
>
> During the surgery, Buterbaugh later reported, he and Dr. Marc Laing, a plastic surgeon, took turns operating.
>
> First, the surgical team reattached the bones with steel plates, screws and pins. Next, the tendons were sutured together.

Using a microscope, the surgeons then used sutures as
fine as a strand of hair to sew the blood vessels and nerves
together. Circulation to the left thumb was established
by 8 p.m. Friday.

Harshberger was attached to a pulse oximeter monitor, which measures circulation to his fingers. "I will lie
awake tonight (Saturday) making sure the fingers are
OK," Buterbaugh said. He said the first 72 hours are the
most critical.

Buterbaugh said that if everything goes well,
Harshberger should have feeling in his fingers in six
months.

Buterbaugh learned his skill at Massachusetts General
Hospital in Boston, where the first retransplantation
procedure was performed 25 years ago this month. He
said that Allegheny General performs an average of one
such operation in a month, although it has done three in
the past week from the tri-state area.

Another variation is the micro-macro story form. In the example
shown in Box 8.2, the micro story is about a lesbian couple who want to
attend a high school prom. But eventually the story shifts away from the
couple and provides a larger, or macro, story about the issue in general. If
necessary, an editor could cut the story right where it begins to discuss the
larger issue without any loss of the micro details.

Both reporter and editor need to make sure that a non-traditional
opening is appropriate. Here is the beginning of a story about four people
who were rescued after being stranded for two days on an island after the
water rose. This is the first news account of the rescue.

Ralph Shaffer and Linda Miller walked two teenagers across the Conewago Creek in East Manchester
Township for a weekend of camping and fishing on an
island.

The creek was ankle high on Friday night as the four
carried a cooler of food, fishing rods, a tackle box, a
small grill, tents and other equipment onto the island,
nearly 300 yards long and 30 yards wide.

Shaffer, 23, Miller, 27, and the two teenagers, all of
York, planned to leave the island Sunday by walking the

A Rite of Passage

Heidi Leiter, a 17-year-old Manassas high school senior, will go to her prom tonight. As she enters the gym, decorated on a Hollywood theme, she expects some of the 300 or so other gowned and tuxedoed guests to stare and whisper. A few, she predicts, might move away if she and her date sit down.

Her date is a woman.

Students at Osbourn Senior High School have been talking about Leiter for more than six months, ever since a classmate began telling people at school that Leiter was dating Missy Peters, 20, a Radford University student who graduated from Osbourn in 1989.

"People make comments. I've seen writing on the wall, 'dyke' and stuff like that," said Leiter, a self-possessed young woman who says she tries to have a comeback ready for every insult.

When she saw "Heidi is a dyke" written on the desk she uses in the yearbook office, she added, "yes and proud of it."

"They kick you when you're down, but if you don't get down they can't kick you," she said.

School administrators believe the pair may be the first openly lesbian couple to attend a prom in the metropolitan area. A Gaithersburg junior brought his boyfriend to Richard Montgomery High School's prom last year.

Leiter and Peters, who have been dating for 17 months, have been talking about going to Osbourn's prom since last spring, when Leiter read about a Cumberland, R.I., boy who won permission in a 1980 federal suit to take a male date to his prom.

"We're not going to the prom to upset anybody else. We're going because we have the right to go just like anybody else," Leiter said. Peters skipped her prom two years ago because she didn't begin telling friends she was gay until she reached college.

"Hopefully, with us going to the prom, it'll make it easier for other gay people in high school so they're not scared," she said.

Before planning to go, Leiter checked with school administrators. They've also discussed their plans with both sets of parents.

Box 8.2   An example of a micro story expanded to macro form. From The Washington Post, *May 19, 1991, B1, B7. Copyright © 1991,* The Washington Post. *Reprinted by permission.*

Continued

"I respect her right to make this decision and I am there for her support and to offer any advice," said John Leiter. "I wish she would have waited a little longer and had some experience with the male side . . . but I don't want to make her decision for her," he said.

Leiter's decision to go to the prom with Peters—to be different at a time in her life when the pressure to conform is perhaps strongest—places her in the vanguard of a new generation of homosexuals.

Perhaps because so few teenagers have felt they could be openly gay, there have been few studies on homosexuality in young people, except among suicides and runaways. A 1988 federal study showed that 30 percent of teens who committed suicide were homosexual. Sexuality experts estimate that more than 10 percent of Americans are homosexual.

Therapists and sexuality experts say adolescents are often confused about their sexual orientation. A 1987 poll of 750 people by the Washington Blade newspaper showed that the average age at which a male realized he was gay was 14. For females, it was 17.

"By the time they reach mid- to late adolescence, what they've done is discover their feelings on the level of fantasy and physical attraction," said James Maddock, a family therapist at the University of Minnesota. Some experts involved with youth caution that young people often experiment during their teenage years, and that it is not uncommon to have both homosexual and heterosexual experiences.

"There's some fear that if [declaring oneself gay] becomes an adolescent, 'in' thing to do, it might influence adolescent women who are dissatisfied with their relationship with men to choose to say, 'To hell with men. I'll be my own person,' " said Mary Lee Tatum, a Falls Church sex education expert.

At Osbourn High School, Leiter has found that being gay is not an "in thing."

She "doesn't really have any friends at school because everybody looks at her as a lesbian and not as a person," said senior Jackie Simpson, 17, who has worked on the yearbook with Leiter. "She has a sense of humor, but it's gone now that everybody teases her."

Leiter usually skips lunch because she doesn't have friends to eat with, and she spends most of her out-of-school hours at work or at the Peters home with Missy, who is taking time off from Radford.

Continued

"They're just like any other couple. I went out with this guy for three years and I see a lot of [similarities] in our relationships," said Candi Schleig, 19, who roomed with Missy at Radford. "Before [I met Missy], I didn't like gay people."

Peters and Leiter have been planning tonight's events for several months. They've rented black jackets and tails and royal purple bow ties. (Neither of them liked the feel of a dress.) They've also hired a limousine big enough to hold friends from Radford and from the Prince William Gay and Lesbian Association, as well as a reporter from Glamour magazine.

Leiter's schoolmates have also been talking about the pair; one class even spent a whole period discussing the issue. "The majority of people think if they want to do it, it's their own business," said junior Nikky Ridnouer. "Some people might think it's gross but they wouldn't try and stop them."

same route they took on Friday. But nature changed their plans when the creek rose nearly 10 feet, leaving them stranded less than 30 feet from shore.

About 25 firefighters from Mount Wolf and York Haven fire companies responded to their plight Sunday afternoon near the Pennsylvania Power and Light Co. on Wago Road. Within an hour, the four were taken to safety, said Lee Bloss, a Mount Wolf Fire Company lieutenant.

The lead is ineffectually vague. This is a first-day story, which normally means the point of the story needs to be presented in the first paragraph. The writer has two options. One is to rewrite the story in the typical inverted pyramid form:

Four county residents stranded on an island in Conewago Creek for two days were rescued late Sunday afternoon by area firefighters. . . .

The other possibility is to drop a hint about the rescue into the original lead.

> Ralph Shaffer and Linda Miller walked two teenagers across the Conewago Creek in East Manchester Township for a weekend of camping and fishing on an island, only to get stranded for two days and require rescue by area firefighters.
>
> The creek was ankle high on Friday night. . . .

The following lead comes from a second-day story. A tornado had struck, and the editor assigned a reporter to do a follow-up story on people's reactions and to see what kind of damage had been caused. Here are the first four paragraphs:

> At 6 years old, Megan Grimes admitted Monday, she used to think it would be neat to live through a tornado or hurricane.
>
> After Sunday night's twister ripped through her hometown of Newberry Township, turning her swingset into a "big, big pretzel" but leaving her neighbor's set unscathed, Megan described the experience as "OK, I guess."
>
> With winds close to 50 mph, the funnel cloud caused more than $500,000 worth of property damage to buildings, said Kay Carman, deputy director of the York County Emergency Management Agency.
>
> Construction workers climbed about I-beam ceiling supports of houses Monday trying to prepare the homes for new roofs.

Later on in the story appears someone whose house, unlike Megan's, was damaged:

> Patrick O'Donnell was visiting his parents in Cumberland County when he heard about the tornado warning, but his wife, Katherine, and their two small children were in York.

When O'Donnell drove his rented car into his driveway, he said, there was a torrential downpour.

"I thought I'd wait for the rains to slow down before I got out and opened my garage door," he said.

As he opened the garage door, he saw the ominous black cloud looming in the background and approaching rapidly.

His 3-year-old son, Christopher, came down to greet him, and O'Donnell ushered his child into the cellar. Then, he said, he called for his wife to come down with their 7-month-old daughter, Shannon.

"Only minutes—no seconds—after she left the baby's room, the roof caved in," O'Donnell said Monday.

Mrs. O'Donnell and her daughter made their way downstairs. They were in the dining room, getting ready to go down another flight of stairs, when the wind kicked up, and glass crashed into the house as the living room window shattered, O'Donnell said.

While he surveyed the damage Monday, he said: "I'm just fortunate we didn't get it as bad as some of the others."

The O'Donnells were one of at least two families who were relocated after roofs were strewn from the four-year-old townhouses. . . .

Given the amount of damage they sustained and the fact that they came close to getting killed, the O'Donnells are more representative than is a 6-year-old with a limp quote. They should be used to lead off the story. Not just any anecdote will do. It must tie to the main point of the story. The O'Donnells do; Megan doesn't.

Endings

One of the virtues of the hourglass structure, Clark notes, is that it enables the writer to complete a story with "a real ending." But whether or not a story is structured like an hourglass, the opportunity to end it rather than just trickle to a close remains. Sometimes it is the event that allows the writer to close a story nicely. Here are the opening two paragraphs and then the close of a funeral story from *The Washington Post:*[7]

> Family, friends, colleagues and top Army officials gathered yesterday in a military chapel at Fort Myer to honor Maj. Arthur D. Nicholson Jr. and eulogize him as a man who had volunteered for a stressful assignment because he wanted to be on "the cutting edge."
>
> Nicholson, 37, a liaison officer to East Germany, was shot and killed by a Soviet sentry near a garagelike storage shed one week ago. Nicholson, whose home was West Redding, Conn., had been attached to the 14-member liaison mission in Potsdam since 1982. . . .
>
> Nicholson's family rose and, one by one, placed roses on his casket. His daughter, then his wife, bent to kiss the lid. The funeral party dispersed quickly, and a few people drifted down the hillside from the Tomb of the Unknown Soldier to stare at the casket, the mounds of flowers and the empty chairs.

The writer, Anndee Hochman, let circumstances (which she observed) dictate her story. This enabled her to write a low-key story that closes strongly.

Another effective way of ending a story is with a direct quotation from someone in the story. These two paragraphs come from a story about the defeat of legislation that would have protected gay men and women from harassment and violence. Some of the people quoted in the story said some rather unkind things. The writer ended the story this way:

> He shook his head sadly at the anti-gay comments of Mr. Foster and other members of the unofficial, bipartisan group that liberal lawmakers have taken to calling "the Neanderthal caucus."
>
> Segal had a kinder description for Foster. "I would call him the dinosaur of diction."

The journalist who starts or closes a story well is usually one who scours his notes for anecdotes and direct quotes and marks the possibilities. Seeing a quote such as the preceding, a journalist might mark it and/or write next to it "good end." Journalists who develop the habit of putting endings on stories will lure readers to read further in stories in search of the interesting endings.

Multiple Speakers

One of the most challenging events to report is the one with multiple speakers, all of whom need to be mentioned in the story. This usually happens when politicians engaged in a race get together. Since no journalist wants to be seen as biased, the journalist mentions everyone. This story from the *Atlanta Constitution* demonstrates how it can be done:[8]

With one candidate warning of a "crisis" in indigent health care, candidates for governor Friday called for local governments to pick up more of the tab for treating the poor.

The story begins with a general lead on a topic on which the candidates agreed. Note that the lead foreshadows one of the candidates.

State Sen. Roy E. Barnes (D-Mableton) opened a candidate forum before health groups with the warning and a vow to stop the "dumping" of indigent patients on public hospitals, particularly regional medical centers such as Grady Memorial Hospital.

The second paragraph follows the lead by naming the candidate mentioned in the lead and explaining his position.

The Republican candidates, state Rep. Johnny Isakson of Marietta and former Superior Court Judge Greeley Ellis of Covington, agreed, and also called for expanded Medicaid coverage for pregnant mothers and youngsters to improve preventive health care.

*The use of the verb **agreed** enables the writer to yoke in two other candidates.*

State Rep. Lauren W. McDonald Jr. D-Commerce, also called for expanded prenatal health services and Medicaid coverage, but offered no specific initiatives.

All four appeared at a joint conference of the Georgia Association for Primary Health Care and the Georgia Rural Health Association. Two other Democratic candidates, Lt. Gov. Zell Miller and Atlanta Mayor Andrew Young, did not attend.

This paragraph functions as the context graph. It tells where the candidates were and who else should have been there. This paragraph enables the writer to mention all the politicians and avoid being accused of bias.

According to Paul Bolster, lobbyist for the Georgia Hospital Association, all of the state's urban counties spend more than one mill of their property tax to fund indigent care. He said about one-third of the state's 159 counties provide some funding.

A background paragraph from a different source, although hardly an impartial one, gives the reader a context for the issue.

Mr. Barnes said, "All government bodies have responsibility for indigent health care," and the next governor should require all local governments to pay a share. He told a reporter that counties that send patients to other jurisdictions could be billed for the care of their residents, or all counties could pay into a pool to equalize the burden.

Now the writer returns to expand on the comments of the politicians who were present.

The senator also proposed the creation of a statewide pool to subsidize medical malpractice insurance for family practitioners in rural areas who agree to continue obstetric services.

Mr. Ellis said every local government should obligate a mill of their property tax to indigent care and to end the "cost shifting" of medical services to private patients.

Mr. Isakson, who is minority leader in the state House, called for fuller funding of an existing loan program to entice doctors to locate in rural areas. He also proposed the creation of a state advisory panel on medical care led by a doctor who could play the role of honorary surgeon general for Georgia.

A variation of the multiple-speaker story is the panel discussion. Panel discussions are especially good assignments for beginning newswriters because they challenge the writer to select newsworthy elements but still make clear to the reader that more occurred. Another challenge arises in deciding which speaker is the most newsworthy. Clearly, leading off with something like, "A group of experts held a discussion on obscenity and the arts last night," will not engage the reader. So the journalist focuses on one speaker but makes it clear that more is to come and eventually yokes in the other newsworthy speakers. This story excerpt is such an example:

Artists are caught in a Catch-22 between art and obscenity, a panel member said last night at Penn State.

By referring to the speaker as a **panel member**, *the writer has foreshadowed that other speakers will appear.*

"Artists won't know that their work is obscene until they are arrested for it," political science professor Bruce Murphy said. He said the Supreme Court has no concrete definition of what is obscene and what is art—and that's the Catch-22 for artists.

By repeating **Catch-22** *at the end of the second paragraph, the writer is developing a thread in the story and effecting transition.*

Murphy said the definition of obscenity is where the real problem lies. "Here we have the problem of defining the nature of obscenity as the Supreme Court sees it and what is the definition of art," Murphy said. He said no one knows the balance between obscenity and art.

The writer wants to get in at least the names of some of the other speakers. Watch how she makes the transition by repeating the word **balance** *in the next paragraph.*

This balance was one of the main points of discussion by the four panel members in the public forum, "Obscenity, Censorship and the Arts." The other panelists were John Kissick, an assistant professor in the School of Visual Arts; Kenneth Foster, director of the Center for the Performing Arts; and Eliza Pennypacker, an associate professor in the Department of Landscape Architecture.

The other panelists are named, and the writer ends the sentence with the name of the panelist she will quote next.

Pennypacker said that the community must define what is obscene. She said the American public and the art community must come to some amicable agreement on the subject.

Now the story can go on. The writer will blend the speakers depending on the topic rather than getting in some comment from all panelists immediately.

Murphy said such interaction becomes difficult because of the public's increasing intolerance toward the arts, individual expression and those ideas that vary from the norm. He said these views have a significant impact on the art community.

Having mentioned all the panelists, the writer can go back to the first speaker, since his remarks fit here.

In addition to the community's reaction toward the arts, Murphy said, the shifting political winds add to the problems faced by artists in defining for themselves the nature of obscene art. . . .

And the story goes on from here.

Stories with multiple speakers challenge writers because the story needs to be more than a tennis match, with each paragraph alternating among the speakers. The preceding story avoids the tennis match approach by giving several paragraphs to one speaker's comments followed by a second speaker's comments. The writer gives information in context rather than jumping back and forth.

Multiple Topics

Just as vexatious to write are multiple-topics stories. Usually, they come from local governmental meetings at which a variety of equally newsworthy topics are discussed. Some newspapers have stopped publishing multiple-topic stories and instead offer two or three stories per meeting, with each story focusing on one issue. That enables the reader to locate topics of interest and ignore other topics.

Other newspapers, sometimes tight on space, cover a local governmental meeting in one story. In those circumstances, the reporter has a couple of choices on how to write the story. Generally, the reporter should look at the story as a stack of inverted pyramids, with each new pyramid starting a new story. Thus, each time the topic changes, the reporter should lead with the action. Another variation calls for a foreshadowing paragraph or paragraphs early in the story.

What follows is a story in the first form, the stack of inverted pyramids, and then a rewrite to show the foreshadowing approach. The original appeared in the *Springfield* (Ohio) *News-Sun*.[9]

Voters will decide in May whether higher taxes will make the city a safer place.

On Tuesday, a 5-year, 3-mill property tax levy was placed on the ballot by city commissioners responding to petitions presented by Citizens for a Safer Springfield.

The tax, which is in the form of a charter amendment, would force the city to add 24 patrolmen to the 100-officer police division. A minimum of six police officers would be assigned to the narcotics unit if voters approve the tax issue. All interest earnings from the levy receipts would remain in the levy fund.

The tax issue would generate about $1.5 million annually and cost the owner of a home with a $60,000 market value about $55.12 each year.

"It's a levy which citizens have begun," said Mayor Warren Copeland, who was joined by Commissioner Nora Parker in personally endorsing the tax issue.

Commissioner Faye Flack, who last week asked that commissioners delay acceptance of the petitions until names could be checked, said she did not intend to imply a lack of trust in the citizens who passed the petitions. Flack said she felt it was the commission's duty to informally review the petitions, which contained 2,022 signatures.

That review showed there were enough valid signatures to indicate substantial citizen support for the tax issue, said Flack.

Also Tuesday, city commissioners heard citizen Kevin O'Neill complain about the commissioners' plan to spend $11,592 on handicapped-accessible playground equipment. He said the money should instead be used to build skateboard facilities.

*The second inverted pyramid starts, with the reader getting the signal from **Also Tuesday**.*

"I think the skateboarders were here first," said O'Neill, who later was reprimanded by City Commissioner Frank Lightle, who said O'Neill was shouting, pointing and showing disrespect to commissioners.

The city has provided space for a skateboard park, but the parents of skateboarders were challenged to raise the funds for the project, a mission which apparently was not successful, said Timothy Smith, director of parks and recreation.

Commissioners have looked into the possibility of using prisoners or welfare recipients to build a skateboard park, said Lightle, disputing O'Neill's contention that the city has ignored the skateboarders.

Copeland said the interested parents should ask the park and recreation board to consider funding a skateboard park. That board makes recommendations to city commissioners, said Copeland.

Given the choice of serving the handicapped and serving skateboarders, Copeland said he would rather help the handicapped.

Commissioners unanimously approved buying the equipment, which Smith said will be among the first in the area. The equipment is unusual because it allows handicapped children to play alongside non-handicapped youth, said Smith.

The ever-popular issue of problem cats was the subject of another citizen complaint.

The next inverted pyramid begins.

Eric Clarkson of 1526 W. High St. said a neighbor of his feeds 20 to 30 cats that he believes create a health hazard by using Clarkson's yard as "their litter box."

Commissioners promised to look into his allegation that the Humane Society refused to pick up the cats, a service for which the city pays.

"This commission needs to pass a cat ordinance soon," said Flack.

State legislators are considering licensing cats, said Lightle.

The topic of George Rogers Clark Park also came up.	*The final inverted pyramid, with the tip-off signaled by* **also.**

Copeland said he is willing to allow the city to help find a solution to the park's financial woes, but he is not willing to accept responsibility for those problems.

County residents freely use city parks, and in return the county and county park board should be responsible for the one park located outside city limits, said Lightle.

Here is the story again, this time with all items of business listed early. Three are handled with single sentences, which foreshadow events later in the story.

Voters will decide in May whether higher taxes will make the city a safer place.

On Tuesday, a 5-year, 3-mill property tax levy was placed on the ballot by city commissioners responding to petitions presented by Citizens for a Safer Springfield.

In other matters, the commissioners:	*These paragraphs foreshadow the rest of the meeting topics and allow readers to decide if they want to read on. The paragraphs also make transition easier by allowing the writer to switch topics without elaborate signalling because the readers have already been forewarned.*
—heard a complaint about spending money on handicapped-accessible playground equipment rather than skateboard facilities;	
—promised to look into how the Humane Society responds to complaints about cats;	
—discussed financial problems at George Rogers Clark Park.	

The tax, which is in the form of a charter amendment, would force the city to add 24 patrolmen to the 100-officer police division. A minimum of six police officers would be assigned to the narcotics unit if voters approve the tax issue. All interest earnings from the levy receipts would remain in the levy fund.

The tax issue would generate about $1.5 million annually and cost the owner of a home with a $60,000 market value about $55.12 each year.

"It's a levy which citizens have begun," said Mayor Warren Copeland, who was joined by Commissioner Nora Parker in personally endorsing the tax issue.

Commissioner Faye Flack, who last week asked that commissioners delay acceptance of the petitions until names could be checked, said she did not intend to imply a lack of trust in the citizens who passed the petitions. Flack said she felt it was the commission's duty to informally review the petitions, which contained 2,022 signatures.

That review showed there were enough valid signatures to indicate substantial citizen support for the tax issue, said Flack.

The complaint about spending $11,592 on handicapped-accessible playground equipment rather than skateboard facilities came from Kevin O'Neill.

Since the topic has already been introduced, the writer can begin with the specific article the.

"I think the skateboarders were here first," said O'Neill, who later was reprimanded by City Commissioner Frank Lightle, who said O'Neill was shouting, pointing and showing disrespect to commissioners.

The city has provided space for a skateboard park, but the parents of skateboarders were challenged to raise the funds for the project, a mission which apparently was not successful, said Timothy Smith, director of parks and recreation.

Commissioners have looked into the possibility of using prisoners or welfare recipients to build a skateboard park, said Lightle, disputing O'Neill's contention that the city has ignored the skateboarders.

Copeland said the interested parents should ask the park and recreation board to consider funding a skateboard park. That board makes recommendations to city commissioners, said Copeland.

Given the choice of serving the handicapped and serving skateboarders, Copeland said he would rather help the handicapped.

Commissioners unanimously approved buying the equipment, which Smith said will be among the first in the area. The equipment is unusual because it allows handicapped children to play alongside non-handicapped youth, said Smith.

On the cat matter, commissioners promised to look into the allegation that the Humane Society refused to pick up the cats, a service for which the city pays.

The writer opens the paragraph by nudging the reader's memory.

Eric Clarkson of 1526 W. High St. said a neighbor of his feeds 20 to 30 cats that he believes create a health hazard by using Clarkson's yard as "their litter box."

"This commission needs to pass a cat ordinance soon," said Flack.

State legislators are considering licensing cats, said Lightle.

In discussing George Rogers Clark Park, Copeland said he is willing to allow the city to help find a solution to the park's financial woes, but he is not willing to accept responsibility for those problems.

As with the previous new topic, the writer begins with a reminder.

County residents freely use city parks, and in return the county and county park board should be responsible for the one park located outside city limits, said Lightle.

The inverted pyramid remains the structure of choice for the basic news story, but journalists soon learn that other approaches may serve them better. A newspaper writer need not be a slave to any particular formula. The first goal is to communicate clearly. Any approach that does not meet that standard should be abandoned.

Review Questions

Name some of the story forms identified by Donald M. Murray.

What is an anecdote?

Clip from your favorite newspaper and bring to class examples of stories that don't fit the inverted pyramid mold. Analyze them.

What is meant by the phrase "show, don't tell"?

Endnotes

1. John H. Boyer, " 'Focus and Dialogue' Urged as Substitute for Inverted Pyramid," *Journalism Educator* (July 1976), 57.
2. Donald M. Murray, "From *What* to *Why:* The Changing Style of Newswriting," *Style,* 16, no. 4 (Fall 1982), 448–451.
3. Peter Passell, "Wine Equation Puts Some Noses out of Joint," *The New York Times,* March 4, 1990, 1. Copyright © 1990 by The New York Times Company.
4. Lauralee Jones, "Local Postal Workers Help out Santa," *York Daily Record,* December 1, 1990, 1. Copyright 1990 © by *York Daily Record.*
5. Theresa Walker, " 'Hobo' Rides Rails to Help the Homeless," *Los Angeles Times,* July 29, 1983, B1. Copyright © 1983 by the Times Mirror Company.
6. Cindy Stauffer, "Citizens: Restaurant Center for Drug Deals," *Lancaster New Era,* March 24, 1990, 1, 5. Copyright © 1990 by Lancaster Newspapers, Inc.
7. Anndee Hochman, "Slain Officer Buried," *The Washington Post,* March 31, 1985, A19. Copyright © 1985 by *The Washington Post.*
8. A.L. May, "Candidates Discuss Health Funding for Poor," *Atlanta Constitution,* November 4, 1989, C3. Copyright © 1989 by Atlanta Journal and Constitution.
9. Lynn Hulsey, "Levy OK'd for May Ballot," *Springfield* (Ohio) *News-Sun,* February 28, 1990, 1, 4. Copyright © 1990 by the *Springfield News-Sun.*

Sources and Resources

Berner, R. Thomas. "The Narrative and the Headline." *Newspaper Research Journal* (Spring 1983): 33–39.

Clark, Roy Peter. "Plotting the First Graph." *Washington Journalism Review* (October 1982): 48–50.

———. "A New Shape for the News." *Washington Journalism Review* (March 1984): 46–47.

Green, Bill. "Dust off the Pyramid." *The Washington Post,* December 5, 1980, A16.

Lanson, Gerald, and Mitchell Stephens. "Jell-o Journalism: Why Reporters Have Gone Soft in Their Leads." *Washington Journalism Review* (April 1982): 21–23. (The October 1982 Clark article was written in rebuttal.)

Shaw, David. "Smoothing out the First Rough Draft of History." *Washington Journalism Review* (December 1981): 28, 32–34.

Chapter 9

Other Story Types

Chapter Objectives

In this chapter you will learn about other types of stories that appear in newspapers. You will also learn their function and something about how to report for them.

Introduction

News story types include features, profiles, in-depth pieces, editorials, reviews and columns. But ultimately journalists should concern themselves with good writing, not labels.

Feature Stories

The feature story is distinguished in part by the way it is written. The feature story's tone and style are more individualized than those of a standard news story, and the feature is plotted. The writer's voice is apparent. A feature story is a break from the routine.

Compare the following stories. Story 1 is, except for the first and last paragraphs, a fairly straightforward report of a court decision. Story 2 is a feature. You can tell the writer enjoyed writing it from an unusual angle.

Story 1

A Howard fisherman can now tell the story of how he was the one that got away.

Kenneth W. Inhoof won an appeal of a fishing law violation Monday because of a missing word in the section of the law under which he was charged.

Inhoof was arrested for throwing a beer can into Spring Creek and charged under a section that prohibits littering "along" state streams.

At one time, the law prohibited littering "in or along" fishing streams, but the section was amended in 1974 and the word "in" was eliminated, according to Centre County Judge R. Paul Campbell.

In reversing the previous guilty decision, Campbell cited a Superior Court decision that says the law must be strictly interpreted.

Campbell said another section of the law "does make it a criminal offense for any person to throw any refuse or rubbish, etc., into or upon any stream."

Story 2

Consider the word "in."

As a preposition, it enables speakers of the English language to say where something is. "In court," for example.

Kenneth W. Inhoof of Howard was in court yesterday because he had been found guilty of littering—of throwing a beer can (empty, of course) into Spring Creek.

In his appeal of the conviction, Inhoof argued that the law under which he had been charged did not specify a person could not litter "in" a stream.

In concurring, Centre County Judge R. Paul Campbell wrote that an earlier version of the law referred to littering "in or along streams in which the public is allowed to fish."

In later years, though, Campbell said, the word "in" was eliminated through an amendment, making it illegal to litter "along" (another preposition) but not "in" a stream.

If that section had been used, Inhoof might not have been the fisherman who got away, according to the judge.

The judge said he didn't know if the dropping of the word was inadvertent or intentional.

Regardless, Campbell said, the law requires a strict interpretation, so he reversed Inhoof's conviction, noting that another section of the law could have been used because it has all the right prepositions.

The writer of Story 1 put a rather clever "kicker" in his lead, a play on the fish that got away. But the second writer chose to make the whole story unusual by plotting it from beginning to end as a discussion on prepositions. Writing a feature story allows a writer to show more individuality of thought and style than is acceptable in a straightforward news story.

Of course, a feature story is not necessarily whimsical. Dennis and Ismach say in their textbook on reporting:

> The feature fills out the space between the lines of the standard straight news report. It adds color and flesh, considers human factors, reports meanings and motivations. The result for the reader is a different level of understanding—a richer, more refined look at the complexity of the story. As the new reporter will learn, no story is really as simple as it may seem at first. And people are endlessly complex. The feature form helps the reporter do a better job for the reader.[1]

In the typical hard news story the reporter would note what happened and what was said, and then accurately convey these unembroidered facts in 10 paragraphs. Beginning with a good lead, she might use a direct quotation in the second paragraph, then with minimum transition alternate between direct and indirect quotations to tell the story. She would draw upon history as needed. This is the basic news story—informative but limited in scope.

In the feature story, the reporter is after more than just the facts and would most likely add details not found in the typical news story. Such details are likely to concern the environment or scene setting. What does a place look like? How are people dressed? What sounds could one hear or not hear? Occasional adjectives and adverb are allowed—to color the story and even to evoke emotions in the reader. Transport the reader from her living room to the scene. Make the story come alive. Paint a picture with words. Let the reader experience the story. Show, don't tell.

A good feature story has a beginning, middle and end. It is plotted. Examine this feature story by Doris Wolf of the *Finger Lakes Times* in Geneva, New York.[2] Note how she uses description and environmental markers to draw the reader into the story. As you read this story, you will be in the vestibule of a clerk's office, walk through large glass doors, sit in someone's kitchen over breakfast, live through the sale of a family farm. You will feel the sadness. The headline writer avoided the typical subject-verb approach and instead put a title on the story. That adds to its specialness.

The Death of a Family Farm

STANLEY—They'd been on life support for years before the plug was pulled. And even now, they hoped. The death of a family farm is slow and agonizing.

For Stanley and Elizabeth Senack of Number Nine Road, hope flickered and died at about 10:30 Wednesday morning in the small vestibule outside the Ontario County clerk's office in Canandaigua when their 235-acre farm was auctioned off.

No casket, no flowers, no organ music eased the passage—just men in white shirts and neckties, carrying briefcases, and farmers wearing plaid woolen workshirts who came to pray, "There but for the Grace of God go I."

In the vestibule, Senack, 44, stood with his back to the wall, looking down at his scuffed and worn brown work boots, his green cap squarely on his head, his middle fingers in the pocket of his dirty jeans with the small holes in the front.

His son, Stanley Jr., 18, who was to be the fourth generation to live in the older brown house and farm on the windswept hill, stood behind Senack. So alike, his feet placed the same, the fingers in the jeans pockets a mirror of his dad's—yet different with his black leather jacket and his white silk aviator-like scarf, his bright blond hair and unlined face.

Young Stanley has dreams, too, of becoming a car salesman. "I want money," he said. But he shares his father's love of the farm, postponing his dream to help scratch out a living cultivating cabbages and grain on the land. For him, the sale is hard, too, but it's liberating. Now he can follow his dream.

Elizabeth Senack was outside, sitting in the pickup truck their son drove to take them to the foreclosure sale. She had walked quickly out through the large glass doors, unable to hold back the tears any longer, as Kathleen Curran, court-appointed referee, began to read from the seven-page document that explained the terms of the auction and described the farm.

Cold and impersonal, the reading continued. An occasional blast of winter air rushed in to chill the vestibule as the door opened to admit strangers, carrying license plates or registration forms, frowning with curiosity as they walked quickly through the group to the Department of Motor Vehicles office.

Earlier that morning, the lingering smell of bacon and coffee had been warm and comforting as Senack sat at his kitchen table, staring at the documents spread in front of him.

After a county sheriff's deputy delivered the official papers with the blue cover last July from the Federal Land Bank of Springfield, Senack spent a frantic four months trying to find a way to save his home.

"When the foreclosure notice came, I went right to the bank," Senack said. "They told me they'd be willing to lend me money if I could catch up what I owed. If I could have done that, I wouldn't have needed to borrow money."

Senack owed more than $296,000—$165,166 to the Federal Land Bank, $75,000 to the Farmers Home Administration and $55,144 to Production Credit Association, a national lending association for farmers.

He pleaded with the FmHA to exercise its second mortgage, to allow him a chance to restructure. Late Tuesday night, FmHA manager Gerald Killigrew telephoned Senack to tell him that wouldn't be possible.

Senack contacted his neighbors, hoping to find one who would buy the farm and let him rent for a few years, with a buy-back option, so they could keep the house.

"I like being here, the people around me," he replied when asked what was the best part of farming. "Every day when I get up, I thank God for being here."

About 9:30 a.m., time to go. Senack joked about taking his beat-up green Dodge pickup, of driving it through the sale, to stop it. "You'll go in my truck," his son said, as he walked toward the shiny black Ford with the white cap.

"When do you start to cry?" Senack was asked. "Right now," he replied, his eyes filling behind his fly-specked glasses.

Senack brightened when he saw Donny Jensen sitting in the pickup in the parking lot in front of the low tan brick building.

"I might be interested," Senack's across-the-swamp neighbor said cautiously when asked if he intended to bid.

"You'll never get a farm any cheaper than you will today," Senack said encouragingly.

Other neighbors filed into the tiny vestibule as though at a wake. They shook Senack's hand, lips pressed tightly together, and quickly looked away as they moved to places near the bright red, white and blue Pepsi machine, or leaned against the window, back to the others, looking out.

Joe Keyser of the Federal Land Bank and his attorney Mark Fandrich stood next to Curran at the front of the room as she read in a monotonous voice, a priest reciting the liturgy at a funeral.

To their left, John Karszes, 26, of Clifton Springs, and his wife, Kelly, a teacher in Gorham, waited nervously. They own a small 90-acre farm in Phelps, Karszes explained, and want to move up to a larger operation. They'd been to Senack's—it might be the right place to follow their dream.

"I've met them," Senack said. "They're nice people."

"We are now open for bids," Curran finally said. "The Federal Land Bank will bid $196,350," Fandrich said.

"I'd like to bid $196,400," said Karszes hopefully. Senack swallowed hard and stared at the floor, lips clamped together tightly.

"I'll go $200,000," said Jensen, as a flicker of hope flashed in Senack's eyes.

"Does anyone want to make a higher bid?" Curran asked. Karszes looked at a small white notebook he held cupped in his right hand. His wife looked up at him questioningly. He bid $202,000. Jensen raised the ante to $205; Karszes whispered with his wife and bid to $210. Jensen talked to his partner, a builder. "I'd like to go $215," he said.

Pointing with his thumb to the bottom line in his notebook, Karszes bid $218. Jensen went to $219. After a long pause, Karszes swallowed and raised the bid to $220.

Senack glanced back at Jensen for the first time—a plea—then looked back at the floor and shook his head slightly.

"Do I hear more bids?" Curran asked. "Are there more bids? Anyone? Sold!"

"I'm sorry, Stan," Jensen said, walking over and shaking his neighbor's hand. "I hoped maybe we could have worked something out. But I had my number and that was it."

"You've got to watch the numbers or you'll end up like me," Senack called after him as Jensen walked quickly away.

"Why wouldn't they buy it from me, so I could have kept the house? I hate to see it go this way," Senack said, his voice choking with emotions, tears welling in his eyes. "I tried, I tried."

Shoulders slumping, Senack walked across the parking lot to tell his wife. Awkwardly, his son reached up to pat his dad's back.

The family sat for a long time in the cab of the truck, Senack shaking his head, tears coming now unchecked. Elizabeth sat between the men, her hands over her face. Stanley Jr. leaned against the door, facing sideways toward his parents, crying, too. Then he wiped his eyes with the back of his hand, turned front and reached for the ignition key.

Slowly, the truck began to drive away, over the familiar back roads, to the home that was no longer theirs.

Some feature stories open more slowly. In this case, Wolf establishes within the first two paragraphs what the story is about and pegs it to an event that occurred two days earlier. The story is rich in detail and contains some evocative phrases and metaphors. One of Wolf's virtues as a writer is her ability to say a lot with few words. The fourth paragraph is but one of many examples of this when she not only tells what Stanley Senack looks like but also conveys his mood.

Wolf is a good observer, unobtrusive, a fly on the wall. She went to the Senacks' home at breakfast instead of meeting them at the auction. That enabled her to provide scenes of the family in more than one setting and to get some background from the Senacks.

Wolf is specific. The clerk's office doesn't have a soda machine; it has a "bright red, white and blue Pepsi machine" and some people stand near it. And once she introduces the players in the story, a form of foreshadowing, she spins out a mini-story about the auction. The reader must stay with her to find out who buys the farm.

Wolf wrote a good story because she is a good reporter.

Profiles

Whereas a feature story may focus on the people in an event and also reveal something about the event, a profile focuses on a person and its purpose is to tell readers about the person. Some profiles share the exigencies of deadline reporting because they are assigned when someone new appears in the news.

But profiles can also be about people who are well known. Then the journalist is aiming to tell something new, to explore a side of the person unknown to the public. "If the person is unknown," Shirley Biagi says, "you completely sketch the person's character." [3]

A good way of approaching a profile is to answer one question: Why is this person worth knowing? That question becomes the frame on which the profile is constructed. The answer becomes the theme of the story.

If a profile is written on deadline, most likely the writer will get information from clips, from the subject of the profile, and perhaps from an acquaintance or two. Deadline profiles tend to emphasize biographical facts more than character sidelights.

But when a journalist has the opportunity to do a longer profile, he has several reporting methods at his disposal. One of those, of course, is the interview. At least two interviews are necessary. The best profiles come from journalists who know their subject.

Observation is another method, one vastly underused in profiles. Go back and read Doris Wolf's feature. She was at the Senacks' home at breakfast; she was at the auction; she was there when the Senack family broke down in tears outside the clerk's office after the sale of their farm.

Observation enables a reporter not only to see a person in action but to describe the person. And description not only tells how a person looks, but also how the person behaves. For example, in a profile on a librarian, one beginning journalist included this paragraph:

> She said she knows people who have gone on sabbaticals. But she cannot do that. "The library is my life. It's crazy." She laughs. She laughs when she says something revealing or personal.

The journalist noticed that trait only after a second interview and through observation. This paragraph appeared early in the profile and established a base for subsequent references to the librarian's laughing.

A great deal of research can be done on people, depending on who they are. Some people have written articles and books or have had public careers. They are fairly easy to research. For less public people, talk to their friends (and enemies). These can be sources of anecdotes which the reader enjoys. If anyone says something critical, give the subject of the profile an opportunity to rebut. In fact, the subject of a profile should be asked for his self-assessment. Also ask what other career he or she may have wanted to pursue. Perhaps the Shakespeare scholar is a stone mason on the side.

Build the story on facts so that readers can draw their own conclusions. The best profiles speak for themselves. Here is an example of one such profile.[4]

> Jeff Ganaposki discovered his life's calling in a discount bin at K Mart.
> Partly by coincidence, partly by fate, a $2.75 paperback book titled "The Big Tax Lie" altered his life. Author William Kilpatrick traced all the nation's problems to income tax and its partner-in-crime—inflation.

After reading the book in February 1989, Ganaposki drafted an amendment to the U.S. Constitution that would abolish federal income tax and replace it with a fairer national sales tax. Now all the Boalsburg resident needs to do is convince a nation.

Ganaposki immediately mailed an outline of his proposal to President Bush and several members of Pennsylvania's legislature. He also sent materials to some of the country's leading television talk-show hosts. Response has been minimal.

"In a nation of 250 million people, for one person to make a difference when he doesn't have any connection to powerful people or the media seems an impossible task," he said. In fact, at times "I feel like Don Quixote."

In October, he formed a group to increase the number of voices asking for changes to the tax laws. His first meeting of the "Committee for Truth in Taxes," of which he is chairman and currently the only member, was a disaster.

On the night of the meeting, Ganaposki's was the only coat to hang in the entrance to Schlow Memorial Library's meeting room. Inside, he methodically arranged spreadsheets, complex computer printouts, charts and bar graphs detailing his findings. Tax information from foreign nations, which he had requested through the mail, was interspersed among his own documents. Finally, Ganaposki sat down behind the information-laden table and waited . . . and waited. A flow chart on which nothing was written during his two-hour wait stood in the corner. A stack of 50 or more chairs leaned patiently against a far wall, but they were not to be disturbed this night. When asked where the Committee for Truth in Taxes was meeting, a library aide snickered.

"It slowed me down, but I just took it in stride," Ganaposki said. "I can't expect the whole world to come beating down my door. If the solution to our tax problem was that easy, someone else would have thought of it by now."

Ganaposki's constitutional amendment would place the burden of taxes on the consumers when they purchase a product or service rather than taxing individuals' income—before they have the opportunity to spend the money.

"Under income tax there is no way you can stop inflation without crippling the economy," Ganaposki said. He later added: "We've been taxing ourselves backwards."

A more unlikely looking savior for the American working class would be hard to find. In his living room, a plaid-covered easy chair swallows his body—a body resembling that of Santa Claus. The beard and mustache that he sports are flecked with spots of gray, but he continues to wear a long, brown pony tail to the small of his back. When he speaks, his hands are folded over his stomach, which periodically escapes from between a faded yellow "Uni-Lube" T-shirt and gray sweatpants.

"I'm not so much an idealist as a technologist," Ganaposki said. "I'm looking for a technique that harnesses the natural financial human urges for profit and the easy way of doing things. And then make it so the goal or result is much better."

Ganaposki lives in a mortgaged single-story home located in a development of similar houses, surrounded by a tidy yard with newly planted shrubs. A single foreign-made car sits in the gravel driveway. He and his wife, Linnette, have three children.

Crayon drawings carefully crafted by children's hands hang in the picture window. The street outside is not heavily traveled. A sign warns drivers to watch for children. Temporarily riderless bicycles and abandoned big-wheels litter the front yards of many of the homes. Ganaposki works 8 to 5 in Boalsburg as a hardware designer at Seven Mountains Scientific, Inc.

In many ways, he is a common man. Yet he is a common man with uncommon ideas.

"The fastest growing group of millionaires are lottery winners," he says as he sinks back into the easy chair. "That just goes to show you, in our system we create poverty. And the only way you can get out is not by hard work but by luck, speculation and gambling."

Ganaposki was a victim of that system. He grew up in the hard-coal mining region of Wilkes-Barre, nurtured by a mother who periodically relied on welfare to raise her two children. As a teenager, he counseled some of his peers at Malabar Drug Rehabilitation Center.

"Drugs were a thrill and a distraction from the pain of their lives," he said.

As a young adult, Ganaposki said he found "anything that was counter to the current way of authority or means of doing things was very attractive." He spent time between high school and college as a stand-up comic, a "professional panhandler," and a street musician. As an electric bass player, he said, "I had delusions of grandeur. An ego the size of a planet."

Like many youth in the 60s, he said, "I used to hitch-hike a lot. One year I racked up 13,000 miles in six months." Those miles were practically all covered on trips from Wilkes-Barre to Butler to see his fiancée.

For a short time he paid $20 a month to share a cabin in the mountains with "a bunch of guys from Philadelphia." The primitive get-back-to-nature setting came complete with outhouses and no running water.

"We were pretty much Bohemians," he said.

Through the assistance of state financial aid institutions, he was able to attend Luzerne County Community College. Later, while holding a part-time job at IBM, he attended the State University of New York at Binghamton.

"To this day, I think a lot of government grants to education are bad because they don't take into consideration the motivation of the student," the former college dropout and financial aid recipient said. The first time he entered college, Ganaposki said he lacked the fortitude and the motivation to handle the course work.

In 1984 he left IBM and started graduate work at Penn State toward a degree in computer science. Lack of money and poor advising forced him to quit and consider suing the university.

"I was firmly convinced it was the university's fault," he said. "But when I tried to sue, the lawyers dissuaded me. Any educational establishment can claim a myriad of reasons why you failed and not that they failed."

After a brief stint as an employee in Penn State's department of computer design services, Ganaposki took his present job at Seven Mountains Scientific, Inc. Co-owner and fellow employee Josephine Chesworth said Ganaposki often bounces new ideas off other employees.

"The last thing he did was to pass around a petition to have the congressmen impeached after giving themselves a raise," she said.

Although Ganaposki's ideas may seem radical, his rebellious lifestyle has slowed somewhat over the years. Other than the pony tail he sports, the only visible reminder of his "hang loose" years is a huge collection of old 45s in the livingroom, and even they are surrounded on his bookshelves by encyclopedias and thought-provoking novels.

Now at age 34, Ganaposki said his life is moving in the direction of becoming a full-time tax advocate.

In January, he will address the Pennsylvania League of Taxpayers at Clearfield. He recently accepted that agency's request for him to be Centre County's regional director. He said with the help of massive petitioning by the 42,000 members of this group, he hopes to begin appearing on national television talk shows. Currently, he is taking his message to local radio programmers and editors of area newspapers. WRSC featured Ganaposki several times during its radio call-in shows that focused on tax reform. He says that other members of the news media refused to talk to him or belittled his proposal.

As the year draws to a close, it appears Ganaposki will not have achieved his goal of eliminating income tax in the 1980s. However, he has no intention of ending the crusade.

"My biggest hope now is to see how much support I receive from the Pennsylvania League of Taxpayers," he said. "If I can get prepaid orders, I'll be able to self-publish my book."

The book, still in the writing stage and yet to be edited by his wife, will provide a detailed explanation of how Ganaposki's proposed tax system works. It will appear in "fine book stores" and K Marts everywhere.

The challenge for the author, Mark Jones, was to profile a person who had a different idea. Since our society frowns on people who are different, it is easy for journalists to dismiss them. So Jones' challenge was to profile this subject in such a way that readers could make up their own minds about the subject. He was sympathetic and fair to his subject, yet leaves no doubt that the person is outside the mainstream.

In-depth Articles

Despite its primary focus on what occurs daily, good journalism also steps back to examine the larger picture, to put daily events into a bigger context of trends or patterns. This is achieved through comprehensive reporting of an issue that results in an in-depth article or articles. The in-depth article provides deeper and broader coverage. It is analytical and evaluative but not opinionated.

Good in-depth reporting is rigorous and current. It can cover where the issue has been or where it is going.

In-depth reporting examines a variety of sources and blends them into a comprehensive account. It is not merely a series of interviews. A reader unhappy with a *New York Times* article complained that most of the sources came from one bar in an industrial town in Pennsylvania and were not representative of the workers of that community. The complaining reader referred to the writer as a "shot-and-beer journalist." Don't be a shot-and-beer journalist. Seek out experts and seek out people who disagree with them.

When seeking experts, make sure you get the right ones. What questions does the following sentence from a newspaper story raise?

> The postmaster noted that the number of letters mailed to Santa Claus via the post office has decreased in recent years as more children send their missives to newspapers and stores promising direct delivery.

What is the postmaster an expert on? Mail. Is he necessarily an expert on why people have changed their use of the mail? Well, he could be. But the preceding example raises some other questions. For one, has the population declined? That could mean fewer couples raising children. The reporter could also check with stores and newspapers. The local department store manager should know. So should the reporter's editor. The reader should be presented with a variety of informed opinions.

Where do ideas for in-depth articles come from? One obvious place is the reporter's beat. A reporter might notice an issue dancing around the edges of the many meetings he or she covers and decide to write about it. Another place is others' shop talk. Good reporters are good listeners. They are also avid readers. Specialized journals are another source of ideas. Ask yourself, "What do readers need to know?"

Every in-depth project has a hypothesis. A hypothesis is in effect the focusing point of the story. It provides the reporter with a guide during the research. A hypothesis can be something as simple as "The new nuclear family does the job" or "A ban on hazing will improve the fraternity system" or "Local governments need to look to regional governments to solve many of the problems facing communities today." One qualification: A hypothesis is a guide, not a dogma. The reporter may find that the hypothesis does not hold up. That's OK. You can disprove your hypothesis and still write a good in-depth article. But you still need a hypothesis from the beginning of the reporting process, because it functions as a navigational aid through the maze of information you gather.

Here is an example of an in-depth story that covers a current issue and has a future orientation.[5]

MINEOLA, L.I., Dec. 26—As the New York metropolitan region's problems with transportation, energy, water, affordable housing and garbage continue to grow, appearing to become more intractable each day, business and academic leaders are renewing calls for some form of regional government.

The calls, which are perhaps being heard the loudest on Long Island, are from some of the most influential people in the region, many of whom are saying that local governments, from municipalities to counties, cannot handle their troubles by working alone.

"We must find a way to govern ourselves as a total, interrelated and interdependent community rather than as a series of independent and competing townships, each with its own bureaucracy," said John C. Bierwirth, chairman of the Grumman Corporation, Long Island's largest employer.

Mr. Bierwirth, who recently delivered a blunt speech about Long Island's future, described municipal handling of solid waste management as "pathetic" and the fight over the Shoreham nuclear power plant as a "depressing spectacle of political and business paralysis."

Even with comments like Mr. Bierwirth's, which were echoed by business leaders across the region, most government officials appeared reluctant to endorse significant change in how municipalities and counties operate. They say they fear the imposition of yet another governmental layer or, just as significant, the loss of home rule.

The calls for regional governing bodies are being made on at least two levels: while some favor multicounty organizations for New Jersey, Long Island or other New York State areas, others argue for one large regional group that would handle problems such as transportation.

The governance problem can be seen clearly on Long Island, which officials say is one of the most heavily governed areas of the country. Authority is divided between 2 counties, 13 towns and 2 cities. Long Island has a total of 666 taxing authorities.

Ingrid W. Reed, an assistant dean at the Woodrow Wilson School of Public Policy and International Affairs of Princeton University, said it is "natural for people to care about their own communities, but the problem we now face is that municipalities are not in control."

"The quandary," said Ms. Reed, who is also the chairman of the Mercer County Planning Board, "is how do you get a handle on the larger than municipal issues without giving up too much of your sovereignty."

The call for regional government throughout the New York metropolitan region has been made many times in the past, with some periods of success. The Metropolitan Regional Council, for example, was formed in 1956 by Mayor Robert F. Wagner of New York. The council was an advisory group of elected officials from 21 counties and 15 cities in the metropolitan region, but it fell apart because of funding questions. And although supporters say their calls for regional cooperation are becoming louder and more forceful, they still question whether they can succeed.

"It is nice to think of some centralized, overarching authority that could guide the development of Long Island," said the president of the State University of New York at Stony Brook, Dr. John H. Marburger 3rd. "But I believe that it would be very, very difficult to realize."

A professor of urban planning at Rutgers University, George Sternlieb, said that although "the logic calls for some sort of regional governance, the reality is that scared people hold onto what they have even if what they have is a declining asset."

Richard C. Hartman, executive director of the National Association of Regional Councils in Washington, said that across the country, "there definitely is more regionalization of government activities."

"The form it is taking," he said, "is through special regional districts and authorities, usually for transit, water or solid waste disposal. it is not a change in governance. It is function by function."

As the year 2000 approaches—with a concomitant flurry of forward-looking studies and analyses, such as the Year 2000 Projects in Westchester County, Fairfield County, Conn., and Morris County, N.J.—many officials are saying that the groundwork for significant change is being laid.

"All these year 2000 programs are new approaches to building civic consensus," said the executive vice president of the Regional Plan Association, Richard T. Anderson. "And when the programs look comprehensively at an area, they can't help but to deal with the governance implications of what they find."

In Westchester County, where a year 2000 committee recently finished its work, several moves have been taken to consolidate some government functions, said Sal J. Preszioso, the executive director of Westchester 2000 and a former county executive.

Officials from village, city and county governments have formed an advisory board for intergovernmental relations, he said, with the hope of finding some way to eliminate government fragmentation. The group will study ways to form a county land-use plan to deal with assessment, planning and zoning, which can vary from town to town.

On Long Island, where a year 2000 study is under way, significant political change is also occurring, change that some officials say could encourage more regional cooperation.

Thomas S. Gulotta, the presiding supervisor of the Town of Hempstead who is widely expected to become Nassau County's new executive in January, has called for strong regional cooperation in solving Long Island's water problems.

Mr. Gulotta, who started a working committee of the Nassau Board of Supervisors and the Suffolk County Legislature, added that many problems, including transportation and solid waste disposal, could benefit from "closer cooperation."

"But I would not support a diminution of local authority," he said. "It's important that we retain local rule."

Suffolk County politicians, however, say that overcoming those provincial feelings will be difficult, if not impossible.

Michael A. LoGrande, who becomes chief executive of Suffolk County on Saturday, cautioned that there is "no simplistic answer to the question of regional authorities."

"Coordination and dialogue are absolutely necessary," said Mr. LoGrande, who previously served as the chief planner at the Long Island Regional Planning Board. "And in many cases, the spirit of cooperation accomplishes a great deal. But when you get into implementation, it gets very difficult."

In New Jersey, the Department of Transportation has introduced a series of legislative proposals that would force counties to approve any large development before a municipal planning board could examine it.

"It would in essence make the county the political entity responsible for planning concerns of regional significance," said Judy S. Berry, the deputy assistant commissioner for policy and regulation at the state transportation department."

"We are trying to force all parties to collectively balance interests and to make provisions for not just what is happening now, but what is expected to happen," she said.

On Long Island, those regional questions are now studied by the regional planning board, but the board does not have the authority to enforce or put into effect its recommendations, although many have been adopted.

"The good part about so many municipalities and authorities is that government is close to the people," said James LaRocca, the president of the Long Island Association, which also serves as a Chamber of

Commerce. "But the bad part is that it is so fragmented that very often it is not possible to bridge all the fragments."

Note the many sources reporter Philip S. Gutis relied on for this story. He did not limit himself to local government officials, but also sought out academic sources and government documents. The article lays out the problem for the reader and suggests ways the issue could be resolved.

Writing any one of the stories described in this chapter requires a more elaborate process than just following the standard inverted pyramid structure. The next chapter discusses the many parts of the process.

Review Questions

What is the function of a feature story? A profile? An in-depth article? Where does a reporter get ideas for such stories?

Endnotes

1. Everette E. Dennis and Arnold H. Ismach, *Reporting Processes and Practices: Newswriting for Today's Readers* (Belmont, Calif.: Wadsworth, 1981), 187.
2. Doris Wolf, "The Death of a Family Farm," *Finger Lakes Times,* December 9, 1988. Copyright © 1989 by *Finger Lakes Times,* Geneva, N.Y. All rights reserved.
3. Shirley Biagi, *Interviews That Work: A Practical Guide for Journalists* Belmont, Calif.: Wadsworth, 1986), 4.
4. By Mark Jones. Written as an assignment for the author's reporting methods class during the fall semester of 1989. Students are required to write a profile of 1,000 to 1,500 words on a subject of their choosing.
5. Philip S. Gutis, "As Problems Grow, So Does the Push for Regional Government," *The New York Times,* December 27, 1986, B1. Copyright © 1986 by The New York Times Company. Reprinted by permission.

Sources and Resources

Best Newspaper Writing. Published annually since 1979 and edited by Roy Peter
    Clark, Don Fry and Karen Brown. St. Petersburg, Fla.: Poynter Institute for
    Media Studies.
Blundell, William E. *The Art and Craft of Feature Writing*. New York: New Amer-
    ican Library, 1988.
Fontaine, André. *The Art of Writing Nonfiction*. 2nd ed. New York: Thomas Y.
    Crowell, 1987.
Garrison, Bruce. *Professional Feature Writing*. Hillsdale, N.J.: Lawrence Erlbaum
    Associates, 1989.
Ruehlmann, William. *Stalking the Feature Story*. Cincinnati: Writer's Digest, 1977.

Chapter 10

Organizing the Longer Story

Chapter Objectives

In this chapter you will learn about the organization of longer news stories. Now that you have advanced beyond the standard story form, planning plays a greater role in the writing of a story.

Introduction

No matter what kind of story it is—a feature, a profile, an in-depth examination of an issue—each story contains parts that can be analyzed.

The Parts

You already know what some parts of a story are. In this section you will read about leads, bodies, scenes, endings, dialogue, and show—don't tell.

Leads

In the standard news story, the lead—typically the first paragraph—is expected to tell the reader what the story is about. That holds true for other types of stories too, but what is different is what is considered the lead.

Outside the standard news story, the lead can be several paragraphs long and foreshadow rather than tell explicitly what the story is about. In all stories, though, the lead focuses the reader on the story; an inept lead blurs the story and confuses the reader.

You read in the previous chapter two feature stories, one of them brief and one of them long. The first paragraph of the shorter story was composed of four words: "Consider the word 'in.' " The story developed from that paragraph, and it was not until the fifth paragraph that you learned the outcome of the case. Three paragraphs followed.

In the longer feature story, "The Death of a Family Farm," Doris Wolf lays out the story in the first two paragraphs:

> STANLEY—They'd been on life support for years before the plug was pulled. And even now, they hoped. The death of a family farm is slow and agonizing.
>
> For Stanley and Elizabeth Senack of Number Nine Road, hope flickered and died at about 10:30 Wednesday morning in the small vestibule outside the Ontario County clerk's office in Canandaigua when their 235-acre farm was auctioned off.

The reader knows what the story is about and has the option of continuing or going on to another story.

The same holds true for Philip S. Gutis' in-depth article. The story's thesis appears in the first paragraph, after which Gutis outlines the problems and the apparent solutions:

> MINEOLA, L.I., Dec. 26—As the New York metropolitan region's problems with transportation, energy, water, affordable housing and garbage continue to grow, appearing to become more intractable each day, business and academic leaders are renewing calls for some form of regional government.

Other opening paragraphs arouse the reader's interest and curiosity without immediately giving the facts. This is the lead from a feature story about a U.S. soldier maimed by a mine in Vietnam. It was written by Martha Miller, then of the Iowa City *Press-Citizen:*[1]

> Two hands lifted the sheet that covered what was left of Dan Vickroy's body.
>
> "You're one tough son of a bitch," the surgeon said from behind a green mask.
>
> "I'm a Vickroy," Dan said. "Take me in and sew me up."

The reader is captured by those three simple paragraphs. What happened? Car accident? A surgeon who swears? Who's Vickroy? Miller engages the reader in the first sentence with a reference to an unidentified pair of hands lifting a sheet. Instead of launching into a description of Vickroy's injuries, Miller uses dialogue to hook the reader.

Some leads establish a contrast. Remember Mark Jones' lead about the tax reformer:

> Jeff Ganaposki discovered his life's calling in a discount bin at K Mart.

The idea that someone could find anything of value in a discount bin is intriguing. Here is a similar approach, this from a profile about an Olympic Games historian:

> In 1968, Joyce Lucas accompanied her husband to the Summer Olympic Games in Mexico City. It was one of the worst experiences of her entire life.

The first sentence suggests that this is a story about how Joyce Lucas enjoyed the Summer Olympic Games. The second quickly changes this proposition and hooks the reader because the reader wants to know why.

Two of the four stories in the previous chapter laid out fairly early what the stories were about. The other two—the feature on the court decision and the profile on the tax reformer—took a little longer. A feature on another court decision or a profile of another tax reformer might not go the same way. A story on regional government might, instead of starting with the thesis, begin with an anecdote that exemplifies the problem. Doris Wolf's story about the farm could have begun with the auction.

Beware the didactic lead. This is the lead that preaches a sermon or delivers a lecture. Here is an example:

> The relationship between rock 'n' roll and religion has been nothing if not topsy-turvy. In rock's infancy, circa 1955, its driving 4/4 beat itself was considered to be a metaphor for sexual rhythms. Rock's history since then can be viewed as one long struggle by its performers to distance themselves from preordained establishment rules.
>
> When Elvis Presley's swinging hips became blasé, a new, more outrageous deed had to be committed. Jerry Lee Lewis marrying his 14-year-old cousin begat the Rolling Stones urinating on the outside wall of a gas station which begat Jim Morrison of the Doors exposing himself during a concert. And so on.
>
> But somewhere out of the 1970s—when the hedonism of rock 'n' roll was at its blown-dry, glossiest height—grew a movement of Christian performers who, instead of spouting rebellious anthems, spouted biblical passages. These performers have concerns not for their fans but for their ministry.
>
> If the idea of Christian rock seems incongruous, consider what critic Robert Palmer had to say in the opening chapter of "The Rolling Stone Illustrated History of Rock & Roll": "The rhythmic singing, the hard-driving beat, the bluesy melody, and the improvised stream-of-consciousness words," he wrote of the music of a rural black church of the South during the 1930s, ". . . all anticipate key aspects of rock 'n' roll as it would emerge some 20 years later."
>
> Translation: What goes around comes around.

The first three paragraphs attempt to establish the story but instead provide history that, if needed, could fit elsewhere. What the reader wants is a quick idea of what the story is about. So cover the first three paragraphs and consider the fourth paragraph as a possible lead. If nothing else, because it is written in the second person, the reader feels invited into the story.

One of the injunctions in lead writing is this: Don't begin a story with a direct quotation. A direct quotation is like a good joke; it needs context to be clear. A direct quotation lacks context.

Given that background, what advice would you give the author of this profile about a popular graduate student who teaches an introductory anthropology course?

> Glenn Storey has found an innovative way to get his students interested in his lectures.
>
> "Anthropology is basically about two things—food and sex," he tells his classes at the start of the first lecture. "You have to have food before you have to have sex."
>
> While that's not a textbook definition of the complex discipline of anthropology, it is an insight into Storey's teaching methods. . . .

That's a good direct quotation. It captures the reader's attention, mostly because of the mention of sex. That's why the teacher uses it; it captures the attention of his students. The advice to the author of this profile was to throw out the first paragraph and start with the direct quotation:

> "Anthropology is basically about two things—food and sex," Glenn Storey tells his classes at the start of the first lecture. "You have to have food before you have to have sex."

The lead points the writer into the body of the story and toward the proper organization scheme for that particular story.

The Body

The body of the story—that is, the information presented between the lead and the ending—represents the writer's success as a reporter. If the reporter has failed to gather enough or the right information, the body of the story will suffer. It will contain holes. It will not fit together. The reader will have questions and, lacking immediate answers, will stop reading.

The writer also needs to organize the facts in a coherent and logical manner. What is logical for one story may not work in another. It sounds almost too simple, but one valuable organization scheme is this: Keep related material together. This advice holds for a five-paragraph or a five-page story. Don't jump around. Develop the organizing principles of the story and then stick to them.

Another simple piece of advice: Define your terms. Too often the journalist gets caught up in the language of the people in the story and forgets the readers. Readers will pay closer attention when they know what the specialized terms mean.

Related to that advice: Be specific. Use concrete examples. One of the great virtues of anecdotes is that they personalize the story, put it in human terms for the reader. Remember the advice on reporting: Always ask for examples. Keep asking "Why?".

Three major organizational devices stand out: transition, tension and foreshadowing. These are creations of the writer, not the reporter; they are created by the writer as needed to maintain the reader's interest.

TRANSITION. Transition is a bridge from one part of a story to another. Transition comes in many shapes and sizes. Simple transition is part of the language. The word *but* is a form of transition or it signals the reader that what follows will disagree with what was just said. Any conjunction, of course, helps the writer keep the subject together or gets the writer from one subject to another.

Repetition of key words aids transition. Those writers who never repeat a word but who go to great lengths to seek out a synonym do not aid transition. The short feature on the court decision (Chapter 9) repeats the word *in* as a way of moving the story along.

But in the story types discussed here, it is the transition created by the writer that needs to be emphasized. The writer creates transition by synthesizing, explaining or summarizing information. Here is a transition paragraph from Philip S. Gutis' in-depth article:

> The calls for regional governing bodies are being made
> on at least two levels: while some favor multicounty or-

ganizations for New Jersey, Long Island or other New York State areas, others argue for one large regional group that would handle problems such as transportation.

Gutis is summarizing what he has learned and is preparing the reader to move from the general introduction to the more specific body of the story. The transition continues for another paragraph, this one a summary of the government structure:

> The governance problem can be seen clearly on Long Island, which officials say is one of the most heavily governed areas of the country. Authority is divided between 2 counties, 13 towns and 2 cities. Long Island has a total of 666 taxing authorities.

Wolf, on the other hand, uses time and motion to effect transition. Look at how she changes from the scene of the auction to the Senacks' house with three words at the beginning of a paragraph: "Earlier that morning. . . ." Here is an example of motion:

> Elizabeth Senack was outside, sitting in the pickup truck their son drove to take them to the foreclosure sale. She had walked quickly out through the large glass doors, unable to hold back the tears any longer, as Kathleen Curran, court-appointed referee, began to read from the seven-page document that explained the terms of the auction and described the farm.

A journalist writes stories based on facts, but the journalist must shape the story—not the facts!—and transition aids in the shaping.

TENSION AND FORESHADOWING. These two attributes often go hand in hand, for as the writer foreshadows or hints at what lies ahead, the writer injects tension into the story.

Tension arises when the writer delays telling the reader about the resolution of some matter. With the matter unresolved, the reader wants to read on to see what happens. An in-depth article by its nature has its own tension, for an in-depth article examines a problem that might have many solutions and that has not yet been resolved.

In a feature story such as Wolf's, it is up to the writer to develop the tension. This she does by the way she arranges the facts. Wolf's story is written in scenes, like a play. She moves each scene to a point, then changes to another scene. The unresolved scenes accumulate, thus creating tension. Here is her story with each scene marked:

Prologue

STANLEY—They'd been on life support for years before the plug was pulled. And even now, they hoped. The death of a family farm is slow and agonizing.

For Stanley and Elizabeth Senack of Number Nine Road, hope flickered and died at about 10:30 Wednesday morning in the small vestibule outside the Ontario County clerk's office in Canandaigua when their 235-acre farm was auctioned off.

No casket, no flowers, no organ music eased the passage—just men in white shirts and neckties, carrying briefcases, and farmers wearing plaid woolen workshirts who came to pray, "There but for the Grace of God go I."

Scene 1

In the vestibule, Senack, 44, stood with his back to the wall, looking down at his scuffed and worn brown work boots, his green cap squarely on his head, his middle fingers in the pocket of his dirty jeans with the small holes in the front.

His son, Stanley Jr., 18, who was to be the fourth generation to live in the older brown house and farm on the windswept hill, stood behind Senack. So alike, his feet placed the same, the fingers in the jeans pockets a mirror of his dad's—yet different with his black leather jacket and his white silk aviator-like scarf, his bright blond hair and unlined face.

Young Stanley has dreams, too, of becoming a car salesman. "I want money," he said. But he shares his father's love of the farm, postponing his dream to help scratch out a living cultivating cabbages and grain on the land. For him, the sale is hard, too, but it's liberating. Now he can follow his dream.

Scene 2

Elizabeth Senack was outside, sitting in the pickup truck their son drove to take them to the foreclosure sale. She had walked quickly out through the large glass doors, unable to hold back the tears any longer, as Kathleen Curran, court-appointed referee, began to read from the seven-page document that explained the terms of the auction and described the farm.

Cold and impersonal, the reading continued. An occasional blast of winter air rushed in to chill the vestibule as the door opened to admit strangers, carrying license plates or registration forms, frowning with curiosity as they walked quickly through the group to the Department of Motor Vehicles office.

Scene 3

Earlier that morning, the lingering smell of bacon and coffee had been warm and comforting as Senack sat at his kitchen table, staring at the documents spread in front of him.

After a county sheriff's deputy delivered the official papers with the blue cover last July from the Federal Land Bank of Springfield, Senack spent a frantic four months trying to find a way to save his home.

"When the foreclosure notice came, I went right to the bank," Senack said. "They told me they'd be willing to lend me money if I could catch up what I owed. If I could have done that, I wouldn't have needed to borrow money."

Senack owed more than $296,000—$165,166 to the Federal Land Bank, $75,000 to the Farmers Home Administration and $55,144 to Production Credit Association, a national lending association for farmers.

He pleaded with the FmHA to exercise its second mortgage, to allow him a chance to restructure. Late Tuesday night, FmHA manager Gerald Killigrew telephoned Senack to tell him that wouldn't be possible.

Senack contacted his neighbors, hoping to find one who would buy the farm and let him rent for a few years, with a buy-back option, so they could keep the house.

"I like being here, the people around me," he replied when asked what was the best part of farming. "Every day when I get up, I thank God for being here."

Scene 4

About 9:30 a.m., time to go. Senack joked about taking his beat-up green Dodge pickup, of driving it through the sale, to stop it. "You'll go in my truck," his son said, as he walked toward the shiny black Ford with the white cap.

"When do you start to cry?" Senack was asked. "Right now," he replied, his eyes filling behind his fly-specked glasses.

Senack brightened when he saw Donny Jensen sitting in the pickup in the parking lot in front of the low tan brick building.

"I might be interested," Senack's across-the-swamp neighbor said cautiously when asked if he intended to bid.

"You'll never get a farm any cheaper than you will today," Senack said encouragingly.

Other neighbors filed into the tiny vestibule as though at a wake. They shook Senack's hand, lips pressed tightly together, and quickly looked away as they moved to places near the bright red, white and blue Pepsi machine, or leaned against the window, back to the others, looking out.

Joe Keyser of the Federal Land Bank and his attorney Mark Fandrich stood next to Curran at the front of the room as she read in a monotonous voice, a priest reciting the liturgy at a funeral.

To their left, John Karszes, 26, of Clifton Springs, and his wife, Kelly, a teacher in Gorham, waited nervously. They own a small 90-acre farm in Phelps, Karszes explained, and want to move up to a larger operation. They'd been to Senack's—it might be the right place to follow their dream.

"I've met them," Senack said. "They're nice people."

Scene 5

"We are now open for bids," Curran finally said. "The Federal Land Bank will bid $196,350," Fandrich said.

"I'd like to bid $196,400," said Karszes hopefully. Senack swallowed hard and stared at the floor, lips clamped together tightly.

"I'll go $200,000," said Jensen, as a flicker of hope flashed in Senack's eyes.

"Does anyone want to make a higher bid?" Curran asked. Karszes looked at a small white notebook he held cupped in his right hand. His wife looked up at him questioningly. He bid $202,000. Jensen raised the ante to $205; Karszes whispered with his wife and bid to $210. Jensen talked to his partner, a builder. "I'd like to go $215," he said.

Pointing with this thumb to the bottom line in his notebook, Karszes bid $218. Jensen went to $219. After a long pause, Karszes swallowed and raised the bid to $220.

Senack glanced back at Jensen for the first time—a plea—then looked back at the floor and shook his head slightly.

"Do I hear more bids?" Curran asked. "Are there more bids? Anyone? Sold!"

"I'm sorry, Stan," Jensen said, walking over and shaking his neighbor's hand. "I hoped maybe we could have worked something out. But I had my number and that was it."

"You've got to watch the numbers or you'll end up like me," Senack called after him as Jensen walked quickly away.

"Why wouldn't they buy it from me, so I could have kept the house? I hate to see it go this way," Senack said, his voice choking with emotions, tears welling in his eyes. "I tried, I tried."

Scene 6

Shoulders slumping, Senack walked across the parking lot to tell his wife. Awkwardly, his son reached up to pat his dad's back.

The family sat for a long time in the cab of the truck, Senack shaking his head, tears coming now unchecked. Elizabeth sat between the men, her hands over her face. Stanley Jr. leaned against the door, facing sideways toward his parents, crying, too. Then he wiped his eyes with the back of his hand, turned front and reached for the ignition key.

> Slowly, the truck began to drive away, over the familiar back roads, to the home that was no longer theirs.

Wolf also foreshadows. She gives hints of what might happen, which add to the tension. There is Senack's desire to try to keep the house and the raising of his hopes when Donny Jensen bids $200,000. Then, later, when Jensen goes to $205,000, everyone's hopes rise again. Wolf introduces the other characters in the play, and the reader gets a feeling about what they might do at the auction.

Foreshadowing usually helps build a story's tension. On a more simple level, foreshadowing establishes a pattern or suggests a story line. The lead about Joyce Lucas' not liking the Summer Olympics foreshadows her behavior in the rest of the story. In another example, a beginning journalist was struggling with her lead on a profile about the director of the senior citizens center. In the draft her editor saw, it was not until the middle of the story that the readers learned that the center's director got there because she could not find a job teaching school 20 years earlier. Her editor suggested this lead:

> Barbara Lindenbaum couldn't find a job as a school teacher and that's when she discovered senior citizens.

That lead, edited to fit the original story, foreshadows a later part of the story that talks about her college degree in art education and her problems finding a job. When the point arises, the reader is not surprised, for the writer foreshadowed it.

The Ending

In some ways, the story serves as a foreshadowing of the ending. The ending should come as no surprise. That does not mean the reader knows how the story is going to end but it does mean that the ending follows logically from the body of the story.

The ending on an in-depth article should point to the future. It must be firm. Ending an in-depth article by saying problems need to be solved is hardly worth the time spent reading the story. People know problems must be solved. They want to know what the options or the impediments are.

Just as the writer makes decisions about how to shape other parts of the story, the writer shapes the ending. A good quotation can sum up the story. An in-depth article on homeless people ended with this comment from a grants coordinator:

> Increased funding and awareness are the keys to fighting hopelessness. "What is important," Hess said, "is that we don't sweep these people under the rug."

When Jeanne Edwards of the *Providence* (R.I.) *Sunday Journal* wrote a story about the death of a couple's teenage son, she included these paragraphs early in the story:[2]

> "Just two weeks before he was shot, he sat in that chair and we got to talking about death and dying," Mrs. Caldwell remembered.
> "He said, 'Mom, if something drastic ever happens to me, don't let them keep me alive on machines.' " Mrs. Caldwell said she told her son that she would "pass the message on to your sister because I'll probably be dead and gone before that."

Eventually, Mrs. Caldwell orders her son's respirator turned off. Edwards revealed in a subsequent analysis of the story that she had used that information earlier in the story but at an editor's suggestion moved it to the end. This is how the published story ended:

> On the night Craig's life ended, Mrs. Caldwell walked into the treatment room at Kent County Hospital.

> She saw her son lying on a table, blood running out
> of his ears. He was hooked up to a respirator.
> She pushed his hair back from his forehead and talked
> to him, knowing he couldn't hear. She told Craig she
> didn't know why anyone would want to harm him. She
> said she was going to miss him terribly.
> Then she remembered the promise she had made to
> her son just two weeks before. And she ordered the
> respirator shut off.

That is a gripping ending, the kind that will stay with the reader for a long
time.

Terrie Claflin of the Medford, Oregon, *Mail Tribune* also wrote an
ending that will stay with readers. She and photo editor Steve Johnson did
a special report about a baby born to a mother who used drugs. The baby
eventually died. Contained in a 28-page tabloid, the report is a collection
of stories and photographs. The last story is eight paragraphs long and ends
with this paragraph:

> Rachel's mother, who declined to be interviewed for this
> special report, is due to have another baby in December.

That one paragraph has tremendous impact on the reader for it recycles the
entire story. That's what a good ending can do.

Dialogue

Dialogue is a verbatim record of a conversation between two or more
people. Dialogue is not quoting one person. There must be at least two
people for a dialogue to take place. Dialogue in a news story shows people
interacting. Doris Wolf uses dialogue in her farm story. Here is one example:

> "I might be interested," Senack's across-the-swamp
> neighbor said cautiously when asked if he intended to bid.
> "You'll never get a farm any cheaper than you will
> today," Senack said encouragingly.

The farm story contains only brief snatches of dialogue, but that does not detract from its usefulness. Obviously, the auction was not a place where an extended conversation occurred. In the next section, however, is an example of dialogue that goes beyond one exchange.

Show—Don't Tell

The ability to show a story rather than tell a story is available to anyone who reports thoroughly. Writing down not just what was said but also seemingly incidental information and descriptions enables the journalist to fill a notebook with the very information needed to show a story. The ability to show rather than tell is the fruit of observation.

Here is an excerpt from a profile on a veterinarian in which the writer both showed and told. Did she have to tell? Is the second sentence necessary?

> Whiskey, an 8-month-old dachshund, stood shivering on the operating table as veterinarian Kathleen Kocher checked its vital signs in preparation for surgery. Concern for the animal is what is most important, she said.
> "Don't worry," Kocher said to Whiskey as she smoothed his fur. . . .

Hasn't the writer shown us the veterinarian's concern? Does she have to tell us the doctor is concerned for the animal? Does she need the second sentence? No. The doctor's concern is evident from the sentence containing the direct quotation and showing the vet smoothing the dog's fur.

When showing something, the writer is usually setting a scene. Here is a scene from a profile. A man is having breakfast with his son and daughter; his wife has already left for work.

> After waking his children, Carter prepared breakfast. This morning, Jeremiah ate fried eggs and Sarah prepared her own oatmeal. Carter had a cup of coffee.
> Before leaving for the 8:10 a.m. bus, father and son sat down to review contractions and spelling for a test Jeremiah had that day.

Two pages later, this paragraph loops back to the breakfast scene: "Carter usually tries to leave work around 5 p.m. but this day he was eager to get home and find out how Jeremiah did on his test."

Here is a more elaborate scene that includes more dialogue than the farm story did:

> A cold wind was blowing under a crystal clear blue sky and the smell of earth filled the air. A backhoe, coughing smoke, was busy digging out the last remaining corner of a pit that would become the foundation of a house. Inside the pit was a series of trenches with wires, rods and plywood sections. Six men were busy lifting rocks from the trenches and throwing them on the piles of dirt that surrounded the pit. A worker wearing layers of flannel shirts, baggy workpants, and a tattered denim baseball cap climbed from the pit and walked toward the inspector standing at the edge.
>
> It was early morning and Harry Burd, a Centre Region Code inspector, was at the job site to inspect the work being done in preparation for the foundation of a townhouse soon to be constructed.
>
> "Come on down, Harry," the worker called out to Burd. "You can't inspect too good from the topside."
>
> Burd was greeted by the workers as he climbed into the pit.
>
> "How long have you worked here?" Burd jokingly asked a worker who was struggling to remove a large rock with a shovel.
>
> "Too damn long," the worker replied.
>
> "You should be able to do that with your eyes closed," Burd said.
>
> "From the looks of his work, you'd think he does," the supervisor said.
>
> The supervisor, Jim Ammerman of the Raybro Construction, had called Burd to the site to answer some questions concerning the construction of a footer—a trench dug into the ground and filled with cement to form the base of a building. . . .

The reporter who uses observation strengthens any story. The details thus gathered create a presence and wrap the story in authority, the authority of fact. Good journalism relies on fact written in a way that engages readers and holds their attention to the end.

The Whole

The overall story works because of the preparation the writer put into the planning stages. For longer stories, outlining helps. Having a theme helps the writer organize the story. Finally, rewriting is critical to the whole story.

The Outline

Putting the parts together usually requires an outline. Some journalists scoff at that suggestion but then admit that while they don't put a outline on paper, they do think the story through before writing.

An outline can take many forms. The writer should adopt the form that suits him. Some writers block off their articles in modules, giving each module a heading and then lumping all relevant information under each heading. As the outline takes shape, the writers begin to see relations they had missed, and information in one module gets linked to information in another with arrows.

Sometimes an entire module can get moved to another part of the article. Go back and examine Doris Wolf's feature. Each scene is a module; the scenes could be moved about merely by tinkering with the transition. Remember, Wolf could have opened the story at the auction. Recall Martha Miller's comment about how she moved a section of her story to create a better ending. She discovered that in the editing process; it could have just as easily happened in the outlining process.

Finding a Theme

A writer can organize a story better if the writer finds a theme, a unifying principle, a spine, a thread—anything that holds the story together. Wolf's story is about the auctioning of a farm, and she never strays from that, even

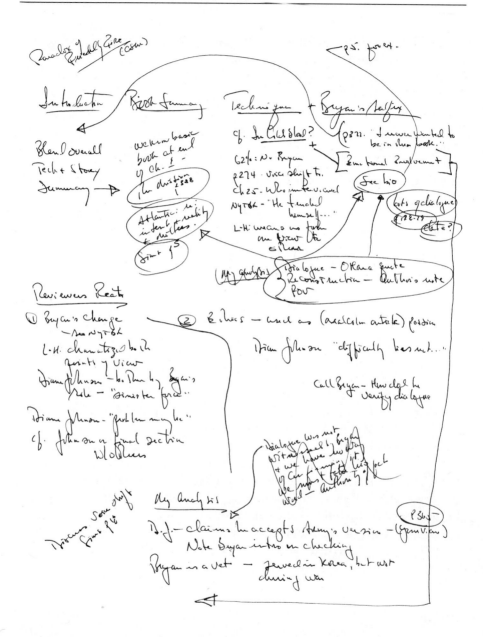

Figure 10.1 The author's outline of his 2,000-word essay on C.D.B. Bryan. The structure allows moving information around simply by drawing arrows from one location to another. Since the entire outline appears on one page, the entire article can still be visualized.

though she undoubtedly gathered other information. The same could be said of Mark Jones' profile on the tax reformer. Jones selected the tax reform angle for his profile, although he could have focused on something else in Ganaposki's life.

An in-depth article can be organized around an individual in the story. This helps personalize the story and gives the readers someone they can identify throughout the story. This approach usually results in an anecdote lead in which the person is introduced. The person surfaces one or two other times throughout the story and then appears in the concluding paragraphs.

Rewriting

As previously noted, rewriting on deadline is virtually impossible, although rewriting any story is a good exercise for beginners. Rewriting non-deadline stories should be a matter of habit.

As Martha Miller put it after meeting Dan Vickroy, the maimed soldier:

> I knew the minute I walked out of it that I had a good story. I rewrote it eight times. Rewriting really works.[3]

Between Fact and Fiction

Journalism is driven by facts. Reporters cannot make up events or assume what people are thinking and report it as fact. If it did not happen, it can't be used in journalism.

Several years ago, a feature writer at a metropolitan newspaper turned in a story that began like this:

> Tcolulhowe picked up the old drum carefully, smoothed his leathery hand over its skin top and banged it slowly. It was as if he was thinking about campfires and tall trees and the sounds of an Indian village as it settled down for the night 300 years ago.

> He was not in the woods, however, but in the base-
> ment of the New Britain Township, Bucks County,
> Recreation Building in Chalfont, which, since 1974, has
> been the old home for the little that remains of the
> Lenape Indian tribe.

A copy editor challenged the second sentence, asking the reporter if
he had asked the subject of the story what he was thinking. The reporter
said he had not. Then, said the copy editor, we can't speculate; we can deal
only in facts. The copy editor proposed the following rewrite, which the
reporter and the chief copy editor accepted:

> Tcolulhowe picked up the old drum carefully, ran his
> leathery hand over its skin top and banged it slowly. But
> rather than being seated under tall trees around a camp-
> fire in an Indian village, he was in the basement of the
> New Britain Township Recreation Building in Chalf-
> ont, Bucks County.

No journalist should make something up. Journalists must adhere to
what Robert H. Woodward and H. Wendell Smith call the "narrative of
fact":

> And whereas fiction is designed to give the illusion of
> reality, factual narration describes reality itself. Indeed,
> the value of a narrative of fact is determined by the extent
> of the writer's adherence to particular truths and to real-
> ity. . . . Documentation of one kind or another is essen-
> tial to factual narration.[4]

How does the following measure up?

> If Jim wants to be a football player—a big-time col-
> lege football player—he's got to be strong, fast and
> quick. And he has to be big. Jim knows that. His high

school coaches know that. More important, college coaches know that.

To attract scholarship offers from the big schools, Division 1-A programs, Jim has to get stronger, faster, quicker—to get bigger. But as a sophomore in high school, Jim figures time is a premium. Even the finest weight-lifting program would take too long to show results. And Jim wants results now.

After school one day, Jim, who lives in a suburban area, heads to a few downtown fitness clubs. He looks up a few body builders—muscleheads he's heard about from friends and from friends of friends—to talk about getting bigger. He returns home that day with his solution in hand.

Steroids.

Anabolic-androgenic steroids are synthetic derivatives of the male sex hormone testosterone. The effects achieved by steroid use include increased aggressiveness, growth of facial hair, deepened voice and a proliferation of other male sex characteristics. But the anabolic effects are what attracts athletes—changes which occur in muscle, bone and blood. In other words, changes which allow an athlete to "build up."

Jim is a fictitious character, but he needn't be created from the imagination. There are an estimated one million adult and adolescent athletes like Jim, people who use steroids. He is far from an isolated case of a high school football player who turns to steroids. Some athletes do it for their egos; others do it to enhance their chances of winning a college scholarship.

You may say that since the reporter said in print that the example was made up, everything is kosher. But if the example was made up, how does the reader know that it describes a real situation? What about the rest of the story? Why can't the reporter find someone who uses steroids and tell his or her story? After all, the reporter says there are a million people like Jim. Why does the reporter have to make anything up? Her lead does not stand the test of truth and reality but fits clearly under the label of imagination, of fiction.

As you write features, profiles, in-depth articles and standard news stories, build your stories on facts. The world is filled with plenty of good stories; journalists don't have to make them up.

Review Questions

Discuss what a lead on a longer story must accomplish.

What is a didactic lead and what problems does it create?

Is there ever a time for a direct quotation lead?

What is one value of an anecdote?

Name three major organizational devices and explain how they are used.

What is dialogue?

What is the difference between showing and telling?

What will having a theme do to help someone write a story?

Endnotes

1. Martha Miller, "An Iowa Soldier's Unending Fight after Vietnam Service." Reprinted in *Best of Gannett 1989.* (Washington, D.C.: Gannett Co., 1990), 33.

2. Jeanne Edwards, "A Death in the Family," From *Providence Sunday Journal,* May 30, 1982. Reprinted in *How I Wrote the Story,* 2d ed., ed. Christopher Scanlan (Providence, R.I.: Providence Journal Co., 1986), 112–114. Reprinted with permission of the Providence Journal-Bulletin.

3. "Iowa City's Miller: Good Story Is More Than Words." Reprinted in *Best of Gannett 1989* (Washington, D.C.: Gannett Co., 1990), 15.

4. Robert H. Woodward, and H. Wendell Smith, *The Craft of Prose,* 4th ed. (Belmont, Calif.: Wadsworth, 1977), 215.

Chapter 11

Writing for Broadcast[1]

Chapter Objectives

In this chapter, you will be introduced to the fundamentals of writing for broadcast. You will learn about some of the differences between print and broadcast writing styles and how broadcast writers write for the ear.

Introduction

Usually, when journalists talk about writing for newspapers and writing for broadcast, they emphasize the differences between newspapers, radio and television. But all three news media have similar requirements that must be stressed. For instance, all three rely heavily on solid reporting; the brevity of a broadcast piece has nothing to do with the amount of reporting that goes into it.

Broadcast writing must be simple, direct and clear. "A writer for radio," says WCUZ executive news director John Bry, "must make short, simple, easily grasped statements because he has only a fleeting shot at one of the listener's five senses."[2] Listeners do not get a second chance to examine an unclear sentence. They cannot go back and rehear something the way a reader can go back and reread something. In broadcast, a moment of ambiguity consigns the story to the refuse heap of obscurity.

Broadcast writing is conversational. The writer is writing for the ear, not for the eye. The writer is always thinking of how a story will sound.

233

Broadcast writing must capture the flavor of actual speech. Actual speech is not stilted.

The successful broadcast journalist is a successful writer. In the words of David Brinkley of ABC:

> Anyone who wishes to be successful in broadcast news must write his own stuff. Otherwise he will never have any style, any individuality; no one will ever recognize him/her as anything more than some voice. If you don't want to write it yourself, you should go and sell insurance. If you can't write it yourself, don't go into the business.[3]

In order to achieve conversational speech, you may use direct address rather than the third person. Because the writing is called conversational, you may use colloquialisms, sentence fragments and vernacular language, but avoid slang and vulgarism.

Broadcast writing uses common words, because they are instantly recognizable, and short sentences, because they are easier on the ear. Broadcast writing uses rounded-off numbers because they are easier for the listener to understand. Frequently, too, broadcast writing does not use middle initials in a person's name.

The emphasis in a sentence is different in broadcast and in print. For newspapers, a writer usually puts the emphasis out front, which means the sentence often ends with something less important, such as the attribution tag. For example:

> Congress will have to raise taxes next year if the country wants to get out of the recession, a White House aide said today.

But because broadcast writing is aimed at the ear, and because listeners remember best what they hear last, the emphasis in a broadcast news sentence is at the end. Broadcast reports usually begin sentences with attribution rather than ending them that way:

A White House aide said today that Congress will have to raise taxes next year if the country wants to get out of the recession.

Broadcast reporting is not a trade for timid people. It demands the stage presence of an actor who has played the role a hundred times, the eye contact of a lover, the voice control of a priest, and the body control of a dancer.

Writing the Story

The Lead

A broadcast lead can be one sentence, two sentences, three sentences, even four, but it must quickly reveal the essence of the story—the most important fact, the crucial element, the nature, the flavor, or the atmosphere. It should be the fact that will be explained by every other fact that appears in the story.

Here is a lead about a new football coach. How many facts does it raise that will have to be explained in the rest of the story?

> BALTIMORE—Former Blue Jays football standout Jim Margraff has been selected as the football coach at Johns Hopkins University.[4]

One fact the lead writer must explain is Margraff's prowess as a Blue Jays football standout. Another fact is what happened to the previous Johns Hopkins coach. A third fact is what are Margraff's credentials for becoming a coach. Here is the rest of the story, with the facts explained:

> Margraff was a four-year starting quarterback for the Blue Jays. He will replace Jerry Pfeifer, who announced his resignation November 21st.

Margraff is the Blue Jays' all-time statistical leader for passing attempts, pass completions, passing yardage and touchdown passes.

He was the leading passer in the Middle Atlantic Conference each year he played from 1978 through 1981. He also held the N-C-A-A Division-Three record in career completions when he graduated.

After coaching high school football, Margraff was named offensive line coach at the State University of New York at Albany in 1985.

In 1987, he became an assistant coach at the University of Pennsylvania.

The following year, he went to coach the offensive line at the University of Rochester, and in 1989 he went to Columbia University.

As an aside, note how nicely the writer effected transition by ending one paragraph with a date and then starting each new subsequent fact with another date. The placement of the dates made the story easier for listeners to follow.

You may need more time to write your lead than the rest of your story, but if your lead sets the tone, the details should fall readily into place.

Tense

Whenever it sounds natural, write your lead in the present tense. It gives the story immediacy.

The Labor Department *says* unemployment *is* down to nine percent.

The Civil Air Patrol *is joining* the search for a missing light plane.

Some administration officials *concede* they've lost the battle of the budget.

If the present tense does not sound natural, try the present perfect tense. Because of its indefinite nature, the present perfect tense has a sense of immediacy about it, which makes it a good tense for the broadcast media. The present perfect tense combines the past participle with the auxiliary verbs *has* or *have*.

> Striking telephone workers and American Telephone and Telegraph *have resumed* their bargaining session.

> Two election losers *have asked* for ballot recounts.

> The County Board of Equalization *has given* taxpayers a two-week extension for property tax appeals.

Even though you do not use the past tense in your lead, you will use it eventually, and that is usually the time to insert the time element:

> An accused murderer says he didn't intend to kill a 17-year-old jail inmate. Matthew Marks *told* the jury *today* he struck Paul Peters, but that was half an hour before Peters collapsed.

> The State Senate has passed a stiff new drunken-driving bill. The senate *voted* 28–12 *this afternoon* to approve mandatory jail terms for motorists convicted of drunken driving.

> Illegal aliens will not get social security benefits. The Social Security administration *ruled yesterday* that no one is eligible for benefits if he/she doesn't have permission to work in this country.

Elements of the Lead

Depending on the twist of the story, the broadcast lead, just like the print lead, can emphasize different elements. Again, those elements are *who, what, why, when, where* and *how*. Here we discuss *what* and *when*.

If a prison riot that has continued for three days is settled, you can get directly to the point in your lead: "The state prison riot is over." Then fill in the background. You can do this with a story that is ongoing for a period of time, since your continual reporting on the event helps the listener retain a sense of the story. The listener will not have the details, but will know, for example, that a prison riot is occurring. That's what enables such a brief lead to work so well when the riot ends.

> One-hundred-forty inmates took over two buildings, held 15 guards and prison workers hostage, and set fire to broken furniture. They were protesting the cancellation of their recreation schedule after an inmate was stabbed during a prison baseball game. They abandoned their strike after the warden sent a suspect to solitary confinement and reinstated the recreation.

Sometimes, when what happened is either unconfirmed or in doubt, you may have to attribute before you detail what happened. For example, if police tell you four students were stabbed at a local high school and they have charged two suspects, you could lead your story this way:

> City police say four students have been stabbed during a fight at South High School, and two students have been arrested.

Then you can attribute the information to the officer who provided it and give the details of the incident:

> Police Lieutenant Talley Keither says the fight followed a South High basketball victory over East High. The wounded students were South High cheerleaders. All four are in satisfactory condition at St. Mark's Hospital.

If you think two aspects of a story are equally important, try writing them both into your first sentence. Perhaps a serious traffic accident has hurt several people, and the wreckage is tying up traffic:

> Highway patrolmen say a four-car accident early this morning injured 12 people and blocked the icy westbound lanes of Interstate 90 near Moses Lake, Washington.

Read the sentence aloud. Does it read comfortably? Will listeners be able to absorb both facts easily. If not, rewrite it as two sentences:

> Twelve people have been hurt in a four-car accident near Moses Lake, Washington. The wreckage has blocked the west bound lanes of icy Interstate 90.

You will write most leads in either the present tense or the present perfect tense, but sometimes, when you want to emphasize how current an event is, stress when it happened or will happen. Start your lead with the time element. This can be done very effectively in broadcast because of the immediate nature of the broadcast media. With radio and television providing sometimes hourly reports, the news takes on those immediate qualities, a circumstance good broadcast writers will exploit. For example:

> *Just minutes ago,* three mysterious explosions rocked a downtown hotel.

> *At this hour,* surgeons at Pittsburgh's Children's Hospital are beginning to transplant a liver into a four-year-old boy.

> *Within the next hour,* Eastern Airlines ground workers are expected to walk off the job.

> *Tonight, Congress adjourns for a month's vacation, leaving behind the President's emergency funding bill.*

> *Today,* winter began, and several northeastern cities are feeling the sting of its first storm.

Story Structure

The traditional newspaper story is structured to allow exit points for readers—points where they can leave the story whenever they have all the information they want. It is also structured so that the information declines in importance as one reads deeper into the story. This is the inverted pyramid structure.

Broadcast newswriters rarely provide exit points. They don't want listeners to become bored or impatient, so they reserve throwaway lines for stories they have to trim if their newscasts are running overtime. They write most of their stories intending to read every sentence.

Because radio and television audiences cannot absorb much detail, broadcast writers limit each story to the main idea, then supplement it with only those subsidiary ideas that help to make that idea clear.

You can write some stories to be read aloud in as few as five seconds; others may require two minutes. But you must discipline yourself to expect that many television news stories will be shorter than one minute, and many radio news stories will be shorter than 30 seconds. The average delivery rate in broadcasting is 150–175 words per minute. That will not fill one piece of $8\frac{1}{2} \times 11$ sheet of paper double-spaced. That is not a lot of space when you have a lot to say, and one of the first challenges the newcomer to broadcast writing faces is writing to time rather than length.

You will have no formula for writing news, but you can develop an instinct for structuring facts into meaningful patterns. In radio and television, your instinct must include a sense of drama—a feeling for the emotion, the conflict, the suspense, and the human qualities that draw your listeners into events to experience them as if they were participants. After all, listeners have other things to do, and so your stories must attract them and hold their attention.

The Hourglass

If you were writing fiction, you would defer the climax until the end of the story. You would explain the background and introduce the participants, and then detail the conflict or the chronological sequence of events that lead to the climax.

But broadcast audiences are impatient. They want to know immediately what happened. In most instances, they need to hear the story's climax before they will focus their attention on background, participants, or chronological details.

Think of the many stories that fit this structure: climax followed by chronological narrative. Begin with the turning point, the change, then write from the beginning. This is the hourglass structure that more and more print journalists are using. It is a good form for telling a story compellingly. Here's an example:

> (*Climax*)   A college student tried to reenact a daredevil exploit from his high school days this morning and fell 200 feet to his death.
>
> (*Chronological Narrative*)   Twenty-one-year-old Rob White was at a party last night when one of his friends recalled how five of them crossed the steel waterline over the Snake River Canyon when they were seniors in high school. They decided to repeat the stunt.
>
> Four men and a woman drove to the south rim of the canyon at about 5 o'clock this morning. White and 20-year-old Mike Adams started across the pipeline first, walking on the steel pipe and holding onto the suspension cables.
>
> About 20 feet from the north end of the line, they encountered a barrier gate that had been erected to prevent such crossing. Adams swung around the gate and scrambled back to the top of the line. White started around the gate but apparently lost his grip on a suspension cable and fell 200 feet to the rocks below.
>
> White's three remaining friends made their way back to the south rim and drove to Ketchum to call the sheriff.
>
> When rescuers reached the bottom of the canyon, White was dead. He suffered multiple fractures and internal injuries.
>
> This afternoon, White's friend Adams called it a "stupid stunt."

Other Story Patterns

Sometimes, a story does not lend itself to a chronological pattern; it may be based instead on a group of important related facts. You must first decide which are the essential facts—the ones that will help your listeners understand the issue—then you must place them in the order of their importance.

The story will begin with its climax or central fact: The state's director of disease control has warned parents to immunize their children against whooping cough.

Now, ask yourself what the listeners need to know or want to know about that fact. Three important questions arise: Why do children need to be immunized now? How does the disease affect children? Is any cure available? Arrange the questions in order of importance and write the answers:

> Disease control director Roger Hudgins says 27 cases have been reported to his office in the last two months. That's one-third of all the cases reported in the last five years. Hudgins thinks the growing number of cases suggest a potential epidemic.
>
> Whooping cough is a highly contagious respiratory disease. Its bacteria can be transmitted through coughs or sneezes or through contact with clothing or toys.
>
> It affects children, especially between two months and four years of age. It starts with sneezing, coughing, loss of appetite, and sometimes fever.
>
> If whooping cough is not treated, the affected children may develop a severe cough, expel large amounts of mucus, vomit, and sometimes choke. It can be fatal.
>
> Hudgins says doctors can treat the disease once they diagnose it, but parents would be safer to immunize their children now. He says 75 percent of the children who die of whooping cough are children under the age of one who haven't been immunized.

The way facts relate to each other may sometimes determine the structure of your story. When one fact raises another question, answer it immediately. As you write, ask yourself what questions your listeners are asking next.

The climax or lead of your story may say:

> A North Terrace woman says she's lost all tolerance for teenagers who cruise Main Street on weekend nights.

Your listeners may be wondering who she is and why she has lost tolerance, so you need to respond to that question:

Convenience store owner Susan Madsen says cruisers use her parking lot as a meeting place and turnaround point.

Why does that trouble her?

They leave empty beer cars and trampled shrubs in their wake, and sometimes they beat neighbors who complain about the noise and debris.

Has she done anything about it?

Madsen says she's called police numerous times, but officers have been unable to control the problem.

Why not?

Police captain Ozzie Roberts says his officers lack the legal power to arrest the troublemakers.

Why?

The parking lot is public, so the teenagers are not trespassing. Officers can cite teenagers for littering, but it's difficult to prove which teenagers are the litterers. Officers can arrest teenagers who assault residents, but most residents are afraid to sign complaints.

What else can officers do?

Roberts says the city needs ordinances to control beer drinking in public places and to prohibit open containers of beer in public places.

Where is the trouble spot?

> Madsen's "all-night shop" is located at 12-hundred
> Main Street, at the north end of the strip where teenagers
> cruise.

You may be able to draw your listeners into a story by letting them emphatically feel what the participants in the story felt. That means you must utilize whatever emotion inherently exists in the event—sorrow, laughter, pathos, love, fear, anger. But remember, the emotion must be a natural, innate characteristic of the event. You cannot force emotion. You cannot inject it into the story artificially and expect your audiences to accept it. They sense the difference between genuine and artificial emotion, and if you try to color the narrative artificially, they will feel only senti-mentality. And sentimentality will affect them negatively.

A reporter or newscaster who first delivers a businesslike, direct report about the president's State of the Union speech, then delivers a story about six people killed in a head-on collision in a lower pitch, slower pace, and deliberate emotional tone will only irritate listeners.

The reporter or newscaster who laughs openly when he delivers the punch line to a humorous story will probably antagonize his audiences.

Avoid temptations to write emotion into your stories. Like a drunk who gets teary when he remembers his misfortunes, your writing may sound maudlin. Use emotions that exist in the event—describe actions that show emotions, include the voices and pictures of newsmakers who show emotions—but resist the urge to be emotional yourself. Write your story straight, and read it straight.

Writing Style

Good writing flows onto paper as it flows from your mind—casually, informally, unpretentiously, conversationally. It conveys to listeners a sense of spontaneity and energy. It is simple, direct, concise, positive, active, and clear. The spoken words fall gracefully from your tongue.

Broadcast writers know that listeners are often inattentive. Consequently, they must compel them to listen. They must attract and hold them long enough for ideas to be absorbed. So, most broadcast writers talk out loud as they write, their words spilling from their minds as if they had just witnessed events they must share immediately with their listeners.

Broadcast writers talk to one person, not to thousands. They know that radio and television audiences are usually alone in their thoughts, if not in their physical space. They know that listeners mentally shut out their surroundings and intimately exchange thoughts and ideas with the voices and faces transmitted by microphones and cameras.

Broadcast writers who think they must impress their listeners may labor over their scripts, searching for sentence structures, words, and phrases that will sound important. When they do, their audiences will probably tune out, because they dislike the oratorical quality of pretentious speech and resist it.

Such writers would be wise to study their notes, organize the important details in their minds, drop their notes in a wastebasket, and ad lib their scripts as quickly as their fingers can encode the words.

By ad libbing their stories into tape recorders, then transcribing those oral stories, some broadcast writers have mastered conversational quality. Such writers must polish their copy—substituting precise, active words, readjusting awkward phrases and sentences to eliminate confusion and wordiness, replacing generalities with specifics—but each time they ad lib their stories, their writing becomes more natural.

You may find another, more effective technique for learning how to talk to listeners, but you must evaluate your progress by reading your stories aloud. If the copy flows easily off your tongue—without awkward pauses for breath, enunciation traps, confusing combinations of sounds, or distracting vocal pops and hisses—listeners will probably understand what you say. But if you pause in places that seem to interrupt ideas, if you stumble over individual words or combinations of words, if you slur through phrases or whistle through your teeth, listeners will probably be confused and discouraged.

Readjust sentences that trouble you when you read them aloud. Substitute or delete words that are difficult to enunciate. Most of all, when you listen to your oral story, listen for the ideas. Ask someone else to read your story aloud. Does that person understand the story well enough to convey the ideas you wanted to convey? If not, you have probably failed to write the story in a way that permits another reader to translate your ideas meaningfully. Rewrite your copy to allow the idea to emerge.

Good broadcast newswriting attracts listeners in the same way that stimulating conversation attracts them. Well-written broadcast copy will flow into your listeners' minds and be immediately understood.

Positive Sentences

Broadcast writers have little time to reiterate facts, and their audiences have little time to think about them. Reporters must speak their ideas clearly the first time. They should write their ideas forcefully and positively because negative ideas tend to confuse listeners. A positive sentence tells your listeners what is happening. A negative sentence tells your listeners what is not happening.

The play-by-play announcer who said, "The coach sent his 230-pound fullback into the center of the line, and he got absolutely not much," led us to believe he was praising the success of the play, then abruptly reversed his field and let us down. He would have been clearer if he had worded the last clause, "and he gained little," or, "he gained only a yard."

Most negative statements are indefinite: "The terrorist plot did not succeed." The writer should have shown us the certainty of the action: "The terrorist plot failed."

One reporter talked about a rock concert at which gunfire erupted and stray bullets killed two fans, then he concluded, "A police spokesman said that, considering the number of people in the stadium, things weren't all that bad." How bad were they? Specifically, how bad were they for the relatives and friends of the dead fans? The police officer probably intended to say that greater violence had erupted at earlier rock concerts, but the reporter carelessly painted him as an insensitive cynic. He could have written the last clause positively: "Things could have been worse."

Positive statements demand that writers be precise rather than evasive. The sentence, "The problem should not be all that difficult to solve," sounds like the writer is uncertain about how difficult the solution might be and he's too lazy or too rushed to investigate it. So he hides his doubt in negative verbiage. He should have asked himself, "Will it be easy to solve? Will it require study? Or am I too blind to see the solution?" Then he could write something like this: "They should solve the problem easily," "They should be able to solve the problem soon," or "They should be able to study the problem briefly, then solve it."

Broadcast writers should also be aware of the confusion that double negatives can create. A sportscaster who said, "We shouldn't be in doubt that Alabama won't win the national championship," would have made a clearer statement this way: "Alabama is unlikely to win the national championship."

Quotation Techniques

Shun Direct Quotations

Broadcast reporters are storytellers; they tell about the fortunes and misfortunes of people their listeners hear about. Since newscasters seldom witness or participate in the events they talk about, they collect information from others and relay it to others. They tell their stories as intermediaries, relating most information in the third person, infrequently using such pronouns as *I, we,* and *us.*

Actors, oral readers, and orators who perform for large audiences like to quote their characters directly. They try to recreate and project the physical and vocal characteristics of the people they represent. But reporters who tell their stories intimately would seem ridiculous if they tried to mimic their sources, so they quote them, for the most part, indirectly. They paraphrase and often condense what eyewitnesses and experts have told them.

Too often, quotation marks tempt reporters and newscasters to dramatize the statements of their sources. If the mayor tells you, "My opponent is full of baloney," you might be tempted to imitate the mayor's vocal force if you quote him directly. If you overemphasize the quotation vocally, however, your listeners and viewers might take the words to be yours rather than the mayor's. You may want to use the mayor's colorful words, but eliminate doubt about who said them, flag the words to make the source clear: "The mayor says his opponent is—and these are the mayor's words—'full of baloney.' " If a resident tells you, "The city council is made up of a bunch of petty thieves," you can remove yourself from the direct quotation if you write indirectly, "Mrs. Brown says the city council is made up of—and this is her phrase—'a bunch of petty thieves.' " If you are giving the story to someone else to read, enclose the strong words in quotation marks to call the reader's attention to the specific words, but quote everything except the strong words indirectly.

Sometimes you may want to include a complete-sentence direct quotation. To do it, some newscasters still use the "quote . . . unquote" or "quote . . . close quote" phrase to set off such quotations, but that technique often sounds hackneyed and unnatural. Use it only when it seems to fit naturally into the context of the sentence, and if the direct quotation is short, flag it at the beginning but not at the end: "The governor says, quote, 'The legislature should fish or cut bait.' " Your listeners can sense when such a short quote ends. If the direct quotation is long, however, you may have to flag it at both the beginning and the end: "The neighborhood city council leader says, quote, 'I'll call down thunder and lightning if the sanitation department doesn't damn soon haul away that stinking heap of garbage,' unquote."

You'll use direct quotations best if you have recorded them on audio or videotape and let newsmakers state them in their own voices. (See Box 11.1 for an example of a broadcast script that contains both taped quotations and the news director's quoting of sources.)

Attribution Tags

Most broadcast newswriters agree that attribution tags should appear at the beginning of a sentence. When you name the source of your information at the beginning of a sentence, you give listeners a foundation for believing or rejecting it. If you report that "the incumbent governor is leading his challenger in preelection polls," listeners will have no reason to believe you because they know you are not a pollster. But if you report that "pollster Dan Jones says the incumbent governor is leading his challenger in a preelection poll," listeners who have heard of the pollster will remember that he has an established reputation for scientific polling and that his findings are usually reliable.

If you allow attribution to dangle at the ends of sentences, listeners may miss it. Too often in oral language, the information at the end of a

KWTO Investigated a Greene County Sheriff's Failure to Report a Deputy's Alleged Molestation of a Boy

News Director Dan Wadlington: Did Greene County Sheriff John Pierpont fail to adequately investigate a child molestation charge against a former deputy sheriff? Was there an attempted cover-up? In mid-June 1988, Sheriff Pierpont learned of the allegations against Shaw from a co-worker. It was almost a month later before Sheriff Pierpont reported the case to Prosecutor Tom Mountjoy. Juvenile and Highway Patrol investigators say that is unusual, and they also point to some other irregularities in the handling of the case. Over the last month, KWTO News has completed extensive research into the Shaw case and found some questionable practices.

Thirty-eight year-old Donald Shaw is accused of molesting one young Willard boy in late 1987, and exposing himself to a 10-year-old boy in early June of 1988.

It was the latter incident that was reported by the boy to his mother, who is an employee in the records office of the Greene County Sheriff's Department. She reported the incident to Willard Police Chief Dwayne Davis.

Davis sent the report to the sheriff's chief deputy on June 13th. It was on June 17th that Sheriff John Pierpont returned to town from a trip and was notified of the incident.

Pierpont called Davis, now a Springfield policeman, for more details. While Davis refuses to discuss the phone call with KWTO News, a confidential memo he prepared does provide some details about that phone conversation.

Unidentified voice: "Sheriff Pierpont expressed great displeasure with the person who went to someone outside the sheriff's office to report incident. The sheriff said that by going outside of his department, could cost the person their job. Sheriff Pierpont was also informed there may be a second case of child molestation involving Shaw, but that there had been no contact with that second victim. Sheriff Pierpont told me to drop my investigation and added that the person who reported the incident had caused problems in the past by disclosing confidential information and telling lies about the department. The sheriff requested I not tell

Box 11.1　This broadcast script contains both taped quotations and the news director's quoting of sources. Copyright © 1988 Dan Wadlington, KWTO Radio.

Continued

anyone about the incident. I was not invited to participate in an investigation of the allegation."

Wadlington: Sheriff Pierpont admits he ordered David to drop his investigation.

Pierpont: "It was a Greene County Sheriff's Department . . . when I talked to him . . . a personnel problem within this department involving two employees. And all I know is what the chief told me he had heard. This happened to be on that weekend when I returned. And I thought—John Pierpont is the sheriff of this county and my background as far as experience, ah, I thought I was capable of taking it under my hands and trying to do the investigation as best I could."

Wadlington: But Pierpont's investigation never materialized. The sheriff says the victim's mother rejected his advice to bring juvenile authorities into the case.

Pierpont: "I told her I thought we should go to juvenile authorities because there was a a juvenile involved. Ah, she did not, at that time, want to proceed that way . . . the employee did not."

Wadlington: The woman later told her ex-husband and others, that she feared being fired by Pierpont for reporting the incident to outside agencies. Pierpont's own notes on the case say, and we quote: "She was very

much out of line to get other people involved in any personnel matter regarding the Greene County Sheriff's office." But the sheriff denies threatening to fire the woman. The sheriff says the woman did not want to broaden the investigation due to a close personal relationship with Shaw. And according to the sheriff's notes on the case . . . he pursued a personnel inquiry rather than a criminal investigation.

Pierpont: "On personnel, to start with, in both, really. We've looked into both phases of it because it involved personnel in this department."

Wadlington: On June 27th, Sheriff Pierpont summoned Shaw, the victim's mother who worked in his department, and two top commanders. The meeting lasted an hour. According to the sheriff's summary of that meeting, Shaw apologized for the incident. The female co-worker approved dropping the incident since there were no life-threatening matters and her son had not been touched. Shaw allegedly masturbated in front of the 10-year-old.

The sheriff's conclusion, and we quote: "All the parties left my office with the understanding the matter would be dropped at this time. And no further action was needed by me as sheriff."

Continued

During that same personnel hearing, Shaw admitted there had been an "accidental circumstance" with the boy. Despite that admission to the sheriff, Pierpont never disciplined Shaw and never checked with the victim about that story.

Pierpont: "The reason I didn't talk to the boy . . . he was a juvenile. I'm a little strict on that . . . I think there should be juvenile people involved when there's anything taken to juvenile. It is not required . . . but here we had a personnel matter . . . two people in my department involved, and I thought that was the proper procedure."

Wadlington: Pierpont never reported that incident to juvenile authorities. In fact a search of files in Greene County Circuit Court on this case finds no criminal or incidental reports about the incident involving Shaw and the boy from the sheriff. Perry Epperly is the chief juvenile officer for Green County.

Epperly: "I have never received any reports from the Greene County Sheriff's office pertaining to the investigation of the report involving Don Shaw. I have not heard one word from the Greene County Sheriff's office regarding their involvement in any investigation of Don Shaw."

Wadlington: Even Greene County Prosecutor Tom Mountjoy, who's prosecuting Shaw, finds no Greene County Sheriff's reports in the case files.

Mountjoy: "We don't have any Greene County Sheriff's reports per se, the reason for that being that it was investigated by the Missouri State Highway Patrol. And, they conducted the investigation. As far as I know, the sheriff's department did not generate any reports concerning it."

Wadlington: But the Highway Patrol entered the case a month after it came to the attention of Sheriff Pierpont and almost three weeks after his personnel inquiry had been resolved. Sheriff Pierpont says he continued to work on the Shaw case after June 27th, in what he terms a "personal" investigation . . .

Pierpont: "As my investigation went on, then I thought that there was more to it and at that time, that's when I contacted the prosecutor to request an outside agency."

Wadlington: But there are no reports on his follow-up inquiry, and still the victim of the incident was never contacted. And Sheriff Pierpont never reported the case to juvenile authorities or to the County Prosecutor's office. Veteran investigators in the Missouri Highway Patrol and juvenile investigators familiar with the

Continued

Shaw case say it appears that the criminal misdemeanor allegations against the deputy sheriff, were allowed to die as a personnel item by the Greene County Sheriff John Pierpont.

Could it be that Sheriff Pierpont believed he could contain the incident . . . keep it a secret and spare his department defaming publicity in an election year? Sheriff Pierpont admits the case against Shaw was shocking and embarrassed both he and his department. But he staunchly insists the case was handled properly.

Pierpont: "I pride myself on being a professional. And I think the two chiefs and I both felt that we did the right thing and handled it the proper way."

Wadlington: It is clear the sheriff ordered the six people who knew about the incident in his department to keep quiet about it by June 27th. It is also clear that the sheriff undertook no effort to report the case to an outside agency for a follow-up investigation after June 27th. There are no notes, files, or records on any criminal investigation in the Shaw case by Sheriff Pierpont. And his detectives were not allowed to work on the case, either.

Tomorrow, we'll explain how the case resurfaced after it was apparently buried, and how the second investigation led to a broadened probe against former deputy sheriff Don Shaw who was still working for John Pierpont at the end of June 1988.

---

sentence seems to be only incidental to the principal thought. So if you report, "It doesn't matter whether Congress balances the budget, says a prominent Republican leader," the audience may hear only that a balanced budget doesn't matter and assume that you expressed your own opinion, not that of a political leader. Don't risk such misunderstanding. Attribute the statement clearly at the beginning of the sentence, where it will get enough vocal emphasis to be heard: "A prominent Republican leader says it doesn't matter whether Congress balances the budget." Now listeners will be alert, waiting for you to identify the prominent Republican.

Attribute a quotation at the beginning of the sentence, especially when it is striking or controversial. If you say, " 'The rumors that I have been unfaithful to my wife are false and scurrilous; they're damned lies,' the vice president told a news conference this afternoon," you are likely to lead audiences to believe that you are rebutting allegations against yourself. Attribute the statement first, then remove further risk of misunderstanding by quoting indirectly: "The vice president has told a news conference that the rumors he had been unfaithful to his wife were, in his words, 'false and scurrilous.' He called them lies."

Occasionally, when you need variety, you might be able to attribute a direct or indirect quotation in midsentence, but be careful not to interrupt the flow of the main idea. For example:

> The convicted murderer accepted the death sentence calmly. "I'm not going to appeal," he told the judge, "but you'll have to accept the guilt for my death."

When you interrupt the main idea for attribution, you may jar listeners and force them to think about your technique rather than the idea. If you think that could happen, rewrite the sentence with the attribution at the beginning.

Sometimes, attribution will fit naturally between the subject and predicate of a sentence:

> Health officials have asked residents to boil their drinking water because it may be contaminated. A sample of water taken at City Hall, they said, revealed an unusually high concentration of bacteria.

But don't wait too long to attribute. The attribution in midsentence in that example may be clear only because you have also attributed in the first sentence. Be sure to attribute before listeners tire of waiting to hear the source.

Once in a while, you can dangle attribution at the end of a quotation, but only if the quotation states an idea that is generally accepted or an idea that is short enough to keep your listeners' attention until you name the source. For example, you might use an indirect quotation in your lead to attract attention:

> Three-fourths of the state's residents believe the oil
> industry is contriving the gasoline shortage, according to
> a statewide poll.

If you have stated an opinion that seems to be shared by many listeners, then you have helped to stir their interest in the story and quickly added the attribution to make it clear that your source is reliable.

When you dangle attribution, choose words and phrases that sound natural, as the phrase *according to* does. Beware of newspaper styles of attribution that sound awkward when they're spoken: "One of the benefits of being mayor is immunity from parking tickets, Mayor Jerry Jacobs said today." Orally, that sentence may sound like one completed sentence followed by the beginning of a second sentence because the newscaster or reporter who reads it must vocally close out the quoted sentence. Read this sentence aloud: "The mayor interfered with police officers when they tried to close a downtown bar last weekend, says Police Chief Charles Mandel." The inverted attribution sounds unnatural because oral readers normally deemphasize attribution verbs vocally. Attribution verbs are merely connecting words, so they almost fade into obscurity when you speak them.

Listen, too, for the sound of monotony in your attribution. If your sentences are alike, following similar rhythmic patterns because your attribution appears too often at the beginning of a sentence, then attribute some sentences in the middle, or even at the end. Whenever you place attribution, however you phrase it, read each sentence aloud to be sure it sounds natural and reads comfortably.

You can also develop a sense of how frequently you need to attribute. No one can write a rule to guide you. You must listen for the sound of monotony, which will occur if you attribute every sentence, but you must also listen for potential confusion that may occur if you attribute too infrequently. Listen to your writing, and ask others to listen to it, so you can develop a sense of how often to attribute.

Do not strain for attribution verbs. Say is a small, common verb that almost disappears into the context of an idea. You will be more conscious of its repetition than listeners will, so attribute with *say* most of the time.

Longer attribution verbs may sound strained unless they fit into the context naturally. Whenever you choose a longer attribution verb, be certain you know its meaning and are using it in a way that fits its meaning. Many attribution verbs sound pompous when used out of context. *To declare* is "to make known publicly or formally, to proclaim," so it is unlikely that anyone would declare anything in an intimate setting. *To assert* is "to affirm positively, assuredly, plainly, or strongly," so it is unlikely that an offhand or casual comment can be an assertion.

On the other hand, *to mention* is "to note or call attention to in a brief, casual, or incidental manner." *To state* is "to recite, report, set forth"—the verb suggests that the speaker is reading or repeating from memory in a formal or pretentious manner. *To claim* is sometimes defined as "to assert with conviction and in the face of possible contradiction or doubt," so it suggests that you are casting doubt on the statement of a newsmaker if you say, "He *claims* he has discovered gold."

Dozens of attribution verbs are available, but be cautious about the verbs you choose. Choose attribution verbs that you would use in conversation, avoiding ones that may seem pompous. If you are in doubt, choose *say*. It's simple, straightforward, and unpretentious.

Names and Titles

To paraphrase Shakespeare, a good name is a jewel. Broadcast newswriters should remember that. The owner of a name holds a proud possession, and if you distort it, you will offend the person.

Use names respectfully: Spell and pronounce them correctly, and employ them conversationally but not frivolously. A radio station that, during the Nixon administration, instructed its announcers to call Secretary of State Henry Kissinger "Henry the K" may have entertained its listeners, but it also diminished the stature of the secretary's office.

Avoid beginning stories with unfamiliar names. Attract listeners to the story with some flavor and essence, then introduce newsmakers by titles that generate interest or show that they have special knowledge about events, issues, concepts, or plans in the story. Unfamiliar names confuse listeners. They stop following the story line while they try to recall whether they have heard the names before. Titles, however, convey information that enables listeners to judge the expertise or qualifications of newsmakers. If you cite someone only by name, Jane Smith, you are not identifying her expertise, but if you cite security guard Jane Smith, you are identifying someone qualified to arrest suspected shoplifters or to protect property against burglars or vandals. The name Jack Horner may remind us only of the nursery-rhyme boy who sat in a corner, but Deputy City Attorney Jack Horner is a man who can tell us whether the city council can legally bar the public from one of its meetings.

Familiar names, on the other hand, may attract attention by themselves. For example, if you start your story, "Robert Redford is standing on a traffic island in the middle of Main Street, waving at passing motorists," you may intrigue your listeners. They will probably stay tuned until you tell them why Redford is standing in such an unlikely place—because he is helping a political candidate conduct a "honk-and-wave" campaign.

Most of the time, you can eliminate middle initials and middle names. Most people can be identified easily without them. Retail merchant Harriet Smith is not the same person as policewoman Harriet Smith, so you don't need to identify the retail merchant as Harriet X. Smith and the policewoman as Harriet Y. Smith. You will sound natural and conversational if you identify Richard M. Nixon as former president Richard Nixon and Eugene G. O'Neill as playwright Eugene O'Neill. Most people use their first and last names only, except on formal documents.

Some people, however, want their middle initials or middle names treated as importantly as their first and last names. Heavyweight boxing champion John L. Sullivan was never known as John Sullivan. Civil rights leader Martin Luther King was never known as Martin King.

Others regularly use their first initials and middle names. Oil billionaire J. Paul Getty might not be recognized if you called him Paul Getty. Atomic scientist J. Robert Oppenheimer always affixed his first initial. Respect such preferences. [R. Thomas Berner concurs.]

Still others, of course, prefer to use only their initials. We know former baseball pitcher James Rodney Richard only as J.R. Richard. Poet e.e. cummings not only preferred using only his initials but always wrote them lowercased.

Avoid nicknames unless you know that newsmakers prefer them. Former President Carter preferred Jimmy Carter to James Earl Carter or James E. Carter or James Carter. Former House Speaker Tip O'Neill was rarely known as Thomas P. O'Neill, Junior.

If you know how other reporters and newscasters read prominent names, you can follow their style; if you are unfamiliar with certain names and cannot determine how newsmakers prefer them read, use first and last names and eliminate middle initials. But if a name is listed with a first initial and a full middle name, or with initials only, or with three full names, read such names as they appear. You can check telephone books, biographical dictionaries, almanacs or encyclopedias to see how they list the names. If names have appeared regularly in the news, wire service pronunciation guides will list them every day.

Of course, when you need initials or full names for precise identification, use them no matter what the newsmaker prefers. If someone has been charged with a crime, or has been seriously hurt or killed, or has been named in a sensitive context, you must use an initial or a second name to distinguish that person from anyone else who might have a similar name. Often you must identify such people by their ages and addresses, too.

In broadcasting, titles usually precede names. If newsmakers' names are unfamiliar, titles identify their competence to speak on issues or concepts in the news. We can visualize architect Maude Gregson as a person who knows something about the design of a new city hall, nursing supervisor Jonathan Mays as one who can give an accurate report on the condition of a hospitalized accident victim, and disc jockey Brenda Davidson as one who knows which records are popular this week. But without titles, we may visualize Maude Gregson, Jonathan Mays and Brenda Davidson as unknowns without reliable knowledge.

Also, if you place titles before names, you can write sentences that flow more conversationally. Thus, "Elm City Mayor Janet Wilson resigned today" is a sentence that flows naturally without pauses, but "Janet Wilson, the mayor of Elm City, resigned today" demands brief pauses where the commas appear and gives the oral sentence a staccato sound.

In most cases, broadcast writers eliminate the articles *a* and *the* before titles. Rather than saying "the speaker of the House, Alma Henderson," they say "House Speaker Alma Henderson." Rather than saying "a convicted strangler, Rusty Farson," they say "convicted strangler Rusty Farson." When they write titles without articles, they need no commas around them, and because they eliminate the commas, they eliminate unneeded pauses.

If a title is long and cannot be simplified, however, you may be able to write a sentence with more natural breathing spaces if you include the article before the title: "A suspect accused of threatening to bomb a bus station, Matthew Traveler," is much easier to enunciate and to understand than "bus station bomb threat suspect Matthew Traveler." Converting natural prepositional phrases into adjectives and stacking them in front of the name only complicates understanding. Whenever you place an article before a title or place a title after a name, commas must surround the name.

Simplify titles. Write them so that they're easy to understand. "Two university freshmen who have been studying astronomy for only two months" is cumbersome. Perhaps you can simply label them "two novice astronomers." "A representative of a mining company that has adopted new uranium mining techniques" is complex and vague. The title "a uranium industry representative" is clearer. Use the other information later in the story as needed.

Some titles of people in governmental agencies and industrial firms are written long deliberately to cover broad areas of authority. For example, "Tri-Cities International Airport Operations, Management, and Facilities Superintendent George Brown" may accurately reflect the title on Brown's letterhead, but it is so unwieldy that it may bore your audience. Simplify the title to reflect the substance of the story, and split it up, placing part of it before his name and part of it after. If your story is about some aspect of airport operations, call him "operations superintendent George Brown of the Tri-Cities International Airport." If your story details some proposed improvements in airport facilities, call him "airport facilities superintendent George Brown." Experiment orally with cumbersome titles to find natural ways to say them without losing their value for identification.

Write only one title at a time. If the newsmaker holds more than one title, choose the one that connects her most appropriately with the substance of your story. Since most university presidents hold Ph.D. degrees, they can be called either "president" or "doctor." But if a university president named Carol Cartwright speaks for the university, refer to her as "university president Carol Cartwright" rather than as "the university president, Doctor Carol Cartwright" or "Doctor Cartwright." Laurence Olivier was knighted. Still, in your first reference to him, you should say "actor Laurence Olivier" rather than "the actor, Sir Laurence Olivier." In a subsequent reference, you might want to call him "Sir Laurence."

Numbers and Other Details

In oral language, meaning must emerge immediately, and it must be unmistakable. Statistics and complex details impede understanding. Our ears are too seldom alert to oral details, so we tend to screen out particulars and rely on impressions.

Broadcast writers must find ways to write information that will leave listeners with impressions of events that do not demand recall of all the complex specifics.

To illustrate, television weathercasters who cover their maps with numbers want to provide temperatures for as many of their viewers as they can, assuming that individuals will focus on the section of the country that interests them most. But those same weathercasters would be foolish to call direct attention to more than a few selected temperatures.

The following newspaper story is packed with information that readers can browse through and select from, but if you were to read the story aloud, you would find that most listeners would remember only one or two details:

> Indiana's energy coordinator has predicted that the impact of the winter's cold—which drove the mercury to a record eleven below zero in Indianapolis Monday—will be felt long into the future.
>
> Dubuque, Iowa, had its 43rd day this winter of zero temperatures and below. Chicago was rounding out its 42nd straight day of freezing weather. Record lows include 17 below at Moline, Illinois, zero at Charleston, West Virginia, 19 at Wilmington, North Carolina, 21 at Charleston, South Carolina, and 27 at Jacksonville, Florida.
>
> The administrator of the National Oceanic and Atmospheric Administration in Washington has warned that heavy flooding could come in March or April.

Radio and television audiences will probably remember the last fact—we can expect heavy flooding in March or April—perhaps one of the temperatures, and maybe the fact that some city has been through 43 days of below-zero temperatures. But most of the story is wasted—its details are too numerous for the ear to absorb.

Avoid offering such lists of numbers. Instead, provide selected details that leave listeners with impressions of lingering cold, and caution them about potential floods that may follow when temperatures rise again.

You rarely need precise numbers. If an earthquake registers seven on the Richter scale, listeners may learn from that figure because they will remember that earthquakes seldom register higher than five or six. But if 52 people were killed and 211 others are missing, round off the numbers: "More than 50 people have been killed, and more than 200 are missing."

You rarely need precise times. The fact that the earthquake struck at 5:33 a.m. will be harder to remember than the fact that it struck just before dawn or just before the city's residents awakened. The fact that the last major earthquake in this city occurred on August 31st, 1927, will be harder to remember than the fact that it occurred more than 60 years ago. The fact that the seismograph recorded minor shocks three days ago, on Monday the 27th, will be harder to remember than the fact that the seismograph recorded minor shocks earlier this week.

Only when you need numbers to identify newsmakers or when you need to pinpoint precise locations will you need to include ages and addresses. But write them in conversational ways. Instead of writing, as newspaper reporters do, that "Billy Brown, 5, is missing," write, "Five-year-old Billy Brown is missing." Instead of identifying, as newspapers reporters do, "Harry Harrelson, 1325 W. Center St.," check the city directory or telephone book to see if it lists any similar names. If no other Harry Harrelson lives in the same neighborhood, identify this one as "Harry Harrelson of West Center Street."

You should also write numbers informally if they don't need emphasis. Instead of *one-hundred*, write *a hundred*. Instead of *two-thousand-500*, write *25-hundred*. Instead of *one-and-one-half*, write *one-and-a-half*. Instead of *12-point-five percent*, write *12-and-a-half-percent*.

Nevertheless, if you need to emphasize a number, write it formally. "*One-thousand* motorists were killed in traffic over the holiday weekend" is more forceful than "*A thousand* motorists were killed in traffic over the holiday weekend."

Help listeners calculate the differences between numbers. If you tell them Candidate A has polled one-million-327-thousand-916 votes and Candidate B has polled one-million-332-thousand-427 votes, they will probably be unaware of who is winning, even if they see the figures on a television screen. Tell them, instead, that Candidate B is leading by about 45-hundred votes.

If you tell listeners that today's high temperature was 92 degrees, and the normal temperature for the date is 87, help them place the information into understandable perspective by adding that today's temperature was five degrees above normal.

Charles Osgood of CBS offers advice to help the broadcast reporter get information that will appeal to the senses of the listeners. He calls it getting "something that is a human thing."[5]

> It's so obvious, and yet you listen to the tapes that come in. "There's a terrible blizzard out there. God, it sounds just awful." And somebody will say, "Yes, we had 34 inches of snow yesterday and we're expecting another 6 inches today." That's a cut. Then they'll say, "It must be very cold." And they'll say, "It's very cold—32 degrees below."
>
> What you really wanted to find out is, "How do you have to dress for this? That sounds like an awful lot of snow. Is it up to the window? Up to the door? Can you open the door? How are you managing during all this? Did you step outside? What does it feel like? Is there wind in your face?" Sense impressions. Tell me about the hot and the cold and, if it hurts, tell me how it hurts.

If you tell audiences that in a public opinion poll 48 percent of the respondents answered yes and 43 percent answered no, add that nine percent were undecided; that will explain why the figures on the screen do not total 100 percent.

Too many facts, other than numbers, can also muddy audience perceptions. In newspaper stories details provide interesting profiles and backgrounds to events because readers can study them. But those same details in broadcast stories would encumber audience understanding. Instead of listing the occupations of all 12 members of a jury, simply say the jurors work at such diverse jobs as housekeeper and used-car salesman. Instead of listing all the experts who will appear at a public hearing on hazardous waste, choose one or two of the most prominent and say something about them. Instead of naming every play the community theater company will produce in the coming season, name only the first one, and say the company will present five others during the year.

You need specific details to make your stories believable, but choose the most important specifics and ignore the rest. Provide listeners with enough information to help them remember the story, but don't burden them with details that may distract from the main idea.

Personal Style

Because broadcast reporters present their news personally, they often become familiar "friends" in the homes of their audiences. Therefore, they can use the unique vocal and visual qualities of radio and television to draw their audiences in to share the news.

You can generate warm, personal relationships with your listeners if you report your news in person-to-person language that shares information with them. Usually, you can create a sense of sharing by using such personal pronouns as *we, us,* and *our.* When you use personal pronouns, however, the substance of your story should have a fairly general impact. Rising consumer prices, changes in postal rates, strikes that interrupt transportation schedules, tax increases, governmental actions that will affect many residents, crime or tragedy that occurs close to home, unusual weather, the fortunes of sports teams familiar to your audiences—all such stories can help you establish links with your listeners.

Very often, second-person pronouns like *you* and *your* help establish a sharing relationship with your listeners. You might attract them with a lead like this:

> If you thought your paycheck was smaller this month, you were right. The government took another half-percent of it for social security taxes.

You could suggest to your listeners that you have them in mind with a lead like this:

> Your bus may be late tomorrow. The Transit Author-
> ity is trying to save money by cutting back the number of
> buses that travel from the suburbs to the city each day.

Be sure you use personal pronouns to set up your relationship with your listeners, not to establish your relationship with other employees in your news department or station. The editorial *we* should have no place in newswriting. The editorial statement, "We believe the tax increase imposed by the state legislature is too severe," should be replaced with a statement such as, "We have a good idea how much the state legislature is going to raise our taxes."

Such a reference as, "The police chief told us reporters that we couldn't look at the scene of the crime," suggests that the chief affronted you personally. But a statement that says, "The police chief says that if too many of us know the details of the crime, we might jeopardize the case when it gets to court," suggests that you are sharing the responsibility with your listeners. "Our reporter says the city council will close the zoo," sounds self-serving and promotional, but "The city council will close our zoo," makes the issue a close, personal one between you and your audience.

You will communicate best through radio and television when you develop a writing and speaking style that is natural and conversational. Remember that you are speaking to each listener individually, so your language must be casual and unpretentious. Resist the temptation to impress your audience; talk to your listeners as you would to a friend. They should remember your voice or your face more readily than they remember the language you speak or the nuances of your reading style. Listeners will accept you more quickly if you talk like one of them, directly but correctly.

Review Questions

What are some of the similarities between broadcast and print journalism?

What are some of the differences between broadcast and print
journalism?

What tenses are common to broadcast leads?

What is the typical length—as measured in time—of a television news
story?

What is the typical length—as measured in time—of a radio news
story?

How does the hourglass structure apply to broadcast stories?

How does ad libbing help the broadcast writer?

Why is the positive sentence preferred over the negative?

What is the preferred verb of attribution?

Where do titles appear with names in broadcast stories, and why?

How do broadcast newswriters achieve a conversational tone in their
copy?

Why should a broadcast journalist attempt to have a personal style?

Endnotes

1. Adapted from Roy Gibson, *Radio and Television Reporting* (Needham
   Heights, Mass.: Allyn & Bacon, 1991). Copyright © 1991 by Allyn and
   Bacon. Adapted with permission.
2. Personal letter to R. Thomas Berner, June 4, 1990. WCUZ is located in
   Grand Rapids, Mich. Berner and Bry met through CompuServe. Reprinted by permission of John Bry.
3. Shirley Biagi, *Newstalk II* (Belmont, Calif.: Wadsworth, 1987), 116.
4. The Associated Press, January 12, 1990, 1327est. Reprinted with permission by the Associated Press.
5. Biagi, *Newstalk II,* 219.

Chapter 12

Responsible Journalism

Chapter Objectives

In this chapter you will learn how journalists should behave and about the legal problems journalists can encounter when they do sloppy work.

Introduction

A very important thing every journalist and news outlet needs is credibility. When people have doubts about the messenger, they don't believe the message. This can result in diminished audiences for print and broadcast media. Journalists strive to maintain credibility through the responsible practice of their craft.

Intertwining Issues

One of the more famous people in modern journalism history is Col. Anthony Herbert. Among other things, Herbert was the United States' most decorated soldier. In 1986, he spoke to a conference at the Gannett Center for Media Studies, sharing the stage with another famous person in modern journalism history, William Tavoulareas, once the president of Mobil Oil. At one point, Herbert said to the audience:

> What the hell you need, not all of you, here and there
> a lawyer and here and there a reporter, is to get your head
> out from between your buns—you need ethics is what
> the hell you need.[1]

In a discussion on libel, the colonel was able to wrap together two issues of major concern to responsible journalists—ethics and libel. Ethics concerns how journalists practice their craft, and libel concerns how they are held accountable for the results. No one who wants to be a journalist should step into a newsroom without some sense of ethics and libel. In fact, this chapter should merely whet the appetite for exploring both subjects in greater detail.

A Primer on Ethics

The principles that underlie a person's or a group's behavior are known as their ethics. Many professional groups have a code of ethics, and violation of the code can bring censure or even removal from the group. A good example of that would be the disbarment of an attorney. But, unlike attorneys, journalists are not members of a licensed profession, and thus unethical behavior by journalists can go unpunished, even uncensured. In fact, various journalism groups have struggled to devise codes of ethics over the past century that do not contravene First Amendment rights, for implicit in any formal punishment of someone who practices journalism is the potential for infringing on the freedoms of speech and the press guaranteed by the First Amendment.

Unethical behavior manifests itself in journalism in many ways. The Society of Professional Journalists' Code of Ethics says, "Journalists must be free of obligation to any interest other than the public's right to know the truth" (see Appendix C). The code then goes on to list areas where journalists need to exercise caution. Among them:

- Freebies. Journalists are discouraged from accepting anything that might compromise their integrity. "Nothing of value should be accepted," advises the code, noting gifts, favors, free travel, special treatment or privileges.

- Divided loyalties. The SPJ code warns against divided loyalties, which can come about when a journalist holds a secondary job or public office or is involved in a political organization. Urging journalists also to avoid any personal behavior that might create a conflict of interest, the code reminds its adherents that journalists serve the public first.
- Source validation. Some journalists suffer from the notion that because they possess information, it should be published. But the SPJ code advises caution when it comes to news communications from private sources rather than public records, urging that such information be substantiated.
- Public business publicly arrived at. Journalists are encouraged to pursue news that is in the public's interest and to stand firm for open government openly arrived at. Implicit in this paragraph is the notion that journalists should not sit in on closed government meetings with the promise not to publish what they learn.
- Confidential sources. The code urges journalists to protect their confidential sources, which has sometimes meant a journalist has had to go to jail rather than reveal a confidential source. The other side of this matter, though, is whether journalists too readily use confidential or anonymous sources.
- Plagiarism. The code says "plagiarism is dishonest and unacceptable."

Other sections of the code discuss accuracy and fair play. What the SPJ code and other codes strive for is a high standard of moral behavior in the gathering and publishing of news. No code can anticipate every questionable situation a journalist might confront. As Ben Johnson says in another SPJ publication:

> Be prepared to handle each situation on a case-by-case basis. Few ethical rules should be drafted that make clearly right and wrong determinations. Most cases are invariably somewhere in the middle.[2]

Still, we have an idea of past practices that journalists have frowned on. In addition to the ones noted in the SPJ Code of Ethics, those practices include listening in on private meetings, stealing documents, not properly identifying oneself as a journalist, fabricating stories. A survey by the American Society of Newspaper Editors produced a list of problems. Among them, made-up quotations, false documentation to support an in-depth article's conclusion, reporters working on the side with governmental or public relations agencies, not crediting a television newscast as the source of a story, accepting payment to speak before groups the reporter might later write stories about.

Another ethical concern arises innocently in the day-to-day business of journalism. Journalists assume too frequently and too readily that everyone they talk to understands how the news media work. Thus, when a journalist calls a source and starts asking questions, the source, especially someone unaccustomed to dealing with the news media, might not realize that what he or she is saying will be published. It is a journalist's obligation to protect unsophisticated sources from their own naïveté. This is a good procedure:

> *Reporter:* I'm writing a story for publication/broadcast about such and such, and I want to ask you a few questions and will most likely quote you by name in the story.

At the end of the interview, the reporter always takes the trouble to confirm some information.

> *Reporter:* Before I leave/hang up, I want to verify some things that you said. Do you have a minute or so for me to do that?

Obviously, such an approach is not necessary with public officials, especially public officials who work with the news media on a daily or almost daily basis. They know what journalists do, and they need no coddling. But many people are thrown into the maelstrom of a news event only once in their lives and, lacking preparation, have no idea how to deal with the news media. An ethical journalist does not take advantage of someone's inexperience with the news media.

What it comes down to is how you would like to be treated if you were the subject of a news story. That's the way you should treat others. You can still get good stories even when behaving ethically.

Cover the News

You are a reporter for a major newspaper stationed at one of the paper's bureaus. It is Sunday, and police in your area have been searching for a man involved in a shooting. You learn that police have zeroed in on the man's whereabouts, and you go to the scene.

Police have surrounded a house and ordered you to stand beyond the roadblock. You do. Bored, you direct traffic. You take some photographs, and you make sure your snub-nose .38 is in its holster. At some point, you look up and see the suspect walk out of the bushes near you and head toward the police, who are looking the other way. The suspect is holding a shotgun over his head, apparently a sign that he is going to surrender.

Believe it or not, the reporter involved in that situation took out his gun and "covered" the suspect as he walked toward the police. (He also took three photographs.) Eventually, the reporter warned police that the suspect was near, and they turned around. The suspect immediately surrendered.

The problem here is that the reporter instead of covering the news became part of the news. He even wrote a sidebar about his adventures, a sidebar that appeared on the front page of the next day's paper. The story that didn't get written, though, was the one about how badly the police had handled the situation. That story did not get written because the reporter, who should have been covering the police, was too busy playing police officer.

Cover the news; do not make it.

Plagiarism

"Plagiarism," Roy Peter Clark once said, "is the skeleton in journalism's closet."[3] The SPJ Code of Ethics devotes one sentence to plagiarism. You would guess that would be enough, since anyone who has ever taken an English course should know what plagiarism is. Plagiarism is always a potential problem in journalism because journalism is the craft of fashioning stories second-hand using (usually) first-hand sources. Attribution is the best safeguard against plagiarism.

Plagiarism means the borrowing—without credit—of the writings or ideas of others. Clark, in the article cited in the previous paragraph, has come up with seven procedures that "now seem dangerous and unprofessional." His list: "robbing the morgue, abusing the wires, lifting from other newspapers and magazines, looting press releases, hiding collaboration in the closet, cribbing from the books, scholarship and research of others, recycling your old stories." [4] In each instance, attributing information to its appropriate source removes the problem.

"Robbing the morgue" is a special problem, a problem compounded by the fact that most newspapers' morgues are now electronic and that journalists can access another newspaper's morgue via a modem. Thus, it is easy to pick up and use verbatim pieces of an old story and not see the problem that is unfolding before your eyes. Remember step five in the writing process:.

> Style is the flavor, quality, spirit, and personality of a written piece. Style is the sum of a writer. In part, it is an attitude: A good journalist wants to write well and interestingly and to use original language. Avoid clichés. Avoid jargon. Be original. Write the story as it has never been written before.

When dealing with material from the morgue—yours or another newspaper's—do not detach the elements that identify the source. If you remove the identifying elements, you might later assume the material is yours and use it without credit. If, by the way, you use something verbatim, put the words in quotation marks. The preference, though, is to paraphrase, using your own language. But verbatim or paraphrased, information must be attributed.

The wire services present an interesting problem. They transmit news, with the understanding that the client will credit them if the client uses the news in the form transmitted. But if the client decides to rewrite the information, there is no contractual obligation to attribute it. Problems have arisen when journalists have lifted parts of a wire story verbatim without credit. Scrupulous editors will advise readers when stories carrying staff bylines include information from a wire service.

Rather than deal with the temptation or the accident of borrowing from another news medium, some journalists prefer not to read other newspapers, listen to the radio or watch television until their stories have been written. That may work under deadline conditions, but that does not preclude reading a day-old newspaper and subsequently borrowing from it. And so the news media have become more careful even about attributing which news outlet served as the initial source of a story. *The Washington Post* advises, "It is the policy of this newspaper to give credit to other publications that develop exclusive stories worthy of coverage by the *Post*."[5]

Columns also present a special problem. A columnist reads someone else's column and then writes a similar column. The similar column mimics the idea of the original but does not use the same language. It is still plagiarism, and columnists have lost their jobs doing it. Again, the injunction to be original can save many a writer.

When you are not being original, say so. There is no shame in acknowledging that an idea came from someone else. When Dennis Hetzel, the publisher of the *York Daily Record,* borrowed a column idea, he concluded his column this way:

> (So I won't be accused of plagiarism, I must thank Jack Keith, managing editor of the Bellingham, Wash., *Herald*. Keith wrote a similar column that made many of the points I've made today.)[6]

It's true that Hetzel's readers probably would never know about the other column, published nearly 3,000 miles away. But Hetzel is a responsible journalist, and acknowledging the source is part of his routine. It also establishes Hetzel's credibility with readers. They see how he behaves, and they can infer that he makes his staff behave the same way.

A quirkier area involves using direct quotations. Take as an example sports columns in two different newspapers published a few days apart in which the direct quotations were the same. The first column suggests that the statements quoted in that column were made exclusively to that writer. But what if the comments were made at a news conference? Then the direct quotations are fair game, some would argue, and one columnist may borrow from another column without attribution. Perhaps not. If the journalist was not present when the statements were made, he or she is better off attributing them to a source than running them without attribution and implying first-hand work.

The attribution advice also holds when rewriting news releases. There's nothing wrong with saying, "In a news release, the president of Company X said . . ." Similarly, when more than one journalist works on a story, all who contributed should get credit, even if only one—the writer—is listed at the top of the story. If not listed at the beginning, the others should be credited at the story's end.

Journalism is not the work of experts. A journalist writing about child abuse is a journalist, not a child abuser or a psychologist. So the journalist relies on experts for information. It happens every day. Relying on others is part of what a journalist does. So the journalist needs to ensure that the experts get the credit. The way to ensure that there is no confusion about who gets credit is to keep good notes. When you sit down with a book or report that you may want to borrow from, first write down in your notebook what the source is. That is better than mistakenly using the information unattributed or trying to find the source later.

A journalist also needs to be careful about recycling his or her work without acknowledging the recycling. This is not a problem for beginning journalists who are writing routine stories. It is a problem, Clark points out, when a writer moves from one news outlet to another, takes his files with him, and then recycles a story from the previous job. Clark calls borrowing from yourself "a low-grade ethical problem."[7]

As a free-lancer, a sportswriter wrote these paragraphs for a magazine:

> The fundamental economic theory of supply and demand.
>
> There are thousands of teachers, but only one Dan Marino. If a math teacher leaves a school system, the system won't fall apart; a replacement of near-equal caliber can be found. When the Dolphins lose Marino, they go from being a good team to an average team.

Approximately a year later the writer joined a newspaper staff and wrote a story on the high salaries athletes receive. It contained this:

Again, the law of supply and demand answers that issue.

There are thousands of teachers, but only one Larry Bird. If a high school math teacher leaves the [name] City School, it won't fall apart; a replacement of near or equal value can be found quickly. However, if Bird is injured, as he was two years ago, then the Boston Celtics go from being an élite NBA team to an average team.

When asked about the similarity, the writer readily acknowledged that he had rewritten himself. He saw no problem, since he was the writer. But beyond the lack of originality in the second piece, there is also the issue of who owns the content of a publication. In some cases, a publication buys freelance work and purchases one-time publication rights. But a newspaper is a different animal and, depending on a contract with each employee, owns the published work. So not only is this an example of an ethical problem, it also reflects a potential legal problem.

What the beginning journalist needs to develop is a hypersensitivity to using others' work and re-using his own, to know when it is proper and when it is not, and to attribute accordingly. There is no shame in attributing information; there is much shame in stealing it.

Sensitive Stories

The editor advises the reporter to get as many details as possible when covering the story and to "show, don't tell" when writing it. But just what does the editor mean? That may be good advice in a feature story about a local veterinarian's handling of stray dogs, but does it apply to a triple murder?

Some stories require sensitive treatment. Sometimes, explicit writing is not the best approach. Take, for example, a story provided by Dick Smyser, a journalism professor and founding editor of the *Oak Ridger* in Oak Ridge, Tennessee. The story comes from the *Anchorage Daily News* and reports the charging of a suspect in a triple murder, which involved the rape and murder of a mother and two daughters.[8] The story goes into graphic detail about the murder scene. It says, "They came upon a grotesque scene, according to court documents filed in the case Friday," and then describes the condition of each victim, from the knife wounds to the damage done by the brutal rape.

The managing editor apologized to the readers, who then responded with a flurry of mostly condemnatory letters. Generally, readers condemned the newspaper for a lack of taste. The graphic detail was not necessary. Some readers also recognized that the detailed coverage would create a problem for the defendant in getting a fair trial.

Smyser argues that journalists need to appreciate that some subjects—gender, race, religion, tragedy, damage suits (medical malpractice, especially)—are inherently more sensitive than others. In a list of guidelines that Smyser uses in his classes, the last one serves as a guide for dealing with sensitive subjects:

> Ask one basic question in each situation: Explicitness to assure that the full story is known, understood? Exploitation—details, tone, emphasis not really to report but rather to excite, titillate? Explicitness, yes; exploitation, no.

Race and Gender

As noted in the previous section, stories dealing with race and gender create sensitive situations. The nonchalant handling of a subject's race or gender can raise questions about a news outlet's impartiality and credibility. What questions does the following story raise?

> PITTSBURGH (UPI)—Pittsburgh Crime Stoppers is offering a reward for information about the April 5 abduction and robbery of a Carnegie Mellon University student.
>
> The victim, James Salsman of Pittsburgh, was attacked by two men from behind and dragged into a small, red two-door car driven by a third man.
>
> Police said the suspects took $2 and an automatic banking card from Salsman's wallet. Salsman was able to escape when the men stopped at a banking machine. He had been beaten, stabbed and suffered a broken nose.
>
> All three suspects are black. Two of them are in their mid-20's, one described as clean-shaven with wire-

rimmed glasses, and the other as being tall, with a medium build and short hair. The third man was about 30.[9]

Do you know the race of the three suspects? What is the race of the victim? If the story mentions the one, it should mention the other. Since this story focuses on a reward, some would argue that the description of the suspects, including their race, is necessary. It's not. So few criminal suspects are identified by the general public, that the written description serves more to indict an entire race than to alert the public to particular criminal suspects.

Problems with race are not limited to the police beat stories. Here is an excerpt from a feature story on a bouncer in a college town bar:

> If you've ever walked past a bar in State College and peered inside, chances are you've seen him. You would remember.
>
> If you saw him working at the All-American Rathskeller in State College, he probably would have been wearing his navy 'Skeller T-shirt, army shorts and white high-top tennis shoes.
>
> He's a Korean, 6 feet and 1 inch tall, and he tips the scales at 285 pounds. He's ticklish. He has a silly giggle.[10]

What does his race have to do with his job as a bouncer? Is it necessary to insert the bouncer's race into the story in such a prominent way? Later, the feature reveals that the bouncer was born in Korea, and the story is accompanied by his photograph.

A journalist must also be sensitive to writing that suggests women derive their standing from men. A woman once lamented to a friend about an article on her husband's hobby of raising honey bees. She was referred to as the "honey queen," as though she had no significance other than being married to the "honey king." Yet she was working full-time and, like her husband, had a Ph.D. degree. Some sexist writing is more subtle. Despite the effort by journalists to use neutral terms, how many times have you heard the word "spokesperson" applied only to females while "spokesman" is exclusively applied to men. Using neutral language does not mean neutralizing terms about women only.

Sexist language is another problem. Consider this lead:

> PETERBORO, Ontario (UPI)—A pretty blonde co-
> ed was evicted from her apartment for her noisy love-
> making sessions with a steady stream of boyfriends.

The story could have been written without the sexist references to "a pretty blonde co-ed." Supposing she had been ugly? Language characterizing a person's physical condition is generally irrelevant. Avoid judgmental writing, a point Richard P. Cunningham addresses in Box 12.1.

References to gender should only be made when necessary and then to the gender of everyone in the story. The best approach is to treat people in any story as individuals rather than as members of a race or a gender, unless this information is clearly relevant.

Age

Ages of news makers are usually mentioned in news stories to aid accurate identification of one individual vs. others who might have the same name. That's no problem. The problem arises when a journalist suggests that because a person is a certain age, the person fits a certain stereotype. Referring to someone over 70 as "doddering" is but one example. A student newspaper once referred to a 32-year-old as "middle-aged." Well, if you're 20, perhaps. But just as a 32-year-old should not be relegated to a stereotype, neither should the 20-year-old journalist—or anyone else.

This is an another example. It comes from *The New York Times* and is the lead on a murder story.[11]

> A 60-year-old woman who sold dresses out of her
> home and a friend who was visiting her were stabbed to
> death early yesterday by an assailant the elderly woman
> apparently let into her Washington Heights apartment,
> the police said.

"Elderly" is a state of mind; 60 may not be not elderly.

Careless Phrasing Blames the Victim

By Richard P. Cunningham

Colleen Patrick, reader advocate at *The Seattle Times,* produced a startling example of what critics mean when they charge us with writing rape stories as if the victim were to blame for the rape.

Patrick focused on a *Times* story she felt, though factual, was not really fair.

Then she rewrote the story in her column to demonstrate what she would have considered a fair approach. Here's the story, slightly abbreviated from the way it appeared in the *Times.*

"Bellevue—Mary Ann Pohlreich, a 27-year-old Bellevue Community College student, went out to a Bellevue bar on Friday and never returned.

"Bellevue police discovered [her] nude body . . . 10 blocks from the bar. Pohlreich had been killed by a blow to the head with a blunt object.

"On the night of her death, [she] went to Papagayo's Cantina, a new restaurant and bar . . . in the Overlake area. Police believe she was alone.

"Bartenders there said she left her yellow sweater and purse behind her. Her black Camaro also was found in the restaurant parking lot.

"She was a regular customer at the month-old bar and at its predecessor, the Saratoga Trunk. 'She used to go dancing several times a week,' her roommate said.

"The roommate said she had warned Pohlreich not to go dancing alone.

" 'It shows you can't go dancing with strangers—even in Bellevue,' she said."

Patrick added, "The article goes on to say Bellevue police are stumped by the case. One officer speculated that 'she could have gone to a subsequent party or restaurant. . . .' "

Patrick noted that a "rather provocative close-up snapshot" appeared with the story on page one with the information about the crime. But then, "The story jumps to page C-9, where a personal portrait is drawn of a church-going, intelligent woman with close family ties."

Here is the story as Patrick rewrote it for her column:

"Bellevue—A 27-year-old Bellevue Community College student was found dead Saturday,

Box 12.1 Preserving a neutral, nonjudgmental perspective is an important goal of newswriters. From The Quill *(October, 1990), 8–9, published by the Society of Professional Journalists. Reprinted with permission.*

Continued

June 23, behind a restaurant in the Crossroads area.

"Mary Ann Pohlreich was killed by a blunt object to the head, according to the Bellevue police, who say the case has them stymied.

"Pohlreich, who had associate business degrees from Green River and Bellevue community colleges, also attended Seattle Pacific University, where she planned to study computer science. She is described as having 'an exceptional aptitude for math' by a family spokesperson and former teacher, the Rev. Stan Hughes. Her 23-year-old brother, Eddie, said 'Mary was not only a sister, she was a friend.'

"According to police, Pohlreich was last seen in the cocktail lounge of Papagayo's Cantina, a new restaurant in the Overlake area, formerly known as the Saratoga Trunk. Bartenders there said her yellow sweater and purse had been left behind. Her black Camaro also was found in the restaurant parking lot.

"Her nude body was found about 10 blocks from where she was last seen. Pohlreich reportedly frequented the establishment, which has been known to be a popular gathering spot for yuppies from the area. Her roommate said she liked to go dancing there several times a week."

Patrick called attention to these differences: "In scenario No. 1, questionable social habits are implied. In scenario No. 2, the victim is established as a person who socializes, but whose death is clearly seen as a mystery.

"The truth is, police have no idea what happened or where, except that Mary Ann Pohlreich was last seen at Papagayo's and later found murdered. There is no conjecture."

Patrick insisted that it does not matter what a woman wears, what her socializing habits are, or where she is.

She criticized a recent *Times* story about the rape of a woman jogger, in which a police officer was quoted as saying the woman was not dressed provocatively. "Murder and rape victims don't have to do anything but be there when the criminal strikes," Patrick wrote.

Patrick also said the *Times* story reinforced a false stereotype by quoting Pohlreich's roommate's caution about dancing with strangers. "The vast majority of murders and rapes are committed by people known to the victim," Patrick wrote. "If it turns out that Pohlreich knew the people with whom she socialized (she did frequent the nightspot enough to make acquaintances), or in fact left with someone she

Continued

> knew, should the lesson be, 'Never dance or leave a cocktail lounge with someone you know'?" Patrick concluded: "I am not encouraging anyone to gloss over facts. If a victim is a dreadful individual, report it. Just make victims real, and don't blame them for their victimization."
>
> "Killers kill. Rapists rape. And victims are just that: Victims.
> "Rest in peace, Mary."

Anonymous Sources

Suggesting that anonymous sources—sources that are not named—are an ethical problem may come as a surprise to budding journalists who see anonymous sources cited day after day. But not all editors are happy with using anonymous sources and from time to time editors inveigh against them.

What's the problem?

Anonymous sources strike at the credibility of the news outlet. The attribution tag "according to a high White House source who declined to be identified for publication" does not give the reader or listener much to go on when deciding how valid that person's information might be. Why doesn't the person want to be named? Does the source have an axe to grind? "Anonymity," writes Gene Miller of the *Miami Herald,* "is an invitation to exaggerate, embroider, embellish, slant, or take the cheap shot. This is true for the reporter, as well as the source. It is a bad habit and it is getting worse."[12] Miller also makes the point that anonymous sources can be the result of sloppy, lazy reporting. Instead of trying to persuade a source to go public, the lazy journalist accepts the path of least resistance by accepting the source's anonymity. One anonymous source leads to another, which weakens the reporting process. Miller argues that a good reporter can get most sources to agree to be identified.

Just the Facts

In the story about steroids in Chapter 10, the lead focused on a young man named Jim, who used steroids. But toward the end of the lead, the writer revealed that Jim was a figment of her imagination, that she had made him up even though there were a million people like him. Then, as now, the argument against making anything up remains. If any part of the story is made up, how can a reader be certain the entire story is not made up? Why can't the journalists write about real situations? Given all the good stories waiting to be uncovered, journalists do not have to make anything up.

Journalists deal with facts. They put them together in the hope that the facts will lead to larger truths. Novelists use their imagination to spin stories that they hope reveal larger truths. It is not the outcome that gets measured, but how journalists and novelists arrive at the outcome. A novel can be dismissed because of a weak imagination, but a news story should never be able to be dismissed because it is not based on fact.

A Primer on Libel[13]

Do you remember when you were a kid and somebody called you a name, say "a left foot from Tuckahoe"? Your equally brilliant rejoinder was: "Sticks and stones may break my bones, but names will never hurt me."

That's not true. In the eyes of the law, calling people names can be harmful—to their reputation and your or your employer's pocketbook. "Libel is injury to reputation," according to *The Associated Press Stylebook and Libel Manual*.[14] And that's what made Col. Anthony Herbert and William Tavoulareas part of modern journalism history, for they sued CBS and *The Washington Post*, respectively, for libel because they believed their reputations were sullied by these news media.[15]

One point budding journalists need to understand is that it does not matter who says something libelous. If a journalist uses a libelous statement in a print or broadcast story, the journalist's employer can be sued, and if the court case is lost, pay damages. A newspaper can be sued for something libelous in a letter to the editor while the person who wrote the letter may be ignored. In libel suits, the person defamed usually goes after the person or company with the most money. To date, the largest judgment awarded was $34 million in damages against the *Philadelphia Inquirer,* followed by

$29 million against Harte-Hanks Communications, Inc.[16] But even if a news medium wins a libel suit, it still loses, for it has to spend money defending its case.

Journalists should always be concerned with not libeling anyone. Journalistic practice is guided by what the courts have determined to be legitimate defenses against libel. For private people, that is, not politicians or other public officials, they are:

- Is the statement true? When your newspaper quoted a woman as saying that her doctor had operated on her 12 times for cancer yet she never had cancer, could your attorney prove that the doctor was in fact guilty of malpractice?
- Is the statement privileged? Official reports and legislative and judicial proceedings have absolute privilege, meaning a witness in a malpractice suit can in fact accuse a doctor of having done something without proving it and not be sued for libel. The news media then have the qualified privilege to report the witness's testimony, as long as the reporting is accurate and fair (not out of context).
- Is the comment part of fair criticism? People have fairly free rein to comment on the public performances of those who regularly work in the public eye, people such as politicians, authors, actors, entertainers, composers, writers and so on. So if you're assigned to review a play by the local theater group, and you think the lead did not perform well, you may say that.

When it comes to public officials, journalists have broader latitude. This stems from a famous Supreme Court decision known as *The New York Times vs. Sullivan,* or just the Sullivan decision. In this case, *The New York Times* published an advertisement that contained 14 fact errors about public officials and police in Montgomery, Alabama. The Supreme Court ruled that because the people in question were public officials, they would have to prove that the advertisement was published with a reckless disregard for the truth or with knowledge that it contained false statements. The court wanted to provide an atmosphere for robust debate on public issues.

A journalist can defame someone in many ways. Suggesting illegal or improper behavior on the part of someone, especially a professional, can draw a libel suit. Linking someone to unsavory elements in society could prove troublesome in court. Reporting someone has been charged with a crime—and giving the wrong crime—can be libelous. Calling a doctor a "quack" is libelous per se, a classification for words that are considered libelous on their face.

In many circumstances, by the way, a quick and prominent correction or apology can head off a libel suit. All the doctor wrongly accused of operating on a woman 12 times wanted was an apology, and when it was not forthcoming, he sued and won a $300,000 judgment. But all he really wanted was his good name restored to him.

Let's go through a series of situations and see what kinds of problems they might cause.

- You are the opinion editor of your college newspaper and publish a letter condemning the health center on campus and one doctor in particular. The named doctor is accused of having diagnosed someone as having indigestion, yet two days later the person was rushed to the local hospital with a case of acute appendicitis. The letter ends by advising readers not to take the doctor's word for anything.

  Fortunately, an apology by the editor saved the college news-paper a lot of money. But what if there was some truth to the charges? One move in a case like this is to wait for the patient to sue and then report the lawsuit. That puts the burden of proof on the injured person, not the newspaper, and puts the debate into a legal arena, with its umbrella of privilege and qualified privilege. Since this was a college health facility, the letter could have been sent to the doctor's superiors in central administration, and their subsequent investigation could have become a news story. The information could have also been forwarded to the local medical society or to state officials.

- A convicted felon files a lawsuit against a state police officer, claiming the officer took personal valuables while conducting an authorized search of his home. The local newspaper, acting on information from the felon, reports that he has filed a private criminal complaint and that the district attorney is investigating the officer. Distressed at this bad publicity, the police officer begins drinking and eventually quits the force for a lower-paying job.

At last word, the resulting libel suit by the police officer against the newspaper had earned him $189,000 (minus attorney's fees). It turned out that no private complaint had been filed and the district attorney was not investigating. What the newspaper published was false. (The newspaper appealed.)

- A story's lead says that police have arrested two men on charges of trying to smuggle drugs to a friend in the city lock-up. The headline says: "Drug smugglers foiled."

  Although we have not discussed writing headlines, this instance is worth noting. A false headline on an accurate story can land a newspaper in court.

- Your newspaper carries a story that the golf pro at the local country club has been fired. He contends he resigned and that your story injured his "good name, credit and reputation."

  That depends. He will have to prove the injuries, and that will be difficult if he has got a new job at an equal or better salary and a good credit rating. The newspaper had better be able to document, through paper or witnesses, that the golf pro was fired.

- An FBI agent sued author Peter Matthiessen because the agent feels he was defamed in *In the Spirit of Crazy Horse,* a book about Indian life in South Dakota and in particular about a fatal confrontation at Wounded Knee in 1975.

  After four years, a federal judge dismissed the suit, saying, in essence, that the FBI agent was a public official and that the public had a legitimate right to question the conduct of FBI agents doing their job. The judge said the book was protected because its author exercised the right of every person to criticize government.

- A group of people has organized as the College Town Consumer Protection Agency, and at one of the agency's meetings someone in the audience stands up and condemns the local television repair business by name as "a fraud that never does anything right and overcharges to boot." The speaker offers no evidence, and no one has ever sued the repair service. Your television station reports the quotation by showing a videotape of the person speaking.

  Of course, the person who made the comment might get sued. But more likely the defamed television repair business will sue the television station that broadcast the comment. Clearly, the news editor had time to think about the comment and made a decision to use it.

- Another person at the same meeting suggests that the city attorney, who also has a private practice, is "an ambulance chaser."

    While it is true that the city attorney is a public person, the speaker was referring to the attorney's private practice. Calling an attorney "an ambulance chaser" is libelous per se. See you in court.

Some journalists see the laws of libel as a burden. But a more constructive examination reveals that our libel laws provide extreme latitude. Libel laws protect people who deserve to be protected, both individuals and the news media. Legitimate questions about a person's reputation are the stuff of news stories, and the law protects the news media when reporting on those. But reckless investigation and scurrilous comment, which no responsible journalist should be interested in anyway, have no place in the news media. Libel laws lead to greater accuracy and thus credibility for the news media. And speaking of credibility, journalists are not doing very well, according to Jack Garner's article in Box 12.2.

The real question about libel is not how does a journalist defend against a lawsuit, but how does a journalist report in a responsible manner so as not to commit libel in the first place? Fair and accurate reporting is a good safeguard. If a private person is criticized in a public forum, seek her out for her response. If the criticism occurs in private, you may still have a story, but you should show it to the company's lawyer first.

Avoid a rush to judgment. Do not publish in haste only to repent in court. The story about the state police officer was accompanied by a note from the reporter to the editor advising that the story needed more investigation, yet the editor went ahead and published the story. That is negligence at least, and in this case the court also said it was malicious.

Distinguish between charges against someone and actual guilt. In the United States, a person charged with a crime is presumed innocent until proven guilty. Thus, a person is arrested *in connection with* a crime not *for* a crime. Good headline writers are careful to state, for example, "Jones held *in* murder," not "Jones held *for* murder."

The overall advice is this: Stick to the facts. If police arrest someone, that's the news. Don't embellish by calling the person a suspect or going

Journalists' Screen Image: Bad News

By Jack Garner

Some things never change—like the lousy way newspaper reporters and broadcast journalists are portrayed in the movies and on TV. Here's how reporter Hildy Johnson described his profession more than 60 years ago in "The Front Page."

"Journalists! Peeking through keyholes! Running after fire engines like a lot of coach dogs! Waking people up in the middle of the night to ask them what they think of Mussolini. Stealing pictures off old ladies of their daughters that got raped in Oak Park.

"A lot of lousy, daffy, buttinskis, swelling around with holes in their pants, borrowing nickels from office boys! And for what? So a million hired girls and motormen's wives will know what's going on. . . ."

And that's exactly how they're depicted in the Ben Hecht and Charles MacArthur play, which has gone on to be the most popular work on journalism of all time—generating at least five major motion pictures and hundreds of stage productions.

But the description by character Hildy Johnson could just as easily describe the broadcast newsman portrayed by William Atherton in the two "Die Hard" films. His persistent pursuit of THE STORY knows no ethical or social bounds, and he twice puts good guy Bruce Willis and dozens of innocent bystanders in jeopardy. The audience typically cheers when Atherton gets slugged by Willis' wife in the films.

"Face it: You're scum," wrote William McKeen, a University of Florida journalism professor, in a recent issue of the ASNE Bulletin. "For 13 years, I've been studying books and movies about journalists, and, as far as I can tell, there are few lines of work that are portrayed as poorly—in the 'fictional world'—as journalism."

"We are all involved in ethical decisions every single day, but they're never depicted in films," says William Florence, executive editor of the *Statesman Journal* at Salem, Ore. (and a major-league movie buff).

"With the possible exception of 'All the President's Men,' we're victims of the classic stereotype, much like the politicians and the athlete."

Politicians are always corrupt, athletes are always dumb,

Box 12.2   Do journalists deserve a better "press"? From The Gannetteer *(November 1990), 6–8. Reprinted with permission of Gannett Co., Inc.*

Continued

and journalists have the integrity and social graces of a groundhog.

The notable exception is "All the President's Men." Alan J. Pakula's 1976 Oscar-nominated film starred Robert Redford and Dustin Hoffman as Watergate reporters Bob Woodward and Carl Bernstein. The film details, with relative accuracy, the way The Washington Post virtually brought down Richard Nixon's government.

Sure, Woodward and Bernstein are depicted playing sly games and going through Machiavellian maneuvers to get at THE STORY, but with a strong sense of moral purpose.

In addition, "All the President's Men" deserves credit for what may be the only truly accurate depiction of how arduous and boring true reporting can be: It's the scene in which they're going through a seemingly endless pile of index cards at the Library of Congress.

Hollywood would like you to believe journalists lead lives that are part cops, part cowboys and part romantic artists. "All the President's Men" dared to show the less glamorous side of the profession.

But the film also set up journalists as knights on white horses vanquishing an evil king and restoring Camelot. For that reason,

"All the President's Men" actually led to a marked increase in journalism school enrollments in the late 1970s. Hundreds of high school graduates dreamt of becoming Woodward and Bernstein (or perhaps, to be accurate, Redford and Hoffman).

Actually, there have been at least three other positive images of journalists on film, though they all took leave of reality at various points:

- "Deadline U.S.A.," a rousing 1952 film by Richard Brooks, with Humphrey Bogart as the penultimate newspaper-editor-as-hero. Even while his paper is collapsing in debt around him, he diligently pursues the truth about corruption in gangsterism in his hometown.
- "Lou Grant," the five-year TV series with Ed Asner as a crusading editor. The popular show of the late '70s was spun off the late, lamented "Mary Tyler Moore Show." Asner was Moore's boss on the classic TV sitcom about a TV station. After "Mary Tyler Moore" ended its run, Asner took the character into an hour-long dramatic format about a Los Angeles newspaper.

  Note that Lou Grant's switch from broadcasting to newspapers also meant a

Continued

switch from comedy to drama. That probably says something about the even-worse way television news is depicted in popular culture.

Anyway, "Lou Grant" and "Deadline U.S.A." get points for integrity, but not for accuracy. For openers, the editors in both stories became too involved in all their stories on the street level. Real editors only wish they could leave their desks or skip the 3:30 budget meeting.

- "30," a piece of 1959 cornball about a "typical" day in the life of a big-city newspaper. The acting among editors ranges from the wooden Joe-Friday style of Jack Webb to the hammy, scenery-chewing histrionics of William Conrad. There isn't an ounce of reality in this film, but it, at least, puts journalists in a positive light, and makes a great movie to show at a newspaper party.

So much for the exceptions. The canon of American films is otherwise relentless in putting journalists in varying degrees of bad light. Consider these films and TV shows:

- "Absence of Malice," in which a reporter played by Sally Field gets into murky ethical territory while investigating possible ties between a businessman (Paul Newman) and organized crime. She uses leaked information, without getting the businessman's side; she throws the public spotlight on innocent bystanders, driving one to suicide; and she has an affair with the same businessman she'd been trying to expose. It's enough to make any self-respecting journalist check the want-ads for jobs in public relations.

"Absence of Malice" stirred debate, particularly because it was written by a veteran newsman (Kurt Luedtke), just as he was leaving the profession to establish himself as a screenwriter.

- "Broadcast News," the Oscar-nominated comedy about TV newscasters that follows the careers and relationships among a hard-driving news producer (Holly Hunter), a conscientious reporter (Albert Brooks) and a manipulative, shallow, but gorgeous anchorman (William Hurt). Of course, the anchorman finds success, in the tradition of air-headed Ted Baxter on "The Mary Tyler Moore Show."
- "Die Hard" and "Die Harder," with the aforementioned ob-

Continued

noxiousness of William Atherton.

- "The Year of Living Dangerously," the saga of an Australian radio reporter (Mel Gibson) who finds himself in the midst of Indonesian intrigue, and who allows himself to be manipulated by his love for a sexy British attache (Sigourney Weaver) and a clever, philosophical Indonesian photographer (Linda Hunt).

- "The Big Carnival," Billy Wilder's cynical look at a newspaperman (Kirk Douglas) who exploits a tragic mine cave-in.

- "Fletch," a comedy with Chevy Chase as a reporter who repeatedly dons disguises and misrepresents himself to get information.

- "Murphy Brown," the current hit TV series which owes a lot of its flavor, and attitude toward broadcasting, to "The Mary Tyler Moore Show." Once again, the show features an anchor who is an airhead, and the concerns of broadcasters are best served through comedy.

- "Under Fire," a taut Latin American thriller with Nick Nolte as a concerned hardhitting journalist. But his heart (and politics) get the best of him: He fakes a photograph.

- The various manifestations of "The Front Page," including three film versions of the original, "His Girl Friday," with sexual role reversals, and "Switching channels," a modern update, in a TV newsroom.

All of "The Front Page" variations revel in showing journalists as colorful wags who'll stop at nothing to get THE STORY. Ethics, the law, hell, even true love, can't get in the way.

It is the story, of course, that drives nearly every journalist on screen. The news photographer portrayed by Jimmy Stewart in "Rear Window" forgets he's bedridden with a broken leg when he tells his editor he's ready to go to the world's latest hot spot.

If there isn't a story to pursue, movie journalists sometimes make them up. The great Orson Welles film, "Citizen Kane," adapts the quote attributed to William Randolph Hearst that he would "provide the war" where there was no Spanish-American War in Cuba.

"Citizen Kane," at least, is one picture whose negative depictions of journalists apparently have some basis in fact. Kane put aside his objectivity when he fell for an opera singer. Reportedly,

Continued

in real life, Hearst insisted that the name of his mistress, the actress Marion Davies be mentioned at least once each day in every Hearst paper even after he died, and after she retired.

However, "Citizen Kane" also helped perpetuate another journalism stereotype—that a bottle of scotch can usually be found next to the typewriter. In that film, the music critic played by Joseph Cotten has the integrity to write an honest negative review about Kane's mistress, only he's too drunk to finish it.

In most cases, the reason journalists aren't treated fairly is probably fairly practical. It's complex and challenging to create honest portrayals of real people, while it's easy to slide into stereotypes. The screenwriter doesn't have to do as much homework, and the characters are more easily manipulated into action sequences, intrigue or romance.

Remember that scene in "All the President's Men," with Woodward and Bernstein hard at work in the Library of Congress? Only journalists probably found that scene interesting. It's much more cinematic to put Woodward in a dark parking garage with Deep Throat.

Fortunately, the Watergate case really had a Deep Throat. But if there wasn't one, maybe the filmmakers would have to make him up.

In some cases, journalists are viewed as the means to satisfy society's needs for heroes. Instead of truth, the goal becomes boosterism.

Consider the western editor in John Ford's "The Man Who Shot Liberty Valance." When he learns that an esteemed senator isn't the hero he was supposed to be, the editor tears up his notes and says, "When the legend becomes fact, print the legend."

It created an endearing motto for John Ford, but it's certainly a questionable way to run a newspaper.

---

off the deep end in reporting all manner of speculation. If the police arrest the wrong person, that's their problem. If you have libeled the person in the meantime, that's your problem.

The general counsel for *The Washington Post* calls libel "the grim reaper of loose journalism."[17] Carelessness paves the path to the courtroom. The reporter who nails down every fact is less likely to have problems with libel. Problems with libel can occur not only in the major stories but also in the "little stories," the accounts of what the police did in the past 24 hours. Make sure you get full names, ages and precise addresses. Some people squirm to see their ages in print, but it's a wonderful way to distinguish between two people with the same name.

The Responsible Journalist

Responsible journalism is the desired outcome in most of the newspapers and television and radio stations in the United States. Responsible journalists behave in a way that does not bring into question their ethical and legal principles. They understand that they have an obligation to report the facts in an effort to get at the truth and that their credibility requires that they do it responsibly.

Review Questions

Generally, what are ethics?

List six areas of ethical problems cited by the Society of Professional Journalists.

Bring to class examples of sexist or racist newspaper writing.

What is an anonymous source, and why are such sources a problem for journalists?

What is libel?

What are some defenses against libel?

Endnotes

1. "Fighting Back: Two Plaintiffs' Views on Libel" In *The Cost of Libel: Economic and Policy Implications*, 21. Conference report. Copyright © 1986 by the Gannett Center for Media Studies.

2. Ben Johnson, "The Problem of Collecting and Presenting Information." In *Solutions Today for Ethics Problems Tomorrow,* ed. Manual Galvan. Special report by the Society of Professional Journalists, 1989.

3. Roy Peter Clark, "The Unoriginal Sin: How Plagiarism Poisons the Press," *Washington Journalism Review* (March 1983), 44.

4. Clark, "The Unoriginal Sin," 45–47.

5. Thomas W. Lippman, ed. *The Washington Post Deskbook on Style.* 2nd ed. (New York: McGraw-Hill, 1989), 5.

6. "Letter Integral to Debate of Issues," from the *York Daily Record,* December 2, 1990, 2G. Reprinted by permission.

7. Clark, "The Unoriginal Sin," 47.

8. Nancy Montgomery, "Police Charge Suspect in Triple Slaying" *Anchorage Daily News,* April 25, 1987, 1, 16.

9. United Press International, April 21, 1990. Reprinted by permission of United Press International, Copyright © 1990.

10. Laura Pace, "A Bouncer's Life Is Not an Easy One." From *Centre Daily Times,* October 12, 1990, 30. Reprinted by permission.

11. "Owner of Dress Business Is Slain in Washington Hts. Apartment," *The New York Times,* August 18, 1990, 29. Copyright © 1990 by The New York Times Company. Reprinted by permission.

12. Gene Miller, "Reader Is Victim When Source Isn't Named." From *The Coaches' Corner,* 3, no. 1 (March 1988), 4. Reprinted by permission.

13. Unless noted, much of this information comes from background material prepared for newswriting students at Penn State. The original material was prepared by Donald L. Smith, now a professor emeritus of journalism. Some of the insight on libel comes from my own experience as an expert witness in three libel suits.

14. Eileen Alt Powell, and Howard Angione, eds. *The Associated Press Stylebook and Libel Manual* (New York: The Associated Press, 1980), 251.

15. "Fighting Back," 20–21.

16. Lee Levine, and David L. Perry, "No Way to Celebrate the Bill of Rights," *Columbia Journalism Review* (July/August 1990), 38.

17. Boisfeuillet Jones, Jr., "Legal Issues." In *The Washington Post Deskbook on Style.* 2nd ed., ed. Thomas W. Lippman (New York: McGraw-Hill, 1989), 9.

Sources and Resources

Bailey, Charles W. *Conflicts of Interest: A Matter of Journalistic Ethics.* A Report to the National News Council. New York: The Council, 1984.

Benjamin, Burton. *Fair Play: CBS, General Westmoreland, and How a Television Documentary Went Wrong.* 1st ed. New York: Harper and Row, 1988.

Bezanson, Randall P., Gilbert Cranberg, and John Soloski. *Libel and the Press: Setting the Record Straight*. Minneapolis: Silha Center for the Study of Media Ethics and Law, School of Journalism and Mass Communication, University of Minnesota, 1985.

————. *Libel Law and the Press: Myth and Reality*. New York: Free Press, 1987.

Brogan, Patrick. *Spiked: The Short Life and Death of the National News Council*. New York: Priority Press, 1985.

Brown, Lee. *The Reluctant Reformation: On Criticizing the Press in America*. New York: McKay, 1974.

Clurman, Richard M. *Beyond Malice. The Media's Years of Reckoning*. New Brunswick, N.J.: Transaction, 1988.

Collins, Keith S., ed. *Responsibility and Freedom in the Press: Are They in Conflict?* Report of the Citizen's Choice National Commission on Free and Responsible Media. Washington, D.C., Citizen's Choice, Inc., 1985.

Fink, Conrad C. *Media Ethics: In the Newsroom and Beyond*. New York, McGraw-Hill, 1988.

Goldstein, Tom. *The News at Any Cost: How Journalists Compromise Their Ethics to Shape the News*. New York: Simon and Schuster, 1985.

Goodwin, H. Eugene. *Groping for Ethics in Journalism*. 2d ed. Ames: Iowa State University Press, 1983.

Grinspan, Mel G. *Ethics, Another Endangered Species?* Memphis, Tenn.: Rhodes College, 1988.

Hulteng, John L. *Playing It Straight: A Practical Discussion of the Ethical Principles of the American Society of Newspaper Editors*. Easton, Pa.: ASNE, 1981. Distributed by the Globe Pequot Press, Chester, Conn.

————. *The Messenger's Motives: Ethical Problems of the News Media*. 2d ed. Englewood Cliffs, N.J.: Prentice-Hall, 1985.

Jones, Syl. "Kill the Messenger." *ASNE Bulletin* (November 1990): 14–21.

Klaidman, Stephen. *The Virtuous Journalist*. New York: Oxford University Press, 1987.

Kowet, Don. *A Matter of Honor*. New York: Macmillan, 1984.

Lambeth, Edmund B. *Committed Journalism: An Ethic for the Profession*. Bloomington: Indiana University Press, 1986.

Malcolm, Janet. *The Journalist and the Murderer*. New York, Knopf, 1990.

McGuire, Tim. "Racial Attitudes." *ASNE Bulletin* (November 1990), 10–13. (This was an explanatory piece that led into Syl Jones' piece cited earlier.)

Meyer, Philip. *Editors, Publishers and Newspaper Ethics: Report to the American Society of Newspaper Editors*. Washington, D.C.: ASNE, 1983.

————. *Ethical Journalism: A Guide for Students, Practitioners, and Consumers*. New York: Longman, 1987.

National News Council. *After "Jimmy's World," Tightening Up in Editing*. Report by the National News Council. New York: The Council, 1981.

————. *In the Public Interest. III. A Report by the National News Council, 1979–1983, with an Index of Complaints, 1973–1983*. New York: The Council, 1984.

Olen, Jeffrey. *Ethics in Journalism.* Englewood Cliffs, N.J.: Prentice-Hall, 1988.

Pippert, Wesley G. *An Ethics of News. A Reporter's Search for the Truth.* Washington, D.C.: Georgetown University Press, 1989.

Rambo, C. David. "Tough Calls." *Presstime* (December 1989): 30–33.

Rivers, William L., and Cleve Mathews. *Ethics for the Media.* Englewood Cliffs, N.J.: Prentice-Hall, 1988.

Schoenbrun, David. *On and Off the Air. An Informal History of CBS News.* New York: Dutton, 1989.

Shaw, David. *Press Watch: A Provocative Look at How Newspapers Report the News.* New York: Macmillan, 1984.

Strentz, Herbert. *News Reporters and News Sources. Accomplices in Shaping and Misshaping the News.* 2d ed. Ames: Iowa State University Press, 1989.

Swain, Bruce M. *Reporters' Ethics.* Ames: Iowa State University Press, 1978.

Winerip, Michael. "Tips from a Times' Columnist on Reporting." *The Coaches' Corner* 3, no. 2, (June 1988), 5.

Appendix A

A Condensed Stylebook[1]

This newspaper stylebook is based on the stylebook jointly developed by the Associated Press and United Press International, which you are encouraged to consult. The author's own style preferences are so identified.

> *abbreviations* Some titles before names are abbreviated, unless they appear in direct quotations. Abbreviate *Dr., Gov., Lt. Gov., Rep., the Rev., Sen.* and most military titles such as *Gen., Col., Capt., Lt., Adm., Cmdr.* When courtesy titles are necessary, use *Mr., Mrs., Ms.* See *courtesy titles.*
>
> Using the first three letters, abbreviate the months of the year (except May, June, Sept.) only when used in dates: *Oct. 12* or *Oct. 12, 1984,* but *October 1984.*
>
> Abbreviate the names of states in city-state combinations (*Joplin, Mo.*) with the exception of Alaska, Hawaii, Idaho, Iowa, Maine, Ohio, Texas and Utah. See *state names.*
>
> *addresses* Abbreviate in numbered addresses (*326 W. Broad St.*) *avenue, boulevard* and *street but not alley, drive, road, terrace* and others. Spell out when no number is given: *West Broad Street.*
>
> Always use figures: *8 Pilsdon Lane* rather than *Eight Pilsdon Lane.*
>
> Numbers used as street names are spelled out: *First Street, Ninth Street;* above *ninth* uses figures: *10th Street.*
>
> Directions that are part of an address are abbreviated (*1015 S. Terrace Ave.*) but are spelled out if no number is given: *South Terrace Avenue.*

ages   Use figures at all times, even if the age is a single digit: *Tommy Thompson, 5, eats an ice cream cone for photographers.*

a.m., p.m.   Always use lowercase letters. Since *a.m.* means morning and *p.m.* means afternoon or tonight, avoid redundancies such as *9 a.m. this morning, 2 p.m. Wednesday afternoon, 10 p.m. tomorrow night.*

Bible   When referring to the Judeo–Christian Bible, always capitalize. In other references, lowercase: *The wire services' stylebooks are the bible at this newspaper.*

Never capitalize *biblical.*

capitalization   In general, follow a down style, in which only proper nouns, names and formal titles before names are capitalized. Titles after names or standing alone without a name are never capitalized.

Work titles or job descriptions are not capitalized: *At the game's end, quarterback Fran Tarkenton threw a touchdown pass to wide receiver Ahmad Rashad.*

Common nouns that are part of proper nouns are lower cased in subsequent references: *the Republican Party, the party.*

century   Always lowercase: *21st century.* Spell out *first* through *ninth* and use figures thereafter.

The 21st century, by the way, begins on Jan. 1, 2001, not Jan. 1, 2000, which begins the final year of the 20th century.

city council/governmental bodies/legislature   Capitalize full names such as *Houston City Council, the Tucson Fire Department* and *the Iowa Legislature,* and capitalize second references to them when it is clear what is being referred to. Houston City Council becomes *the City Council, the Tucson Fire Department* becomes *the Fire Department* and *the Iowa Legislature* becomes *the Legislature.*

Condensed further, though, it is *the council, the department.*

congress   When referring to the U.S. *Senate* and the *U.S. House of Representatives* or to a foreign body that includes *congress* in its name, capitalize. Lowercase *congress* when it is not part of an organization's name or when used as a second reference to a group or as a substitute for *convention.*

congressional districts   Always use figures and capitalize: *the 3rd Congressional District, the 23rd Congressional District.* But use lowercase in subsequent references: *the district.*

congressman, congresswoman Acceptable gender-neutral references include *House member* and *senator, but not congressperson*. (Author's preference)

constitution Capitalize whenever referring to *the U.S. Constitution, the Constitution*. When referring to other state's or nation's constitutions, capitalize only with the state or nation's name: *the Oregon Constitution, the French Constitution, the state constitution*.

An organization's constitution is always lowercase.

constitutional Always lowercase.

county Capitalize in names of counties and county government units: *Schuylkill County, the Clive County Sheriff's Department*. Subsequent references in a clear context always take capital letters: *the County Sheriff's Department*.

Lowercase *county* when it stands alone or as a subsequent reference to a proper name.

courtesy titles Avoid courtesy titles. A person's gender or marital status has nothing to do with that person's newsworthiness. However, apply courtesy titles to situations where confusion might result, as when writing about a married couple and referring to one of them. Does the reference to *Jones* mean Mr. Jones or Mrs. Jones (or, if preferred, Ms. Jones)? Then a courtesy title is needed. (Author's preference)

datelines Newspapers use datelines only on stories from outside the newspaper's immediate circulation area.

Generally datelines consist of a city name followed by the state name (abbreviated per style): *Laramie, Wyo*. Well-known cities do not need to be followed by a state.

State names are not used in newspapers published in that state unless the city name by itself might cause confusion: *Washington, Pa., Cairo, Ill*.

In roundup stories, state names might be necessary within the story proper to make references clear: *Altoona, Iowa,* and *Altoona, Pa*.

(Datelines are so called because at one time they included the date the action in the story took place. The two major wire services now put the time element in the lead, but some newspapers still use datelines.)

dimensions/weights   Always use figures, but spell out *feet, inches, yards, meters, pounds, grams, ounces: The newborn baby weighs 8 pounds, 7 ounces and was 21 inches long.*

The only exception to this rule is *millimeter* (use *mm*) when used in reference to film widths (35 *mm*) or weapons (50 *mm*).

directions/regions   Lowercase compass points when standing alone. Capitalize regions known specifically by direction: *the West, the South, the Middle West, the East, the Northeast, the Southwest.*

Lowercase general directions when part of a proper name, such as *southern Texas,* unless the section is well known, such as *South Philadelphia* and *Southern California.*

distances   follow the general number rule: Spell out *one* through *nine* and use figures for *10* and above. *The proud parents of the 8-pound, 7-ounce, 21-inch baby took their child on her first trip—a five-mile drive to Grandma's.*

fractions   Below *1,* spell out; above *1,* use figures or convert to decimals. To convert $3\frac{1}{4}$ into a decimal, divide the 4 into the 1 and affix the answer with a decimal point to the whole number: *3.25.*

hurricane   Capitalize when part of a storm's name: *Hurricane Hugo.* A storm is not a hurricane unless the sustained wind speed is 74 miles an hour. Lesser blowing attempts are called *tropical storms.*

Although hurricanes have female and male names, all subsequent references to them are made with the neutral pronoun *it.*

incorporated   Although seldom needed in a corporation's name, *incorporated* is abbreviated and capitalized *Inc.* Do not set off with a comma: *NL Industries Inc.*

initials   When a person chooses to be known by his or her initials, respect that usage. Use periods but do not space between initials because video display terminals and typesetters use space codes as guides in justifying lines and a space between initials could place them on separate lines.

it/she   Modern usage does not use gender pronouns to refer to neutral objects. Ships, nations and hurricanes are *it,* not *she.*

names/nicknames   Refer to people as they prefer to be known: *J. Edgar Hoover, Jimmy Carter* (whose full name is James Earl Carter Jr.).

The same guideline applies to nicknames, except when the nickname is intended as derogatory: *"Fats" Olson.*

Some people acquire nicknames because their given names are uncommon. Thus, Amandus Lutz was always known as "Bud," which he preferred.

Nicknames are set off with quotation marks except on the sports pages.

No. Always the abbreviation for *number* when referring to rankings: *The No. 1 ranked football team in the pre-season poll finished No. 19.*

numbers Generally, spell out *one* through *nine* and use figures for *10* and above.

Numbers at the start of a sentence are spelled out if the result is not ungainly: *One thousand six hundred fifty-two students collected money to help fight cancer last year.* The sentence works better this way: *A total of 1,652 students. . . .* However, don't carry that rule to extremes. It's all right to begin a sentence *Five people . . . A total of five* wastes words.

For exceptions to the general numbers rule, see *addresses, ages, century, congressional districts, dimensions/weights, fractions, No., temperatures.*

party affiliation Three possible approaches form the basic application of this guideline:

Republican Sen. Barry Goldwater of Arizona said . . .

Sen. Barry Goldwater, R-Ariz., said . . . (note punctuation and abbreviation)

Sen. Barry Goldwater said . . . The Arizona Republican also said . . .

The choice often seems based on what goes best with the rhythm of the sentence.

pope/pontiff Capitalize *pope* only in a formal title, but never when used alone: *Pope John Paul II, the pope. Pontiff is not a formal title and is always lowercase.*

post office Do not capitalize; the correct name is *U.S. Postal Service* although *post office* may be used when referring to the building where mail is distributed from.

president Capitalize only when part of a title, not when standing alone: *President Lincoln,* the president.

race   Identification of anyone by race should be avoided. Consider the subjects of stories as individuals rather than as members of a race and avoid unnecessary racial references. (Author's preference)

seasons   Unless part of a proper name, the seasons of the year are always lowercase.

slang   Don't use. People may use slang when they talk, but when they read, they expect precision, not flippancy. Given the generational differences in interpreting many slang words, their use impairs communication.

spouse   When referring to marriage partners in general, use *spouse* to avoid the implication that only men occupy work roles and only women are homemakers.

state names   Always spell out state names when they stand alone, but with the exception of eight states, abbreviate when used with town and city names in datelines and stories. Accepted abbreviations are: Ala., Ariz., Ark., Calif., Colo., Conn., Del., Fla., Ga., Ill., Ind., Kan., Ky., La., Md., Mass., Mich., Minn., Miss., Mo., Mont., Neb., Nev., N.H., N.J., N.M., N.Y.., N.C., N.D., Okla,, Ore., Pa., R.I., S.C., Tenn., Vt., Va., Wash., W.Va., Wis., Wyo. (Do not use U.S. Postal Service abbreviations; they are confusing.)

temperatures   Except for zero, all temperatures are given as figures. Use the words *minus* or *below zero* to report such temperatures. Do not use a minus sign.

time element   Except when referring to the current day (the day of publication), use the day of the week. Thus, a Thursday newspaper would refer to *Wednesday* and *Friday* where appropriate, not *yesterday* and *tomorrow*.

TV   Television is more acceptable, especially in noun usages.

United Nations/U.N.   Use *United Nations* as a noun; use *U.N.* as a modifier. *The United Nations met today to debate a U.N. resolution.*

United States/U.S.   Use *United States* as a noun; use *U.S.* as a modifier. *The United States sends many U.S. products overseas.*

vice president   As a formal title, capitalize; standing alone, lowercase.

women/men   The two sexes are equal and should be treated as such. Copy should not assume a group of people is all male or female, or refer to a person's physical appearance: *attractive, muscular.* Copy should not mention a person's family relationship (*mother of five*) unless relevant.

In other words, treat men and women with equal respect and with a total lack of condescension and stereotyping.

Endnote

1. Adapted from R. Thomas Berner, *The Process of Editing*. Needham Heights, Mass.: Allyn and Bacon. 1991.

Appendix B

Glossary[1]

advance A story announcing an event that is to occur, such as a speech or government meeting; a story written and made available to an editor days before its publication date. Typically, such stories are features that do not have to appear immediately.

advertising The solicited and paid-for sales pitches that appear in a newspaper. The revenue from advertising helps pay the bills, but the work of the editorial department attracts the audience for the advertiser.

anecdote A short amusing or revealing narrative about someone that a journalist might use to illustrate a story.

anonymous sources A source of news that is cited but not named in a news account.

art Any graphics element on a page, including line drawings and photographs.

Associated Press, The A news-gathering cooperative.

attribution The act of identifying the source of information for a story.

attribution tag A phrase containing a identified source of information: *the president said, according to the president.*

beat An area or specialty assigned to a reporter to cover. A reporter who checks police activities daily and writes about crimes and accidents is said to be assigned to *the police beat.*

bias An unreasoned attitude in favor of or against a subject that could affect the way a journalist gathers information.

body The part of a story in which a journalist lays out specific information and details to develop the story.

box A border surrounding a story or other page element.

brite A light-hearted or humorous story.

broadsheet The format/size of a standard newspaper.

bullet   A dot used at the beginning of each paragraph that is part of a list. Some editors use dashes.

bureau   A subordinate office of the main newspaper office.

byline   At the beginning of a story, the name of the reporter who wrote it or of the wire service that provided it.

cliché   A word or phrase used so many times it has lost the warmth and glow of originality. Avoided in good writing.

column   A short essay expressing a viewpoint. Also, a vertical arrangement of lines of type on a page; the width of such lines.

computer   A piece of equipment capable of storing millions of bits of information and processing that information speedily upon command.

conversational speech   An informal speaking style, used to attract radio and television audiences. Often achieved by writing news copy in the second person (*you*) rather than the third (*he, she, it*).

copy   Newsroom jargon for "story."

CPU   Central processing unit, or the brains of the computer. The area of a computer where all the calculations take place.

crash   A computer breakdown.

cursor   A blinking rectangular light that shows a VDT user's place on the screen. For example, a letter to be removed must appear under the cursor before the computer will delete that letter on command. The cursor moves in the four directions—up, down, left, right.

database   An electronic library that can be accessed from a computer and over telephone lines.

deadline   The final moment in any department of the newspaper after which productive, economical work can no longer be accomplished.

dialogue   A written representation of a conversation.

direct quotation   A written or oral repetition of a person's exact words; signaled in writing by quotation marks around the exact words. See also *indirect quotation.*

discretionary time   Periods of free time when readers and viewers can bestow their attention as they please. A newspaper competes with other leisure activities for this attention.

disk   The physical device on which information is stored.

document   A physical (non-human) reliable source of information.

editing   The process of revising copy so that it conforms to the news medium's style and the usage of readers or viewers; the reworking of a story to make it flow smoothly.

edition   A press run's worth of newspapers, not a day's worth. An edition is usually focused on a particular locale (city edition) or time of day (early edition). See also *zoned edition.*

editor   The person with overall responsibility for the editorial content of a newspaper. All other editors report to the editor; the editor reports to the publisher.

ending   The closing paragraph(s) of a story.

ethics   The moral principles that underlie a person's or a group's behavior.

feature   A human interest, or soft news, story written in a narrative or other non-inverted pyramid structure. See also *inverted pyramid, soft news*.

floppy disk   A disk (similar to a phonograph record) on which computer programs or newsroom-generated information are stored for later accessing.

graphic   A visual element designed to enhance the communication of a story. Drawings more than photographs qualify as graphics, although when editors refer to "graphic elements," they include photographs.

hard news   News that occurs and is reported within a 24-hour or shorter cycle; information that is timely. See also *soft news*.

hardware   Computer equipment.

headline   The larger type appearing (usually) above a story and telling what the story is about.

home   A VDT command that returns the cursor to the top left-hand corner of the screen or to the beginning of a line.

hourglass   A story in which the basic information is told in descending order of importance in the first two or three paragraphs and then, after a transition paragraph, in chronological order.

in-depth story   A story that examines the larger picture, that comprehensively explains the flow of news rather than a particular event.

indirect quotation   A paraphrase of a person's words.

insert   A VDT command that allows a user to insert a word or letter without erasing other words or letters. When not in the insert mode, a VDT is in the overstrike mode.

International Typographical Union   The union that represents members of the production department; at some newspapers the ITU also represents members of the editorial staff.

interview   To ask questions of a news source, usually in person but also over the telephone.

inverted pyramid   A news story that tells the most important information first and then records other facts in descending order of importance.

investigative reporting   The process of examining an issue in depth until the truth is known.

issue   A single copy of a publication or the entire publication for a particular day. Not to be confused with edition, which is a particular part of an issue: *The local edition of Monday's issue contained fewer than the normal number of typos.* See also *edition*.

journalese   The jargon of journalism; not fit to print.

jump   To continue a story from one page to another; the continued story.

lead   The beginning of a story; usually only the first paragraph.

libel   Anything published or broadcast that defames a person.

library   A newspaper's collection of reference works and the newspaper's own stories. Older journalists call it the "morgue."

localize   To rewrite or edit a wire story so that the angle of interest to the newspaper's audience appears at the beginning of the story.

media   Agencies of mass communication like newspapers, magazines, radio and television. A plural noun (the singular is *medium*).

memory   The area of a computer that holds information, usually described in terms of capacity.

microcomputer   Also known as personal computer. Microcomputers began as standard home models but were taken on in newsrooms around the country because of their increasing capability and low cost.

modem   A device attached to a computer or affixed inside a computer that allows access to telephone circuits. "Modem" is the acronym for modulator-demodulator.

morgue   A newspaper's library.

nameplate   The name of the newspaper and other publishing information found at or near the top of Page One. Also called a flag.

news   The timely content of a newspaper or broadcast. Information that is fascinating and interesting to readers and viewers.

news hole   The amount of space devoted to the news, usually determined as a percentage of total space after the advertisements are dummied.

news release   An announcement written in news style from an organization seeking publicity. News releases can provide tips on possible stories.

Newspaper Fund   A non-profit foundation supported by various newspapers and news organizations and dedicated to encouraging young people to consider careers in journalism. Two programs provide internships for minorities and students interested in copy editing.

newsprint   The paper on which a newspaper is printed.

obit   Journalese for "obituary." An obituary is an account of a person's death and facts about the person's life.

ombudsman   A member of the newspaper staff whose main function is to process reader complaints against the newspaper and to serve as an in-house critic of the newspaper.

open   A VDT command that tells a computer to produce a story from its files.

page A VDT screenful of type. A page is composed of about 20 lines, or what a reporter would normally type on one sheet of $8^1/_2 \times 11$ inch paper.

para A VDT command given at the end of a paragraph so that the following paragraph will be indented.

para del A VDT command for "paragraph delete."

peg A story's *raison d'être*; the main point on which the story hangs.

photojournalism The melding of words and pictures into a coherent story told mostly with photographs.

plagiarism The use without credit of the writings and ideas of others.

profile A feature story that focuses on a person and whose purpose is to tell about the person not about an event.

program Computer instructions.

publisher The chief officer of a newspaper. The publisher oversees all phases of the newspaper but does not get involved in day-to-day decisions in any one department.

Pulitzer Prize Journalism's most prestigious honor bestowed annually on the best journalists and newspapers (and plays and books).

readability The clarity of the written word.

reporting The process of gathering factual information for a news story.

revising The process of changing a story to make it better.

rewriting the process of making a story flow better. Rewriting frequently occurs after editing and represents an opportunity for a reporter to amplify the story by doing additional reporting.

scroll up/scroll down VDT commands that move lines up or down on the screen. On personal computers *Pg Up* and *Pg Dn* do the same thing.

second-day lead A lead on any version of a story except the first in which the news is originally reported. A second-day lead generally takes a feature angle or highlights a new and important action in a continuing story.

sent del A VDT command for "sentence delete."

sidebar A story related to a major story, but focusing on one special point.

sign off A VDT command telling the computer that the reporter or copy editor is through using the terminal.

skip to start A VDT command key that sends the cursor to the beginning of the story, thus causing the beginning of the story to appear at the top of the screen with the cursor. On personal computers, *Ctrl Pg Up* has the same effect.

slug The name or identifying tag for a story. Usually the slug tells something about the story: *hotel/fire*. Also called slugline.

soft news   the timeless or feature content of a newspaper that usually bears some relation to a recent news event.

software   A particular program, such as a spreadsheet or a word processing program.

source   A person or document on which a reporter relies for information.

split screen   The VDT capability of displaying two stories side by side. Also called windows.

stereotype   An oversimplified view of members of a group of people which assumes that all individuals in the group behave the same way.

stet   A printer's term (derived from the Latin *stare*) to advise the person setting type to disregard a correction or to let a word stand as is even if it appears incorrect. The word has no use in computerized typesetting, but every generation of writers and copy editors should know what it means.

structure   The organization of a story. See also *hourglass, inverted pyramid.*

style (news medium)   The prescribed way of processing ambiguous usage in a news stories. Style should always be consistent.

style (writing)   The flavor, quality, spirit and personality of a written piece. Style is the sum of a writer.

subsumption   The process of choosing the most comprehensive word or description that conveys subsidiary meanings or events in one stroke.

tabloid   A newspaper format that is half the size of a standard newspaper. Also, a phrase used to describe a sensational newspaper.

take   A portion of a story, usually one page; for a wire story, 450 words.

theme   The unifying principle in a long story.

time element   Usually the day of the week on which a news story takes place. Yesterday, today, tomorrow, last night, this morning, in addition to the days of the week, are acceptable time elements.

transition   A word, phrase or paragraph that alerts the reader to a change of subject in a story.

typo   A typographical error.

United Press International   A privately owned news-gathering organization.

verification   The process by which a reporter checks information with other sources to verify its accuracy and validity.

VDT   See *video display terminal.*

video display terminal   A television screen connected to a typewriter keyboard; commands typed on the keyboard appear on the screen.

window   A segment of a computer screen in which text appears. Using two or more windows simultaneously is a handy way of comparing related stories side by side or checking information at the end of a long story with information early in the story.

zoned edition   An edition of a newspaper that includes a page or section emphasizing news of a small geographical area within the newspaper's larger circulation area.

Endnote

1. From R. Thomas Berner, *The Process of Editing*. Needham Heights, Mass.: Allyn and Bacon, 1991. Copyright © 1991 by Allyn and Bacon.

Society of Professional Journalists Code of Ethics[1]

Society of Professional Journalists believes the duty of journalists is to serve the truth.

We believe the agencies of mass communication are carriers of public discussion and information, acting on their constitutional mandate and freedom to learn and report the facts.

We believe in public enlightenment as the forerunner of justice, and in our constitutional role to seek the truth as part of the public's right to know the truth.

We believe those responsibilities carry obligations that require journalists to perform with intelligence, objectivity, accuracy and fairness.

To these ends, we declare acceptance of the standards of practice here set forth.

I. Responsibility

The public's right to know of events of public importance and interest is the overriding mission of the mass media. The purpose of distributing news and enlightened opinion is to serve the general welfare. Journalists who use their professional status as representatives of the public for selfish or other unworthy motives violate a high trust.

II. Freedom of the Press

Freedom of the press is to be guarded as an inalienable right of people in a free society. It carries with it the freedom and the responsibility to discuss, question, and challenge actions and utterances of our government and of our public and private institutions. Journalists uphold the right to speak unpopular opinions and the privilege to agree with the majority.

III. Ethics

Journalists must be free of obligation to any interest other than the public's right to know the truth.

1. Gifts, favors, free travel, special treatment or privileges can compromise the integrity of journalists and their employers. Nothing of value should be accepted.

2. Secondary employment, political involvement, holding public office, and service in community organizations should be avoided if it compromises the integrity of journalists and their employers. Journalists and their employers should conduct their personal lives in a manner that protects them from conflict of interest, real or apparent. Their responsibilities to the public are paramount. That is the nature of their profession.

3. So-called news communications from private sources should not be published or broadcast without substantiation of their claims to news values.

4. Journalists will seek news that serves the public interest, despite the obstacles. They will make constant efforts to assure that the public's business is conducted in public and that public records are open to public inspection.

5. Journalists acknowledge the newsman's ethic of protecting confidential sources of information.

6. Plagiarism is dishonest and unacceptable.

IV. Accuracy and Objectivity

Good faith with the public is the foundation of all worthy journalism.

1. Truth is our ultimate goal.

2. Objectivity in reporting the news is another goal that serves as the mark of an experienced professional. It is a standard or performance toward which we strive. We honor those who achieve it.

3. There is no excuse for inaccuracies or lack of thoroughness.

4. Newspaper headlines should be fully warranted by the contents of the articles they accompany. Photographs and telecasts should give an accurate picture of an event and not highlight an incident out of context.

5. Sound practice makes clear distinction between news reports and expressions of opinion. News reports should be free of opinion or bias and represent all sides of an issue.

6. Partisanship in editorial comment that knowingly departs from the truth violates the spirit of American journalism.

7. Journalists recognize their responsibility for offering informed analysis, comment, and editorial opinion on public events and issues. They accept the obligation to present such material by individuals whose competence, experience and judgment qualify them for it.

8. Special articles or presentations devoted to advocacy or the writer's own conclusions and interpretations should be labeled as such.

V. Fair Play

Journalists at all times will show respect for the dignity, privacy, rights and well-being of people encountered in the course of gathering and presenting the news.

1. The news media should not communicate unofficial charges affecting reputation or moral character without giving the accused a chance to reply.

2. The news media must guard against invading a person's right to privacy.

3. The media should not pander to morbid curiosity about details of vice and crime.

4. It is the duty of news media to make prompt and complete correction of their errors.

5. Journalists should be accountable to the public for their reports, and the public should be encouraged to voice its grievances against the media. Open dialogue with our readers, viewers, and listeners should be fostered.

VI. Mutual Trust

Adherence to this code is intended to preserve and strengthen the bond of mutual trust and respect between American journalists and the American people.

The Society shall—by programs of education and other means—encourage individual journalists to adhere to these tenets, and shall encourage journalistic publications and broadcasters to recognize their responsibility to frame codes of ethics in concert with their employees to serve as guidelines in furthering these goals.

Endnote

1. Adapted from *The Quill,* March 1991. Code of Ethics adopted in 1926 and revised in 1973, 1984 and 1987.

Index